A Pillar by Day

365 Daily Meditations from the Pentateuch

Jon Courson

A Pillar by Day
365 Daily Meditations from the Pentateuch

Copyright © 2005 by Jon Courson

Published by Calvary Chapel Publishing (CCP),
a resource ministry of Calvary Chapel Costa Mesa
3800 South Fairview Road
Santa Ana, California 92704

First printing, 2005

All Scripture quotations in this book are taken from the King James Version of the Bible.

ISBN 1-59751-011-4

Printed in the United States of America.

INTRODUCTION

What great patience God had with His people in the Old Testament! Imagine Adam and Eve disobeying when they lived in a perfect environment! And remember how the Israelites complained so often? As we read God's Word, we wonder how they could have been so faithless. And yet, what about us?

Maybe we don't complain about eating manna, but how often are we dissatisfied with a worn-out wardrobe, upset because of a crummy car, or joyless in our jobs?

God's message to His people long ago is His instruction for us today: find contentment in Me. God invites us to rest in His shade, discover comfort in His Word, and grow more in love with Him. When we find ourselves surrounded, God says, "Don't panic—follow My cloud. Watch Me miraculously dry up deep waters. See Me drown your enemies. Trust Me to lead, and you will find sweet waters among the bitter brooks."

Together we will walk from Genesis through Deuteronomy, observing how God's Old Testament work points to New Testament truths. Like God's children of old, let us follow the Pillar by Day, each day. Let us go and meet with Jesus.

JANUARY 1

In the beginning God . . .

Genesis 1:1

The word *genesis* means "beginning." Therefore, Genesis is a fitting title for the book before us, for its pages record the beginning of everything—the beginning of creation, man, sin, family, culture, and industry. It deals with the beginning of everything one could possibly imagine—except it does not deal with the beginning of God.

Why?

First, because God has no beginning.

Second, the Bible being, in a sense, the autobiography of God, He needs no introduction. Think about it. If you were to write your life story, you would not spend chapters trying to prove that you exist because the very fact that you were writing the book would verify your existence.

The more I study the Bible, the more I realize it was composed supernaturally. Comprised of sixty-six different books written by forty different authors over a span of sixteen hundred years in three different languages, yet, there isn't one contradiction. Instead, there is a unified theme that begins here in Genesis, the book of beginning, and extends through the book of Revelation. That theme is the story of God's gracious, glorious work of redemption.

A number of years ago, due to a previous commitment, I wasn't able to see one of my son Benjamin's Little League games.

"How did it go, Ben?" I asked eagerly upon my return.

"Well," he answered, "before I got up to bat the first time, I went to the end of the dugout, got on my knees, and prayed."

"Atta boy!" I said. "You probably parked it over the fence, huh?"

"No, I struck out," he said, as a huge grin spread across his face. "But I got to pitch the next inning!"

How often we pray, "Lord, change my husband," or "Lord, help my boss see my talent," or "Lord, let me hit a homer"—only to strike out. But there's a next inning, folks—a big inning, a new, big inning—a new beginning. That's always the way it is. For, although our God has no beginning, He gives us new, big innings, and new beginnings every time we call on Him.

JANUARY 2

And darkness was upon the face of the deep. And the Spirit of God moved upon the face of the waters. And God said, Let there be light: and there was light. And God saw the light, that it was good: and God divided the light from the darkness.

Genesis 1:2–4

Throughout Scripture, water is a symbol of the Word. How does the Spirit of God move?

Upon the face of the water—upon the Word.

In the beginning, God created the heavens and the earth. But when Lucifer launched his rebellion and was cast out of heaven, the earth became dark. Then the Spirit moved on the face of the water, and God said "Let there be light."

That's *your* story. You were created in God's image, but sin wiped you out and your world was dark. The Spirit of God moved in through the Word. You attended a Bible study, listened to a radio program, watched Billy Graham on TV, or heard from a friend—and the Spirit of God moved. You saw the light, and you were born again. Then God separated the darkness in your life and good things began to happen—not only in creation physically, but in your life personally because of God's sovereign grace and mercy.

If you feel tongue-tied when sharing your testimony, try using this short passage to tell others how God brought light to your life and how He can do the same for them.

JANUARY 3

And God made two great lights; the greater light to rule the day, and the lesser light to rule the night: he made the stars also.

Genesis 1:16

Jesus is the Light of the World (John 8:12). He said we are also to be lights (Matthew 5:14). He is the greater light—the sun. We are the lesser light—the moon—reflecting His light to our dark world.

As I recently watched the moon appear smaller and smaller due to an eclipse, I was reminded that to whatever extent the world gets between the sun and the moon is the extent to which the light of the sun upon the moon is diminished. The same thing is true with you and me. Jesus is the sun; we're the moon. And to whatever degree we allow the world to come between us, His light in our lives will fade proportionately.

If you were to chart your own life tonight, would you be a full moon, a three-quarter moon, a half moon, a quarter moon, or an eclipsed moon? It all depends on how much of the world you allow to creep in between you and the Son.

JANUARY 4

So God created man in his own image, in the image of God created he him; male and female created he them. And God blessed them, and God said unto them, Be fruitful, and multiply, and replenish the earth, and subdue it.

Genesis 1:27–28

Before things went haywire after the fall, God assigned Adam and Eve the job of subduing the earth. From whom were they to subdue it? Satan.

You see, from the very beginning, it was as if God said, "This little rock called earth is the place where there is to be a cosmic showdown between Me and Satan. So I'm going to use you, mankind, to partner with Me as part of the process to drive out the Enemy."

How? By being fruitful and multiplying.

How are you to subdue your earth, your world, or your family which seems to be in the grasp and grip of the Enemy? By being fruitful.

Because the fruit of the Spirit is love (Galatians 5:22), and because love covers a multitude of sins (1 Peter 4:8), you'll be fruitful if you don't criticize, gossip, or find fault with things, people, or situations. You'll be fruitful if you speak words of love and peace, patience and gentleness, for such is the fruit of the Spirit.

James talks about the tongue being an instrument of fire (James 3:6). If you find fault with your neighbor, your job, your school, your church, or your family, you will hand your world over to the hellish flames of the Enemy. But if you speak words of affirmation and encouragement, of faith and joy, you will replace the fires of hell with the fruit of heaven.

How do we multiply?

Acts 6:7 tells us the Word of God increased and the number of disciples multiplied when the Word was shared.

If you talk to your kids, your classmates, or your co-workers about the Word, you will see multiplication of life and love. And eventually the world in which you live will be subdued—won back from the Enemy.

JANUARY 5

And God said, Behold, I have given you every herb bearing seed, which is upon the face of all the earth, and every tree, in the which is the fruit of a tree yielding seed; to you it shall be for meat.

Genesis 1:29

Our God is awesome. He could have said, "For nourishment, take a pill." Instead He said, "For food, here's a thrill. The colors and textures and tastes of bananas, mangoes, guavas, avocados, tomatoes, and celery are all yours to enjoy."

"He satisfies our mouth with good things," David declares (see Psalm 103:5).

"Every good and perfect gift is from above," James echoes (1:17).

"He has given us richly all things to enjoy," Paul affirms (see 1 Timothy 6:17).

"If you being evil know how to give good gifts to your kids, how much more will the heavenly Father give good things to them that ask Him?" Jesus says (see Matthew 7:11).

"Then why haven't I received what I've been asking for?" you ask.

The answer is, because it's not a good gift. If it were good, God would give it to you, for He withholds no good thing from them that walk uprightly (Psalm 84:11).

JANUARY 6

And the LORD God commanded the man, saying, Of every tree of the garden thou mayest freely eat: but of the tree of the knowledge of good and evil, thou shalt not eat of it: for in the day that thou eatest thereof thou shalt surely die.

Genesis 2:16–17

Why would God place in the garden a tree from which Adam and Eve were not to eat?

Because God desires a loving relationship with man, and true love is built on choice. Therefore, in placing the tree of the knowledge of good and evil in the garden, it was as if God said to mankind, "If you want to kill our relationship, if you want to turn your back on Me, I must provide this opportunity. All you have to do, Adam, to end our relationship is to eat from that tree."

The Lord is so good because He made it as scary as possible. He said, "If you eat from that tree, it's going to kill you." What else could the Father have done? He provided a choice, but He also made the right choice obvious.

Notice God did not say, "If you eat of that tree, *I'm* going to kill you." He said, "If you eat of the tree, *it* will kill you." Perhaps there was something carcinogenic in the fruit of the tree of the knowledge of good and evil, something that would cause men to begin to die. For many years, I thought that if I did something wrong, God would track me down. No, the Bible says, "Be sure your sin will find you out" (Numbers 32:23). It is *sin* that tracks us down; it is our *sin* that wipes us out. Wise is the man and of utmost intelligence is the woman who stays as far away from sin as possible, and instead draws ever nearer to the side of the One who gives life.

JANUARY 7

And the LORD God caused a deep sleep to fall upon Adam and he slept: and he took one of his ribs, and closed up the flesh instead thereof; and the rib, which the LORD God had taken from man, made he a woman, and brought her unto the man.

Genesis 2:21–22

When Adam was in a deep sleep, a bride came forth from his side. Down the tunnel of time, another bride would come forth from the side of another Adam, the last Adam, Jesus Christ. When a Roman soldier stuck a spear in His side and the birthing fluids of blood and water poured forth, a bride was born: the church—you and me.

"Husbands, love your wives, even as Christ also loved the church, and gave himself for it," Paul instructed the Ephesians (5:25). Husband, you are to love your wife as Christ loved the church. In other words, you're to die—to your needs, your desires, your dreams—because that's what Christ did for us.

Wife, you came from the side of man, and you will find fulfillment at the side of your man—neither leading him nor lagging behind him, but standing by him, standing with him, submitting to him. But know this, wives: Your husbands will never be all you want or need them to be. A rib was taken from Adam, and men have been missing something ever since! There is only One who has it all together. He's not called the second Adam, which would mean that there might be a third one. He is called the last Adam because there is no other. And He's not missing a thing. Therefore, He will be the One who will listen to you by the hour and walk with you in the garden in the cool of the day. He will be the One who will hear not only the words of your lips, but the cry of your heart. He will be the One who will truly understand you.

Gang, as we spend time with the last Adam, with the Altogether One, with Jesus Christ, we take pressure off our mates and are then able to enjoy them without expecting something from them that they cannot give to us.

JANUARY 8

And Adam said, This is now bone of my bones, and flesh of my flesh . . .

Genesis 2:23

"Bone of my bone, flesh of my flesh" is a Hebrew idiom meaning, "exact counterpart." I believe it was a matching of body, soul, and spirit that caused Adam to realize Eve was truly bone of his bones.

"Marriage and misery go hand in hand," wails the world. Not God. He says, "I want marriage to be a taste of heaven for you. If you'll go My way, it can be just that."

"It's a little late for me to hear this," you might be thinking. "I married the wrong person."

That's what Jacob could have said . . .

After seven years of working and waiting, he woke up to find he had wed Leah instead of Rachel—the older sister instead of the girl of his dreams. But at the end of his life, when deciding where he would be buried, Jacob again had to choose between the two women. And this time, with eyes wide open, he chose Leah. Why? Because Leah produced a son whose name was Judah, from whom would come Yeshua, Messiah, Jesus.

So too, I have known people who have difficult marriages. However, they have developed, out of necessity, a deep walk with the Lord which never would have been developed if they had had an easier, simpler marriage. I know people who have hung in there and now say, "If I could do it all over again, I would willingly choose my husband or wife because our marriage has brought me to a richness with Jesus I never would have known had it been easier."

If you have gone through a divorce, if you have dropped the ball, if you have missed the mark, know this: We all have. Every one of us has totally blown it (Romans 3:23). But the good news is that the work of the cross completely takes care of my failure, my shortcoming, my sin. And it takes care of yours as well. All we have to do is say, "Lord, I've failed. I determine by Your grace and with Your help to walk rightly to the greatest possible degree. And if my hurts or mistakes can help others, use my wounds." If we confess our sins rather than cover them up, excuse them, or justify them, our points of failure can be our points of greatest ministry.

JANUARY 9

And the serpent said unto the woman, Ye shall not surely die: for God doth know that in the day ye eat thereof, then your eyes shall be opened, and ye shall be as gods, knowing good and evil.

Genesis 3:4–5

After questioning the Word of God, Satan questions the way of God, intimating that God is withholding something good from Eve. This is the same strategy Satan uses today. He slithers up to our friends, our children, and our neighbors and hisses in their ears, saying, "You know why you're not *ssss*upposed to do that? Because it's really fun. And God doesn't want that for you. He wants you to be re*ss*tricted and mi*ss*erable."

Not true. As I tell my kids, "If you think sin is fun, if you want to eat from the tree of forbidden fruit, look first at another tree—the tree of Calvary—and you'll see what sin ultimately does: it crucifies. And if you think God is holding something back from you or doesn't want the best for you, look at that tree again, and you'll see Him with outstretched arms and nail-pierced palms, unequivocally proving that He loves you passionately."

JANUARY 10

And when the woman saw that the tree was good for food,
and that it was pleasant to the eyes, and a tree to be desired
to make one wise, she took of the fruit thereof, and did eat,
and gave also unto her husband with her; and he did eat.
And the eyes of them both were opened.

Genesis 3:6–7

"In the day ye eat thereof, then your eyes shall be opened," said Satan to Eve, "and ye shall be as gods, knowing good and evil." Unfortunately, Satan was right. You see, before man ate of the tree of the knowledge of good and evil, he had to ask the Father about every matter and about every situation in order to discern good from evil. God and Adam walked together in the cool of the day in constant communion because Adam had to depend solely upon God for his knowledge. After the fall, Adam grew independent from God, and knowledge apart from God is always deadly.

The tree of the knowledge of good and evil is as deadly for us as it was for Adam. It can squeeze the life out of our relationship with the Lord if we're not oh, so careful. Even Bible knowledge can be deadly to anyone who says, "I've been to Bible school; I've been to seminary; I've been reading the Word for years. I know good from evil."

"But aren't we supposed to know the Bible?" you may ask.

Yes. But as we study the Word, we are to fellowship with the Lord intimately, talk to Him personally, worship, praise, commune, and listen to Him constantly.

You see, as parents, our job is to help our kids to become independent. When they take their first steps, we say, "Way to go!" When they learn to tie their shoes, ride a bike, drive a car, or move out, we say, "Hooray!" But our heavenly Father wants just the opposite for you and me. He wants us to be totally dependent upon Him. He wants us to be constantly talking to Him just as Adam did before he ate of the forbidden fruit.

JANUARY 11

Unto the woman he said, I will greatly multiply thy sorrow and thy conception; in sorrow thou shalt bring forth children; and thy desire shall be to thy husband, and he shall rule over thee. And unto Adam he said, Because thou hast hearkened unto the voice of thy wife, and hast eaten of the tree, of which I commanded thee, saying, Thou shalt not eat of it: cursed is the ground for thy sake; in sorrow shalt thou eat of it all the days of thy life; thorns also and thistles shall it bring forth to thee; and thou shalt eat the herb of the field; in the sweat of thy face shalt thou eat bread, till thou return unto the ground; for out of it wast thou taken: for dust thou art, and unto dust shalt thou return.

Genesis 3:16–19

The desire of the woman would be for her husband. The man, on the other hand, would work by the sweat of his brow. And therein lies a foundational dilemma in marriage to this day.

"Why won't my husband slow down? I want him to take a walk with me, talk to me, listen to me," she cries.

"I show my love most clearly by providing for my family," answers the weary husband. "That's why I work three jobs."

She wants to talk. He needs to work. She wants to enjoy. He can't wait to get going. It's all part of the curse. When husbands and wives realize what the curse has done and how it works, no longer will they try to change each other. Lowered expectations will replace futile ideas of transformation. Don't raise the bar for your marriage. Lower it. And as you lower your expectations on earth, raise your sights toward heaven.

This is what Paul meant when he said, "Let those who are married be as though they're not" (see 1 Corinthians 7:29). In other words, "Life is short. Keep your focus on the kingdom, your eyes on eternity." What will setting your sights on the Lord do? It will make you a better husband or a better wife because as His love flows from you, time with your husband or wife will be sweet and rich.

It's amazing what happens when we do what the Lord tells us to do. When we seek first the kingdom, everything else will be added to us (Matthew 6:33). When a woman and man both deeply love Jesus Christ, they each find their ultimate satisfaction in their walk with Him. The pressure is removed. The bickering stops. They are a joy to be around.

JANUARY 12

Unto Adam also and to his wife did the LORD God make coats of skins, and clothed them.

Genesis 3:21

To replace Adam and Eve's itchy fig leaves, a sacrifice was made—illustrating the fact that mankind's sin and nakedness would never be covered by his own efforts, but by the sacrifice of an innocent One, the Lamb of God, Jesus Christ.

There is nothing you can do to make God love you more. Nothing. There's nothing I can do to make God love me one ounce more than He already loves me right now. If I pray all day today; if I fast for a week or a month; if I worship constantly, He will not love me anymore than He loves me right now. Likewise, there is not one thing you could do to make Him love you less.

This amazes me because, like you, I am under the impression that I have to do something to earn God's favor.

"No," says God. "Your efforts will be like fig leaves. They will be scratchy. They will crumble. They won't work. Let Me give you that which you could never provide for yourself: matchless grace and infinite mercy to cover you completely and eternally."

JANUARY 13

So he drove out the man; and he placed at the east of the garden of Eden Cherubims, and a flaming sword which turned every way, to keep the way of the tree of life.

Genesis 3:24

A sacrifice had been made to cover Adam and Eve's nakedness. Cherubim and a flame followed. This same picture will be painted again in the tabernacle, for over the mercy seat, sprinkled with sacrificial blood, were cherubim and the bright *shekinah* glory of God.

But the place we see this picture painted most powerfully is not in the garden, nor in the tabernacle, but in an empty tomb where two angels clothed in light sat at either end of a slab stained with the sacrificial blood of the Lamb of God.

Genesis 3 keeps man away from the Tree of Life. Jesus Christ, however, invites mankind to eat of the Bread of Life (John 6:57). And as we do, we begin to experience power over the curse as well as a sneak preview of coming attractions, when the curse will be obliterated in heaven. Oh, glorious day!

JANUARY 14

And the LORD said unto Cain, Why art thou wroth? and why is thy countenance fallen? If thou doest well, shalt thou not be accepted? and if thou doest not well, sin lieth at the door. And unto thee shall be his desire, and thou shalt rule over him.

Genesis 4:6–7

Although I feel like a prophet crying in the wilderness as I go against the flow of what our culture says about depression, I remain biblically persuaded that many people today are seeking medical help for depression when in reality it is often a spiritual issue. You see, the psychiatrist and the pastor differ not in the diagnosis of depression, but in the cure.

The psychiatrist says, "Take a pill." The pastor says, "Make a choice."

That is, we can *choose* to put on the garment of praise for the spirit of heaviness (Isaiah 61:3). We can *choose* to rejoice in the Lord (1 Thessalonians 5:16). We can *choose* to pray without ceasing (1 Thessalonians 5:17). We can *choose* to give thanks in everything (1 Thessalonians 5:18). We can *choose* to think on whatever is pure and lovely and praiseworthy (Philippians 4:8).

"Why art thou cast down, O my soul?" David asked when he faced depression like ours. What was his prescription? "Hope thou in God" (Psalm 42:11).

"My bones ache. My eyes weep. I feel as though there's gravel in my teeth," cried Jeremiah in his own deep, dark depression. His cure? "I will lift up my heart with my hands unto the heavens" (see Lamentations 3:41).

Although I am increasingly convinced that there are people who, because of difficulties in life, can benefit from wise and prudent medical help in this arena, such is not the norm, because as you read the Bible from cover to cover, it becomes clear that the issue regarding depression is primarily an issue of choice.

God didn't say, "I know you're sad, Cain. Here, drink this; swallow that; and you'll be better in the morning." No, He said, "Your bitterness is causing your countenance to fall. If you don't choose well, you'll be eaten up. But if you choose to do well—to obey My Word—you'll be lifted up."

JANUARY 15

And he said, What hast thou done? the voice of thy brother's blood crieth unto me from the ground.

Genesis 4:10

Unforgiveness, hatred, and bitterness have repercussions far greater than I might think. That is why in the book of Jude, God specifically says to watch out for the way of Cain, which is bitterness, unforgiveness, and hatred (verse 11). Make sure there's no one you're mad at, upset with, or angry about because it only takes one person to affect many. Ask Cain.

"The blood of your brother cries out to Me." The writer of Hebrews picks up this metaphor when he declares, "Jesus' blood speaks better things than the blood of Abel" (see 12:24). What does Abel's blood cry? It's a message of condemnation, judgment, and accusation. What does Jesus' blood cry? It cries, "Forgiven."

If there is an old boyfriend, ex-spouse, parent, or boss you're mad at, whose name still comes up when you talk to people, God would say, "My Son was slaughtered on the cross for the very sin that person committed against you. Let it go. Give it up. Put it under the blood that speaks better things. Lay it at the cross."

JANUARY 16

This is the book of the generations of Adam. In the day that God created man, in the likeness of God made he him; male and female created he them; and blessed them, and called their name Adam, in the day when they were created.

Genesis 5:1–2

In calling Adam and Eve "Adam," God called them one. You see, knowing our propensity to think the grass is always greener on the other side of the fence, and knowing our tendency to want to trade this year's car for next year's model, God made it really simple for us. He ordained marriage for life. Those who understand this find glorious peace and freedom when they look at their spouse, because they know there's no one down the line or around the corner who will give them a greater thrill. There's not another person on earth who will make them happier, more content, or more fulfilled. Such is the amazing mystery of matrimony.

I have known couples who weren't perfectly matched body, soul, and spirit—but they stayed together because they understood the way of the Lord. And as I've watched them over the years, as I've seen their hair turn gray and their backs bow a bit, as I've seen them blessed with children and grandchildren, I've heard them say, "Wow. It's worth it to go God's way."

There is no greater joy than watching your kids grow and walk in the way of the Lord. But all that is thrown away by the one who says, "If I have an affair, I'll be forgiven." But there is no thing and there is no one worth losing your family for. God talks more about the sin of adultery than about any other single sin because adultery uniquely brings long-term, irreversible repercussions.

If you have been one of the fortunate few who have experienced a miraculous resurrection of your marriage following the deathblow of adultery, rejoice. You have been graced. Go your way and sin no more.

Dear people, determine that no matter what you've been through, no matter where you've been, you will do whatever it takes to guard the sanctity of your family.

JANUARY 17

And Adam lived an hundred and thirty years, and begat a son in his own likeness, after his image; and called his name Seth.

Genesis 5:3

So begin the "begats"—the genealogy from Adam to Noah. Often, people come to sections of Scripture like this and become frustrated and wonder why the Lord made some Scriptures so seemingly tedious and mysterious. Why didn't He simply write a section on marriage, a section on finances, and a section on parenting? Why all the stories and rules and ordinances and parables and pictures and types and illustrations?

Solomon shed light on this question when he wrote, "It is the glory of God to conceal a thing: but the honour of kings is to search out a matter" (Proverbs 25:2). God purposely conceals some things because even though initially a certain story, passage, or section of Scripture might not make sense to you, as you meditate on it, pray about it, and wrestle with it, a week, or a month, or a year later, when a light goes on and you finally understand it, you'll never forget it.

I have often found that the passages I wrestle with the most are the ones I learn the best. How many wonderful truths I would have missed had I not read the Word consistently—even when I didn't necessarily understand it. Jesus promised the Holy Spirit will "bring all things to your remembrance, whatsoever I have said unto you" (John 14:26). In other words, the Holy Spirit will bring to our minds and make application of that which the Lord has said to us in His Word. He cannot, however, bring to mind that which we haven't read.

Wondering why God was doing certain things and why He wasn't doing other things, Habakkuk said, "I will go up into a high tower and I will wait and see what the Lord will say unto me" (see Habakkuk 2:1).

The Lord did indeed speak to Habakkuk, saying, "Write the vision" (Habakkuk 2:2), and Habakkuk didn't have to borrow a pencil.

What does it mean to read with expectancy? I believe it means you come to your devotions, to Bible studies, or to church with pencil and paper in hand, ready to take note of what the Lord would speak to you.

I wonder if, in our morning devotions and study times, we're not speaking volumes through our casual, lethargic approach. "Ho hum, Lord," our actions say, "I don't expect You to say anything to me today. You never do. So let's see, where should I read today . . ." No wonder the Lord doesn't speak to us. No wonder the Word isn't real to us.

I want you to do well, gang. Approach the Word with anticipation and expectation. "For he that cometh to God must believe that he is, and that he is a rewarder of those that *diligently* seek him" (Hebrews 11:6, italics added).

JANUARY 18

And Enoch walked with God: and he was not, for God took him.

Genesis 5:24

"Who shall I say sent me?" asked Moses of God.

"Say I AM that I AM hath sent you" (see Exodus 3:14).

And with this, Moses must have come to realize that if God is "I AM," like Enoch, he "was not."

John the Baptist must have come to the same conclusion, because when he was asked if he was the Messiah, he emphatically declared, "I am not" (John 1:20). Oh, how we as a culture, as a body, and as individuals need to grasp what Enoch, Moses, and John the Baptist understood so clearly: that God is, and we are not. You see, I believe the problem for most of us is that we are constantly trying to figure out who we are, what we should do, how we should minister, where we should go. Yet the more we think about how we're doing, where we're going, or what we're thinking, and the more we talk about ourselves, make reference to ourselves, or draw attention to ourselves, the more misery we heap upon ourselves.

Do you ever get tired of hearing your own voice, of dealing with your own stuff, of taking your own pulse? I do. That's because we were created not for self-indulgence or introspection, but solely to give pleasure to God (Revelation 4:11). It is only logical, then, to join Enoch, Moses, and John the Baptist in losing our lives in the wonder of His glory (John 3:30) and in decreasing so that He might increase.

Because Adam sinned, and because the wages of sin is death, everyone in Adam's family tree ends up the same way: dead. There is, however, one exception. There is one guy who never dies. After walking with God three hundred years, one day the Lord simply snatches, grabs, raptures Enoch.

The wages of sin is still death. But, like Enoch, there will be a people who will not die. Paul put it this way: "Then we which are alive and remain shall be caught up together with them in the clouds, to meet the Lord in the air: and so shall we ever be with the Lord" (1 Thessalonians 4:17). I believe we are the generation who will see the rapture of the church. But even before that glorious day, you and I can experience rapture in our hearts presently. You see, the Latin word *raptus* speaks of the physical event that will take place when Jesus comes to call His church home. But it also speaks of an emotional event that can take place right now.

"I was enraptured by that music," we say. Or, "The poem she sent me enraptured me." Is your heart enraptured? Maybe you've walked with the Lord for ten years; maybe you've been a believer for twenty years; but maybe you haven't found the Lord to be all that enthralling lately. Instead, maybe you're discouraged, defeated, or depressed. Maybe you've read that happy are the people whose God is the Lord (Psalm 144:15), and the joy of the Lord is my strength (Nehemiah 8:10), but you're feeling anything *but* happy and joyful.

Why is this?

It is because you're not doing what Enoch did. Look at our text: Enoch pleased God. That is, as he walked *with* God, Enoch brought pleasure *to* God. The closer you walk to God today, the more you'll be enraptured, taken, caught up with Him. The godliest people I know don't talk about themselves. The happiest people I know are not focused on themselves. The folks I truly admire are not those who live to please themselves. The people who are the most godly and happy, the people who are just a joy to be around are those who live for one reason: to simply walk with and please God. May we be such people.

JANUARY 19

But Noah found grace in the eyes of the LORD.

Genesis 6:8

That Noah found grace in the eyes of the Lord does not mean that God showed grace to Noah exclusively. Yes, a flood eventually wiped out everyone else, but not before God gave them one hundred years to repent of their wickedness and receive salvation. Yes, the planet was deluged, but every man had opportunity to hear His message as they observed Noah building the huge barge. But the world refused to grab hold of the good news of salvation, and they drowned in their sin. It wasn't that God looked at Noah with grace and everyone else with condemnation. God looked at *everyone* with eyes of grace and mercy. It's just that Noah *found* the grace.

The question I want to ask you today is this: What have *you* found in the eyes of the Lord?

> The story is told of the time a London traffic jam prevented C. S. Lewis from arriving at a certain religious symposium on time. The panel, comprised of the world's most highly esteemed religious thinkers, began without him, their first question being: What is unique about Christianity? Although the Buddhist, Muslim, Jew, and Taoist discussed the question, they could arrive at no conclusive answer. In the midst of their debate, C. S. Lewis burst into the room.

> "Dr. Lewis," said the moderator, "tell us what is unique to Christianity."

> "That's easy," Lewis is said to have replied. "It's grace."

C. S. Lewis was right. No other religion or philosophy provides unmerited, undeserved, unearned favor. Every other religion, every other philosophy says there are things we must do—devotional exercises, good deeds, or righteous acts—to earn blessings from Allah or to gain favor from Buddha. Only biblical Christianity says, "It's all grace, nothing more, nothing less, nothing else."

JANUARY 20

These are the generations of Noah: Noah was a just man and perfect in his generations, and Noah walked with God. And Noah begat three sons, Shem, Ham, and Japheth.

Genesis 6:9–10

Noah walked with God because he found grace in the eyes of the Lord. Peter was another who, like Noah, looked into the eyes of the Lord. And what he saw therein caused him to weep. What did Peter see in the Lord's eyes? I believe your answer is a good indication of where you are in your relationship with God. You see, Peter fell asleep when he should have prayed, denied the Lord when questioned by a young maid, and forsook the Lord because he was afraid. Thus, it would be natural to think that it was the look of disappointment in the eyes of the Lord that caused Peter to weep. But such was not the case, for Jesus had already told Peter that Satan sought to sift him like wheat, but that he would eventually make it through, regardless of his failure (Luke 22:31–32). No, Peter didn't find disappointment or discouragement in the Lord's eyes. He found the same thing Noah found. He found grace.

The writer to the Hebrews says, "Let us therefore come boldly unto the throne of grace, that we may obtain mercy, and find grace to help in time of need" (Hebrews 4:16). If you want to experience the blessings of God in a world that's falling apart, if you want to experience the blessings of God no matter your situation, you have the privilege of gazing constantly in the eyes of the Lord. You have an invitation to find grace.

JANUARY 21

Make thee an ark of gopher wood; rooms shalt thou make in the ark, and shalt pitch it within and without with pitch.

Genesis 6:14

Not coincidentally, I believe, due to its density and strength, gopher wood was used to make coffins. "If any man will come after me, let him deny himself, and take up his cross," Jesus declared (Matthew 16:24). Salvation begins with death. It begins when we say, "I'm dying to self, Lord. I no longer demand my own way, but rather give myself completely to You."

The Hebrew word translated "rooms" is literally "nests." On the good ship salvation, there is an abundance of rooms, where Episcopalians and Presbyterians, Baptists and Lutherans, Catholics and Methodists alike can nest. How careful we must be to allow room, to give our fellow brothers and sisters in Christ space to "work out their own salvation" (see Philippians 2:12). Each of us thinks we see clearly. But Paul reminds us that on this side of eternity, each of us only sees "through a glass, darkly" (1 Corinthians 13:12). Therefore, we need each other. The ark had plenty of room. So does the kingdom.

This is the only time in the Old Testament where the Hebrew word *kapher* is translated "pitch." In many other passages this word is translated "atonement"—a wonderful word that essentially means "at-one-ment." Just as the salvation God provided Noah was surrounded by the pitch of atonement, so God provided us "at-one-ment" with Him by sending His Son to die for our sins.

In whatever storm faces you today, be assured, fellow sailor, that there is no safer place to be than in the ark of God's election and provision, in the hold of His astounding mercy and amazing grace.

JANUARY 22

A window shalt thou make to the ark, and in a cubit shalt thou finish it above; and the door of the ark shalt thou set in the side thereof.

Genesis 6:16

Because it was God who shut him in (Genesis 7:16), Noah had no control over the door of the ark. But he did have control over the window. So too, I control how much illumination and understanding I have in life by how much I allow the Word of God to be in my thinking (Psalm 119:105). I can either remain in the dark, or I can gain light and insight by opening up the window of the Word. Sure, sometimes it would be easier to just watch Jeopardy. Sometimes it would be easier to sleep in and skip morning devotions. Sometimes it would be easier not to take the time to study Scripture, but I will walk in light only to the extent that I choose to open the window and allow the light of the Word to flood my soul and renew my thoughts.

There was only one door in the ark. There was no back door, no emergency exit. "Why can't you just be broad-minded? Why can't you just say there are many ways to enter into a relationship with God?" people ask us. The reason is because Jesus said, "No man comes to the Father but by Me" (see John 14:6). And I'm real glad about that. You see, if God had five ways to enter into salvation, five ways to be able to make it to heaven, five ways to cultivate a relationship with Him, Satan would come back with twenty-five counterfeit ways. If God had ten ways, Satan would come back with ten thousand. God says, "I don't want anyone to choose the wrong door. I'm going to keep it real simple. There's only one."

JANUARY 23

But with thee will I establish my covenant; and thou shalt come into the ark, thou, and thy sons, and thy wife, and thy sons' wives with thee. And of every living thing of all flesh, two of every sort shalt thou bring into the ark, to keep them alive with thee; they shall be male and female. Of fowls after their kind, and of cattle after their kind, of every creeping thing of the earth after his kind, two of every sort shall come unto thee, to keep them alive.

Genesis 6:18–20

Eight souls were to enter the ark. Yes, there would be some bobbing up and down, some noise and confusion, some questions and concerns, but guess what? They would be headed to a fresh start, a new beginning, a new world. And that's what's happening with you and me. The reason we have morning devotions, the reason we keep plugging away in Bible study is because we're saved. And when all is said and done, that's all that matters. Let's never lose sight of that. Let's never get so caught up in the esoteric understanding of Scripture that we miss the underlying base of all things—that God so loved the world that He gave His only begotten Son, that whosoever believes in Him should not perish but have everlasting life (John 3:16).

Three-storied, the ark contained 97,000 square feet of space. How big is that? It's equivalent to 520 boxcars. Would this be enough space to hold all of the animals? Taxonomists tell us that on the earth today there are 3,500 species of mammals; 8,600 species of birds; 5,500 reptiles and amphibians. (Fish obviously weren't on the ark; and the 25,500 species of worms could fit in the cracks.) Added together, there were 17,600 species of animals. Double that to include male and female, and the figure becomes 35,200. The average size of the 17,600 species of animals on the ark is equivalent to a full-grown sheep. Thirty-five thousand, two hundred sheep would easily fit within only 120 boxcars. Even doubling the number to include species which may have become extinct since Noah's day would only require 240 boxcars—leaving 280 boxcars worth of space for Noah's family and food.

"But what about dinosaurs?" you ask. Due to the biblical account in Job 40 and 41, as well as the discovery of fossilized footprints of dinosaurs adjacent to footprints of men, I believe dinosaurs and men lived simultaneously. If that is true, dinosaurs would have to have been on the ark.

Wouldn't they take up the whole ark? Not if they were babies.

JANUARY 24

Thus did Noah; according to all that God commanded him, so did he.

Genesis 6:22

What if Noah hadn't done all that God commanded him to do? What if he had completed the sides of the ark, but hadn't put the roof on? If Noah had given it a pretty good shot, but then said, "Oh well, close enough," then we wouldn't be here. Noah did *all* that God commanded him. He finished the ark. As great as Noah's accomplishment was, however, God's Word speaks of a far greater accomplishment by another carpenter—the Carpenter from Galilee, Jesus Christ.

Noah held a hammer in his hand.

Jesus absorbed the blows of a hammer upon His hand.

Noah built with wood.

Jesus was pinned to wood.

Noah constructed a door.

Jesus said, "I am the door" (John 10:9).

Noah covered the ark with pitch.

Jesus covers us with His blood.

May God give us the ability to understand and remember that we are of all people most blessed. No matter what's happening in our lives today, we're most blessed because we're saved.

JANUARY 25

And Noah was six hundred years old when the flood of waters was upon the earth.

Genesis 7:6

Based on Genesis 5:32, Genesis 6:3, and Genesis 7:6, we know that Noah was 480 years old when he began building the ark, 500 years old when his first son was born, and 600 years old when the flood began. This means that when God instructed Noah to make a place for his sons in the ark, He did so twenty years before Noah's first son was even born!

Twenty years before his sons were born, God said to Noah, "As the leader of the family, as the patriarch of the clan, as the father, Noah, you are to expect your sons and their wives to be in the ark—the place of salvation—with you and your wife."

> Could this be why blood on the doorposts during Passover spared not only the one who applied it but the entire house (Exodus 12:13)?
>
> Could this be why the Holy Spirit fell on Cornelius *and his house* (Acts 10)?
>
> Could this be what Paul meant when he said to the Philippian jailer, "Believe in the Lord Jesus Christ, and thou shalt be saved, *and thy house*" (see Acts 16:31)?
>
> Could this be what the writer of Hebrews referred to when he wrote: "By faith Noah, being warned of God of things not seen as yet, moved with fear, prepared an ark to the *saving of his house*" (Hebrews 11:7, italics added)?

I believe so. Am I suggesting a new doctrine: Dad, get saved and everyone else is included? No, I'm not talking about a doctrine—but about a dynamic. By faith, Noah prepared a place for his family on the ark even before his kids were conceived. So too, open your heart, Dad, to the Lord Jesus Christ, and by faith say, "I am believing my sons and daughters and their spouses and our grandchildren will be on board the good ship salvation."

Certainly, each man, woman, and child must make his or her own decision regarding salvation—but they do so more easily when they see the reality of faith lived out before them, just as Noah's family observed him pounding away on the ark day after day.

JANUARY 26

And Noah went in, and his sons, and his wife, and his sons'
wives with him, into the ark, because of the waters of the
flood. Of clean beasts, and of beasts that are not clean, and
of fowls, and of every thing that creepeth upon the earth,
there went in two and two unto Noah into the ark, the male
and the female, as God had commanded Noah.

Genesis 7:7–9

"There went in two and two unto Noah." In other words, Noah didn't have to round up the animals. As He did in the garden of Eden when He brought the animals to be named by Adam (Genesis 2:19), God brought the animals to Noah. How could the wolf and the pig, the fox and the rabbit come together into the ark? Second Corinthians 5:17 declares that if any man be in Christ, he is a new creature. So too, somehow in preparation for the new creation which would take place after the flood, the Lord caused the animals to enter the ark by twos and sevens without antagonizing each other. This shouldn't be that hard to understand, however, since similar miracles occur daily in the animal world . . .

Sitting on ice floes, dressed in identical tuxedoes, millions of emperor penguins are mirror images of each other. And yet, after she lays her egg and dives into the Arctic waters for a three-month eating binge while the father incubates the egg, Mama Penguin is able to pick her husband out of the look-alike crowd upon her return.

From the North Pole, terns fly to Hawaii for the winter. But they leave their young behind because the young aren't ready to fly.

Several months later, having gained enough strength to make the journey, the young terns fly in formation on their own—without a single travel agent or map—straight to their parents in Hawaii.

I can't explain terns or penguins, but I do know this: God can do whatever He chooses to do with the animal kingdom, just as He can do whatever He chooses to do with you and me if we simply give Him permission to change our beastly behavior.

JANUARY 27

In the selfsame day entered Noah, and Shem, and Ham, and Japheth, the sons of Noah, and Noah's wife, and the three wives of his sons with them, into the ark.

Genesis 7:13

When it was time for Noah and his family to enter into the ark, Noah went first. He didn't say, "There's the ark, kids. Go ahead. I'll catch up." No, Noah led the way. He was an example, and that's the key. Mom and Dad, what you are personally will be communicated to your kids individually, and it will impact them very powerfully.

Think with me. When David was a young man, he killed a giant. The list of David's "mighty men" in 2 Samuel 23 includes those who also killed giants. This means that, even though most of David's men didn't see him kill Goliath, they became giant-killers simply because of their link to David.

Dad, you be a prayer warrior and watch how your kids will be prayer warriors too. You be a witness at work, and watch your kids follow your example at school.

Who we are very definitely affects what our kids become. Therefore, if I am a man who loves the Word, who is devoted to prayer, and who is committed to the kingdom, my kids will be impacted deeply. Your kids will either be spiritual wimps who get wiped out and are intimidated by the Enemy, or they will be giant-killers who overcome and are successful in the things of God.

Mom and Dad, lead the way in the things of God, and your family will follow.

JANUARY 28

They, and every beast after his kind, and all the cattle after their kind, and every creeping thing that creepeth upon the earth after his kind, and every fowl after his kind, every bird of every sort. And they went in unto Noah into the ark, two and two of all flesh, wherein is the breath of life. And they that went in, went in male and female of all flesh, as God had commanded him: and the LORD shut him in.

Genesis 7:14–16

Now the door is shut, and Noah and his family are sealed in the ark. There's no way for them to open the door to escape or to change their minds. This speaks to me because the One who said, "I am the door" (John 10:9) lets us know we are likewise secure in our salvation. "You are in My hand," Jesus declares, "and no man can pluck you out" (see John 10:28).

Do I believe in eternal security? Yes, I do. I am absolutely secure, because the Lord has "shut me in." You see, it wasn't Noah who shut the door of the ark, hoping he latched it right and that it would stay shut. *God* shut the door of the ark—just as He seals our salvation on our journey to heaven.

"Wait a minute," you say. "I thought there will be some who won't make it into heaven even though they once made a profession of faith."

That's also true. And I believe the story that most clearly explains this dichotomy deals with a ship like the ark and a storm like the flood . . .

On a ship bound for Rome, Paul advised the captain to winter in a port due to bad weather. Ignoring Paul's advice, they sailed on, right into a storm that grew so fierce that the sailors feared for their lives. "Be of good cheer," Paul said. "There stood by me this night the angel of God, whose

I am, and whom I serve, saying, Fear not, Paul, thou must be brought before Caesar: and lo, God hath given thee all them that sail with thee" (Acts 27:22–24).

When the storm continued, some of the sailors decided to bail out. But just as they were about to leave, Paul said, "Except these abide in the ship, you cannot be saved" (Acts 27:31). In other words, "If you choose to go overboard, you'll be wiped out. You are secure, safe, and sealed only as long as you stay on board."

Gang, no one can pluck us out of God's hand—but that doesn't mean we can't leave on our own. I'm shut in the good ship salvation because I have no intention of going overboard, of sailing off in another direction. Yes, I sin. But I am determined, and have decided that I will love the Lord all the days of my life. I pray you have too.

JANUARY 29

And the waters prevailed upon the earth an hundred and fifty days.

Genesis 7:24

Although Noah had heard the voice of the Lord telling him to go into the ark, there is no record of God speaking to Noah while he was on the ark. In fact, he would not hear the voice of God again for a total of 377 days.

Maybe that's your situation presently. Maybe 377 days ago, the Lord made Himself known to you through a very real revelation of some sort and you said, "Okay, Lord. This is awesome!" And you did what you knew you should do. But now, as you are cooped up and bouncing around on rough seas, you wonder why God isn't speaking.

Folks, all of us wish God would speak more frequently than He does. But unlike some people, God isn't a chatterbox. Why doesn't He speak with greater regularity on specific issues? It's not because He is callous. It's not because He doesn't care. It's because there's a bigger issue at stake: "But we glory in tribulations also: knowing that tribulation worketh patience; and patience, experience; and experience, hope: and hope maketh not ashamed" (Romans 5:3–5).

Bobbing around on the ark, sometimes there's nothing to do but learn patience. Then, when I finally settle down, when I finally quit squawking, God says, "Good. Now you're getting it." And it is then when I begin to gain some experience.

Looking back over the years, I have discovered that the things I've done, the words I've said, and the attitudes I've held of which I'm ashamed are all directly linked to a loss of hope. I suggest the same is true for you. What you are ashamed of today happened during the times you thought, "What's the use? Why even bother? Why try so hard to follow the Lord?" That's precisely why hard times—times when we feel shut up in an ark with no word from God—are vital to our development. They make us patient, which gives us experience, which leads to hope.

JANUARY 30

The fountains also of the deep and the windows of heaven were stopped, and the rain from heaven was restrained; and the waters returned from off the earth continually: and after the end of the hundred and fifty days the waters were abated. And the ark rested in the seventh month, on the seventeenth day of the month, upon the mountains of Ararat.

Genesis 8:2–4

What took place on the seventeenth day of the seventh month? The resurrection of Jesus Christ.

Our faith rests on the fact of the resurrection. If Christ is not risen, then we are, as Paul said, most miserable (1 Corinthians 15:19). We don't know what to say to the Taoist, to the Mormon, or to the Buddhist. If Christ did not rise from the dead, we do not know if we're headed in the right direction. If, on the other hand, He did rise from the dead, He did something no one else in history has every done. The resurrection is conclusive proof that we are on the right track. Our ship of faith rests on the mountain of the resurrection.

I visit Israel almost every year. Every time I go, I check the tomb. And guess what? It's empty.

"That *sounds* good," says the scoffer, "but maybe it's the wrong tomb."

Believe me, when the word started spreading that Christ had risen, the enemies of Jesus would have searched frantically to make sure that the empty tomb was not a case of mistaken identity. You see, the leaders of Judaism desperately desired to see Christianity wiped out. All they would have had to do would be to say to the Christians, "Here's the body of this One who claimed to be the exclusive way to heaven. Here's proof He couldn't validate His claim." But they didn't.

"Well, maybe the disciples stole His body to perpetuate the myth of a resurrected Jesus," claims the cynic.

Peter was crucified upside down. Thomas was speared in the back. James was sawn in half. Matthew's brains were beaten out with a club. With the exception of John—who was banished to the isle of Patmos after an unsuccessful attempt to boil him in oil—each of the disciples died a torturous death. To believe that eleven men would have allowed their wives and children to be martyred, and their own bodies slaughtered to propagate what they knew to be a lie requires an incredible leap of faith.

"It was the Romans who took the body," declares the doubter.

Christianity was such a threat to the Roman Empire that they launched ten waves of persecution in which sixty million Christians were killed. Indeed, Christianity would eventually cause the Empire to split in two—East and West—and ultimately fall. Certainly the Romans didn't have the body, for producing it would have saved their Empire.

"No one stole the body because Jesus didn't really die," muses the mocker. "One of the disciples put some drugs in the vinegar that was lifted up to Jesus as He hung on the cross, which caused Him to go into a coma. After the cool air of the tomb revived Him, it appeared as though He had resurrected."

The scourging Jesus suffered before His crucifixion was in itself enough to kill a man. Jesus went on, however, to endure spikes through His hands and feet and a spear thrust into His side. Then He was put in a tomb for three days without food, water, or medical attention. To suggest He then stood up, single-handedly rolled away a two-ton stone, and took on the Roman soldiers guarding His tomb requires infinitely more faith than I could possibly muster.

He who studies the resurrection honestly and intellectually must rest finally on the mountain of evidence that says, "He is risen. He is risen, indeed!"

JANUARY 31

And the waters decreased continually until the tenth month: in the tenth month, on the first day of the month, were the tops of the mountains seen.

Genesis 8:5

The act of the resurrection impacts my entire understanding of spirituality and Christianity. Paul put it this way: "I am crucified with Christ: nevertheless I live; yet not I, but Christ liveth in me: and the life which I now live in the flesh I live by the faith of the Son of God, who loved me, and gave himself for me" (Galatians 2:20).

The resurrection means that Christ lives *in* you. It's not imitation—trying to be a "good little Christian boy or girl." It's impartation . . .

As a high school discus thrower, I constantly watched a film loop of the world record throw of four-time Olympian Al Oerter. Over and over, I'd watch him drive his hip, thrust his shoulder, cock his arm, steady his grip, and make the toss. Then I'd go out to the rink and I'd try to do it all, just like Al. But although I knew exactly what to do, did I ever do it like he did? I didn't even come close.

And that's the problem with religion and philosophy. They tell you what to do, but fail to give you the power to do it. Not so with Christianity. If Al

Oerter could have squeezed into my body and thrown the discus through me, I could have set world records just like he did. So too, because Jesus is risen, His Spirit lives *in* me. It's not a matter of me trying to figure out what to do, reading certain books, going to certain seminars, or listening to certain tapes. It's a matter of Him living in me, giving me the power to do what the Word tells me to do.

FEBRUARY 1

And it came to pass at the end of forty days, that Noah opened the window of the ark which he had made.

Genesis 8:6

In the seventh month, on the seventeenth day of the month, on a mountain named Ararat, the ark came to rest. The seventh month would become the first month in the Hebrew religious calendar to mark when the Jews were delivered from their Egyptian bondage (Exodus 12:1–5). And it was on the fourteenth day of the first month—Passover—that Jesus Christ, the Lamb of God, was nailed to a cross.

The ark rested on the seventeenth day—three days after Passover. What took place three days after Jesus was crucified? He rose again. "Because I live, you shall live also," declared Jesus. "It's a pact I'm making with you." If Christ had not risen, we would have no hope of eternal life ourselves. But because He lives, we shall rise as well.

Jesus is risen, and He is returning. And while that gives me great peace, it also stirs me. You see, Peter tells us that when the Chief Shepherd shall appear, we will receive a crown of glory (1 Peter 5:4). The events in the Middle East indicate to me that Jesus' coming is very near. And even if it's not as soon as I think it's going to be, life goes by oh, so rapidly. Very soon I'm going to face Jesus personally. I will stand before the Chief Shepherd to give an account for what I did with all that He so graciously gave me. So will you.

God has given you money, talent, time, ability, freedom, health, opportunity, and calling. He's given you vision, direction, and instruction. And, because He lives within you, He's given you power. One day, you will give an account of what you did with the graces and gifts He has given you.

"I hear what you're saying," you might be thinking, "but I'm still young. As soon as I get married, I'll serve Jesus."

So you get married, and then not too much later, you hear yourself saying, "We're really serious about serving Jesus. But right now, we've got a home to build and diapers to change. When our kids are in elementary school, then we'll get busy and serve the Lord."

But with elementary school comes Cub Scouts, piano lessons, and Little League. And church gets shoved down further because, after all, who's going to cheer junior on if you're not there? So he misses Sunday school because he's learning to hit a curve ball!

Then you say, "As soon as our kids are out of the house, we're really going to get serious about serving God."

But then a funny thing happens. I have discovered that right about the time the kids leave is the time people start to remodel their houses.

Gang, there will never be a day easier than this one for you to say, "I will seek first the kingdom."

FEBRUARY 2

And he sent forth a raven, which went forth to and fro, until the waters were dried up from off the earth. Also he sent forth a dove from him, to see if the waters were abated from off the face of the ground; but the dove found no rest for the sole of her foot, and she returned unto him into the ark, for the waters were on the face of the whole earth: then he put forth his hand, and took her, and pulled her in unto him into the ark.

Genesis 8:7–9

Most of us need pictures and stories to understand theology. I know I do. The text before us provides just such a picture, for it pointedly and powerfully portrays what it means to be empowered by the Spirit ...

The first animal to leave the ark was a raven—a black bird that goes "to and fro" eating the carcasses of dead animals.

When Satan came before the Lord one day in heaven, the Lord said, "Where have you been?"

"I've been going to and fro," said Satan, cruising around just like the raven (see Job 1:6–7).

Peter tells us Satan is always on the lookout for those whom he may devour (1 Peter 5:8). But the good news is that, as the raven circled, Noah released a dove, which throughout Scripture, speaks of the Holy Spirit.

Why?

The dove is the purest of all birds, for not only is it white in color, but it secretes more dirt-repelling oil on its feathers than any other flying bird. The dove is also sensitive because it is one of the few animals that mates for life. Finally, the dove is a symbol of peace because, unlike vultures or buzzards, doves vacate places of frenzy or fighting.

As Noah saw the dove circling overhead, he could have said, "If the dove wants to land on me, he can. I'm open." But that's not what he did. Noah extended his hand, grabbed the dove, and brought it in.

So often, with regard to the power and presence of the Spirit, people say, "If the Holy Spirit wants to bless me and empower me, I'm open." But that kind of passivity will never bring the potency of the Spirit in the greatest possible degree. If you want to be empowered by the Spirit, you cannot be passive about the work of the Spirit any more than you were passive about the work of salvation.

This is where so many people err. You see, God is looking for those who will partner with Him, and not just be passive about Him. Noah didn't simply fold his arms and watch. He stretched forth his hand and reached.

FEBRUARY 3

And Noah builded an altar unto the Lord; and took of every clean beast, and of every clean fowl, and offered burnt offerings on the altar.

Genesis 8:20

"Noah, what are you doing?" the world would say. "There's a whole planet to repopulate, and you're burning up limited, valuable resources. It's a waste, Noah. Be practical."

Whenever I find myself thinking this, I realize I'm in very bad company.

> A woman poured an alabaster box full of perfume upon Jesus. "Wait a minute," said Judas. "That's a waste of resources. The poor could be helped with that money."
>
> "What she has done, she has done unto Me," said Jesus (see Matthew 26:12).

And in this I begin to understand that God values worship more than work.

"Thou shalt worship the Lord thy God, and him only shalt thou serve," declared Jesus (Matthew 4:10). Did you notice the order? Worship comes first, service second. You might not be a missionary to Africa, an evangelist in a big stadium, or a singer on the radio, but every person can do that which most blesses God, for the highest priority of ministry is not work, but worship.

Worship is the highest, most precious ministry you will ever perform.

Worship will bless you the most, and honor God in the greatest way.

Worship will "altar" your life—it will change who you are.

FEBRUARY 4

> *And the LORD smelled a sweet savour; and the LORD said in his heart, I will not again curse the ground any more for man's sake; for the imagination of man's heart is evil from his youth.*
>
> Genesis 8:21

Even though the external flood couldn't deal with the internal depravity of man, the fragrance of Noah's sacrifice—a sweet-smelling savor unto the

Lord—overpowered the stench of sin. A burnt offering was made, and that made all the difference.

Every Old Testament sacrifice points to Jesus Christ—the ultimate sacrifice, the Lamb of God slaughtered on the cross for the sin of the world. It's the fragrance of the work of Christ that overrides the stench of my depravity. The flood didn't clean up the culture. The flood didn't solve the problem. No, it was the sacrifice that caused God to say, "Neither will I again smite every living thing" (Genesis 8:21).

You might feel terrible. You might feel like you've blown it badly. But even now you can worship God, and He will smell a sweet savor. He knows our imaginations are evil continually, yet He still finds sacrifice sweet. God doesn't command you to worship Him today, but some of you will. He won't command you to worship Him tomorrow, but some of you will. And in so doing, you'll bless Him.

FEBRUARY 5

And God blessed Noah and his sons, and said unto them, Be fruitful, and multiply, and replenish the earth. And the fear of you and the dread of you shall be upon every beast of the earth, and upon every fowl of the air, upon all that moveth upon the earth, and upon all the fishes of the sea; into your hand are they delivered.

Genesis 9:1–2

God blessed Noah, for in building an altar, Noah had blessed God. So too, if you choose to bless the Lord by sacrificing to Him, like Noah, you will be blessed, for God will be a debtor to no man. You will always get back more than you give.

Noah, here, is essentially told to start over. Even as God had initially told Adam and Eve to be fruitful and multiply, Noah and his sons and their wives are hearing the same command. This time, however, earth is not paradise, but neither is it perdition. Due to man's perpetual propensity toward sin, our planet is not what it was in Adam's day, but neither is it as bad as it could have been.

I say this to remind you that although you may not think your life is going great, it's going a whole lot better than you deserve. We deserve to be frying in hell. God is so good to us. Anything we have, everything we enjoy is due to His mercy and kindness. We're headed for heaven, where all things are right and perfect. Yet even in the meantime, we have so much today for which to be thankful.

FEBRUARY 6

And Noah began to be an husbandman, and he planted a vineyard: and he drank of the wine, and was drunken; and he was uncovered within his tent.

Genesis 9:20–21

How could this be? After all, Noah was the one who preached for one hundred years to the whole world. Noah was the one who built the ark, and who didn't complain when he was sealed for 377 days within a floating zoo. Noah was the one who built an altar, who blessed God, who found grace in the eyes of the Lord.

When he was going through challenging times, difficult days, and thundering storms, Noah walked with God. But when things became normal, he became vulnerable. And the same is true with us. It's when everything is going well, when our vines are growing, when our jobs are going fine, when life is on "automatic pilot" that we are in danger. No longer are we on guard, no longer are we dependent upon the Lord or desperately crying out to Him.

It's when things are going well that we must be especially careful. When the storms are brewing and when trials are coming, we have a tendency to pray and seek the Lord. But when things are on "automatic pilot," we, like Noah, often fall into trouble.

FEBRUARY 7

And Ham, the father of Canaan, saw the nakedness of his father, and told his two brethren without. And Shem and Japheth took a garment, and laid it upon both their shoulders, and went backward, and covered the nakedness of their father; and their faces were backward, and they saw not their father's nakedness.

Genesis 9:22–23

Ham saw his father's nakedness. That's always the way it is, for whether it's regarding our birth family or our church family, those closest to us are those who will see our weaknesses. Why Ham talked about his father's nakedness, I do not know, just as I don't know why we are so eager to talk about one another's weaknesses. But this I do know: Shem and Japheth wouldn't look at their father's nakedness themselves. Why did they stretch a garment between them? Because they didn't want anyone outside the tent to look in and see their dad's nakedness. They didn't want those outside of the tent to be distracted by their father's condition.

Folks, people are looking for reasons not to believe our message of hope and salvation. And hearing us talk about each other's weaknesses gives them reason not to come in and join us.

But not only did Shem and Japheth keep others from viewing their father's nakedness, they did not look upon it themselves.

Why?

Because even though I know someone may be forgiven, and even though I know sin is common to everyone, looking at someone's sin or listening to reports of someone's iniquity taints the way I view him in the future. You see, if you come home from work upset with your boss and you start complaining and exposing his mistakes and weaknesses to your wife, although you end up feeling much better, your wife stores that information away. And the next time she sees your boss, there are daggers in her eyes, and you wonder why she no longer wants to go to the company picnic. So too, if I listen to reports of the sin or iniquity of another, it will taint the way I view that person. Malicious exposure is damaging, destructive, and divisive.

Shouldn't we talk about problems? If it's *your* problem, yes. But if it's someone else's problem, someone else's sin, someone else's weakness, nakedness, or vulnerability, follow Shem and Japheth's example: walk in backwards and conceal it from others. Not only will this protect the one who sins, but it will protect you as well, for the person who talks to you about someone else will invariably also talk to someone else about you.

How do I know this?

Because Paul warns, "Take heed that you do not bite and devour one another because you will be consumed one of another. On the other hand," Paul continues, "the entire law is fulfilled in the one word: love" (see Galatians 5:14–15).

FEBRUARY 8

And Noah awoke from his wine, and knew what his younger son had done unto him. And he said, Cursed be Canaan; a servant of servants shall he be unto his brethren.

Genesis 9:24–25

When Noah awoke from his drunken state, he knew what Ham had done and cursed Ham's son. No doubt Ham thought, "I've got big shoulders. I can handle the repercussions of my sin." Unbeknownst to him, however, was the fact that the repercussions didn't fall on him. They fell upon his son. How bad were the repercussions? The Canaanites were the worst culture in the history of the world. Totally immoral and completely perverted, they were eventually annihilated.

Dad and Mom, if we sin, we must not think we alone will pay the price. Sin doesn't work that way. The consequences will often come in ways that will break your heart as they relate to your family. The children of parents who expose the weaknesses of bosses and neighbors, of sisters and brothers; the children of parents who are dour and sour and critical grow up unmotivated to go to church, bitter about the things of God, and uninterested in the Bible.

So what are we to do?

We are to say, "I've been forgiven of so much that I will not talk about the weakness of my boss, my neighbor, my pastor, the person sitting next to me, my friends, or my enemies. I will not speak or listen to negativity." Every one of us will fail at some point or another. But if you choose today to be like Shem and Japheth—to cover the nakedness of others—you will likewise be covered when you fail.

FEBRUARY 9

And the whole earth was of one language, and of one speech. And it came to pass, as they journeyed from the east, that they found a plain in the land of Shinar; and they dwelt there. And they said one to another, Go to, let us make brick, and burn them throughly. And they had brick for stone, and slime had they for morter.

Genesis 11:1–3

Man builds with brick. But because brick is man-made, it cracks and chips easily. That's why God uses stone.

The massive stones used for the temple were cut to size in a rock quarry a mile away from the temple site so that when the stones arrived at the building site, the Bible says the sound of neither hammer nor chisel was heard (1 Kings 6:7). How close did the stones fit? So close that not even a knife could fit between them. There was no need for cement or mortar, for the stones fit perfectly.

God still uses stones to build His temple. We are living stones being fit together for a spiritual house (1 Peter 2:5). This means the world is the rock quarry wherein the chipping takes place so that when we get to the true temple in heaven, there will not be the sound of a hammer or chisel heard.

Therefore, we should not be surprised when the living stone we're sitting next to or married to rubs us the wrong way. It's all part of God's plan to knock off our rough edges so that when we get to heaven, we'll fit together perfectly.

FEBRUARY 10

So the Lord *scattered them abroad from thence upon the face of all the earth: and they left off to build the city.*

Genesis 11:8

No matter how hard they tried, no matter how sincere their attempts might have been, people could no longer communicate. So they separated into language groups and began to form their own cultures. The good news, however, is that the necessary curse of Genesis 11 was reversed in Acts 2 when one hundred twenty believers in an upper room began to praise God in languages they had never learned, causing the people from Mesopotamia, Cappadocia, Egypt, Arabia, Galatia, and from all parts of the world on the streets below to hear the gospel in their own language.

And now I begin to understand that the only way for people to truly communicate cross-culturally is to be focused on the cross of Christ and to be empowered by His Spirit, for apart from Christ, all of our efforts at unity are nothing more than slime and chipped brick. Without Christ, we can try to build a foundation of unity; we can have all kinds of rallies and seminars and marches, but there will be no unity apart from the power and person of the Holy Spirit coming upon us. It is only in Christ that there is neither male nor female, bond nor free, Jew nor Gentile (Galatians 3:28). It is only in Jesus that division is obliterated.

FEBRUARY 11

And I will make of thee a great nation, and I will bless thee,
and make thy name great; and thou shalt be a blessing: And
I will bless them that bless thee, and curse him that curseth
thee: and in thee shall all families of the earth be blessed.

Genesis 12:2–3

God said to Abram, "I'm going to give you a name, make you a nation, and protect you. Those who bless you will be blessed; those who curse you will be cursed." In other words, you're going to have primacy, identity, and security.

I find this intriguing because those were the three things man had wanted so desperately at Babel (Genesis 11:4). "Let us build a tower," said man, "whose top may reach unto heaven (primacy); and let us make us a name (identity), lest we be scattered abroad upon the face of the whole earth" (security).

The same is still true. We want something meaningful to do in life—primacy. Or we want to discover who we are—identity. Or we need security relationally or financially. Jesus said, "If you seek first the kingdom, *all* these things will be added to you" (see Matthew 6:33).

FEBRUARY 12

So Abram departed, as the LORD had spoken unto him; and
Lot went with him: and Abram was seventy and five years
old when he departed out of Haran.

Genesis 12:4

Abram was fifty years old when he initially heard God's call. But he didn't leave Haran until he was seventy-five. Obviously, Abram faltered in his obedience. But guess what? God didn't give up on Abram. Rather He waited *for* Abram.

"Lord, why aren't You directing me?" we cry.

"I already did," He answers. "Twenty-five years ago, I told you what to do. And I won't give you more to do until you do what I've already told you."

Many people are confused about God's will because, like Abram, they've delayed doing what He has already asked of them. It might concern intercessory prayer, witnessing, or Bible study. I encourage people to keep journals—to write down things God lays upon their hearts because so often we ask, "What's going on?" when, if we would just look back at what God had told us previously, we could see the problem.

God wasn't mad at Abram—and He's not mad at you. When your kids take their first steps, you don't yell at them when they fall down. You celebrate their steps rather than berate their stumbling. God is the same way. He knows this is how we learn to walk by faith. Take hope, stumbling saint, Abram was in a twenty-five-year slump, and God didn't give up on him. God gives us a second chance, and a third, and a ninety-ninth. His mercy is new every morning. His grace is limitless.

FEBRUARY 13

And the Lord *appeared unto Abram, and said, Unto thy seed will I give this land: and there builded he an altar unto the* Lord, *who appeared unto him. And he removed from thence unto a mountain on the east of Bethel, and pitched his tent, having Bethel on the west, and Hai on the east: and there he builded an altar unto the* Lord, *and called upon the name of the* Lord.

Genesis 12:7–8

When the astronauts went to the moon, they planted a flag. So too, upon entering the Promised Land, Abram leaves a mark. As we will see, wherever Abram goes he leaves two marks: he builds an altar, which shows he's a worshiper; and he pitches a tent, which shows he's a pilgrim. Abram never builds a house. Why? Because "he looked for a city which hath foundations, whose builder and maker is God" (Hebrews 11:10). He realized that what he really craved was heaven.

Abram—the father of faith, the friend of God—shows us the real way to live. Wherever you go, build the altar of worship. It will alter who you are, how you feel, and the way you think. Wherever you go, go with a "tent" mentality. We may think we're looking for a ranch in the country or a house on the lake, a ski boat or a ski cabin, a dream car or a dream date. But what we're really craving is heaven. No other city has foundations. Everything else is shaky and wobbly.

Abram pitched his tent with Bethel on the west and Hai on the east. *Bethel* means "house of God." *Hai* means "heap" or "dump." Therefore, Abram had the house of God ahead of him and a dump behind him. That's basically where you and I live. With heaven before us, and the world behind us, we're camped out in the middle, waiting for the culmination.

FEBRUARY 14

And there was a famine in the land: and Abram went down into Egypt to sojourn there; for the famine was grievous in the land. And it came to pass, when he was come near to enter into Egypt, that he said unto Sarai his wife, Behold now, I know that thou art a fair woman to look upon: Therefore it shall come to pass, when the Egyptians shall see thee, that they shall say, This is his wife: and they will kill me, but they will save thee alive.

Genesis 12:10–12

Throughout Scripture, whenever people go to Egypt, they always go *"down to Egypt"* because Egypt is a type or symbol of the world. Abram was doing well, but now he falls again because he didn't remain in the land God showed him. A famine made him think he had to take matters into his own hands—always a dangerous thing to do.

Here's the father of faith faltering in the arena of faith because man always struggles and stumbles in his area of strength . . .

Righteous Noah fell when he got drunk in his tent (Genesis 9:21).

Moses, the meekest man on the face of the earth, struck his rod against a rock and said, "You rebels, must we fetch water for you?" (see Numbers 20:10).

Unsheathing his sword, Peter was ready to take on a whole army in order to defend Jesus in Gethsemane. Yet, only hours later, he faltered when a young girl asked him, "Aren't you one of His?" (see Mark 14:67).

The area in which you think you're strongest is the area you'll be most vulnerable because you'll depend on your own strength. At the point you say, "That's not a problem for me; I'll never fall there," watch out because that's the very area in which you'll experience difficulty. Where you know you're weak, you rely on God. So consider yourself weak in all areas, and instead, rely solely on His strength.

FEBRUARY 15

And Abram went up out of Egypt, he, and his wife, and all that he had, and Lot with him, into the south. And Abram was very rich in cattle, in silver, and in gold. And he went on his journeys from the south even to Bethel, unto the place where his tent had been at the beginning, between Bethel and Hai; unto the place of the altar, which he had made there at the first: and there Abram called on the name of the LORD.

Genesis 13:1–4

There is no record of Abram pitching a tent or building an altar in Egypt. Here, however, we see him return to the place where he had pitched his tent; we see him going to the altar once more.

When you find yourself in Egypt, when you know things aren't the way they're supposed to be, what do you do? To the church of Ephesus—a group of believers who had strayed from their passion for Him—Jesus said, "Remember therefore from whence thou art fallen, and repent, and do the first works . . ." (Revelation 2:5).

Maybe your relationship with the Lord was great five years ago. Maybe things were really happening spiritually four months ago. Jesus' word to you is the same as it was to the church of Ephesus. Remember, repent, and repeat: go back and do what you used to do. Perhaps you were enjoying a season of morning devotions. Maybe you were attending mid-week worship services. Maybe you were memorizing Scripture or aggressively sharing your faith. What were you doing when you were on fire, when things were really cooking? Do it again.

FEBRUARY 16

And there was a strife between the herdmen of Abram's cattle and the herdmen of Lot's cattle: and the Canaanite and the Perizzite dwelled then in the land. And Abram said unto Lot, Let there be no strife, I pray thee, between me and thee, and between my herdmen and thy herdmen; for we be brethren.

Genesis 13:7–8

Notice how Abram emerged from Egypt a wiser man, for here he shows *directness.* That is, he goes to Lot and deals with the issue directly. "There's strife between our herdsmen," he says, "and the heathen are watching us fighting. It ought not be." Such is often the case today. Christians fight and bicker while the world watches and wonders. It ought not be.

Notice also Abram's *deference*. He doesn't place blame on Lot. He says, "Let there be no strife between *me* and thee, between *my* herdsmen and thy herdsmen." While he will assume the secondary position when it comes to choosing the land, Abram assumes the primary position when it comes to shouldering responsibility for the problem.

Notice finally Abram's *discernment* when he says, "We be brethren." In other words, "There is more that unites us than divides us. Sure, there are some complications with the cattle and some hassles with the herdsmen, but we're brothers."

How we need to realize the truth of this within the Christian community, in our country, and around the world. Because we all embrace the person and work of our Lord Jesus, there is more that unites us than could possibly divide us. If there's a "Lot" in your life who is causing a lot of problems, follow Abram's example, and see how peace will follow you.

FEBRUARY 17

And Lot lifted up his eyes, and beheld all the plain of Jordan, that it was well watered every where, before the LORD destroyed Sodom and Gomorrah, even as the garden of the LORD, like the land of Egypt, as thou comest unto Zoar. Then Lot chose him all the plain of Jordan; and Lot journeyed east: and they separated themselves the one from the other. Abram dwelled in the land of Canaan, and Lot dwelled in the cities of the plain, and pitched his tent toward Sodom. But the men of Sodom were wicked and sinners before the LORD exceedingly.

Genesis 13:10–13

Contrast the wisdom of Abram with the worldliness of Lot. First, Lot was weak in devotion, for we never read of him building an altar. Like Lot, you may possess a "tent mentality," knowing you're headed for heaven. You may even have a ministry, with herds to tend. But if you're not an altar builder, you'll be weak in devotion, which will lead to real problems.

Second, Lot was worldly in desires. He lifted up his eyes, but not high enough. He didn't lift his eyes to heaven and say, "Lord, show me the best place for me and my family." Instead, he lifted up his eyes only high enough to check out the financial possibilities and the greenest pastures. Lot saw a good place to raise cattle, but failed to see that it would be a lousy place to raise kids because he fixed his gaze short of heaven.

Third, Lot was wrong in decision, as seen in the series of wrong decisions he made based on his own reasoning . . .

In verse 10, he looked toward Sodom.

In verse 12, he pitched his tent toward Sodom.

In chapter 19, he became a leader in Sodom.

Lot left Ur, but he became entrenched in Sodom. A lot of people are like that. They say yes to heaven, but they never say no to the world. And, like Lot, they end up in a terrible predicament.

FEBRUARY 18

And he blessed him, and said, Blessed be Abram of the most high God, possessor of heaven and earth: . . . And he gave him tithes of all.

Genesis 14:19–20

From cover to cover, the Bible calls us to set our hearts on things above and not on things of this world (Colossians 3:2). Jesus put it this way: "Seek ye first the kingdom of God, and his righteousness, and all these things shall be added unto you" (Matthew 6:33).

How do we practically seek first the kingdom and set our hearts on heaven? Jesus told us when He said, "Where your treasure is, there will your heart be also" (Matthew 6:21). If your treasure is on earth, that's where your heart will be. So God in His wisdom, kindness, and love for you and me says, "Lay up your treasure in heaven where neither moth nor rust destroys, where thieves don't break in and steal. Put your treasure in heaven because, in so doing, your heart will follow" (see Matthew 6:19–21).

If your treasure is in your house, your retirement account, or your Mercedes, that's where your heart will be. Knowing this, the Lord demands that the first tenth of whatever we make on any given day or in any given week be given to Him in order that our hearts will be set on our heavenly destination.

Jesus talked more about money than He did about heaven. He talked more about money than He did about hell. In fact, He talked more about money than He did about heaven and hell combined. Why? Because He knows it's a huge issue for you and me, and that it speaks of larger principles. One of the things Jesus said about money was this: "And I say unto you, Make to yourselves friends of the mammon [money] of unrighteousness; that, when ye fail, they may receive you into everlasting habitations" (Luke 16:9).

In other words, the money you have "made friends of," that you have used rightly, will greet you when you die. Now, the old adage is true: You can't take it with you. But you *can* send it ahead. And what you send ahead—through the tithe that God demands, and through the offering which He deserves—will meet you there.

"But I don't make much money, so there won't be much to greet me," you say. Consider this: When Jesus saw a widow giving two mites—less than a penny—He told His disciples that she had given more than they who, out of their abundance, had given much, because she gave all that she had (Mark 12:41–44). Jesus acknowledged just two mites, given by a woman who will receive a "mite-y" big welcome in heaven!

FEBRUARY 19

And blessed be the most high God, which hath delivered thine enemies into thy hand. And he gave him tithes of all.

Genesis 14:20

In Malachi, we see three promises God makes to those who tithe . . .

> Bring ye all the tithes into the storehouse, that there may be meat in mine house, and prove me now herewith, saith the LORD of hosts, if I will not open you the windows of heaven, and pour you out a blessing, that there shall not be room enough to receive it.
>
> Malachi 3:10

"I will reward your faith." Immediately after lending Jesus his fishing boat for use as a floating podium to teach the multitude on the shore, Peter caught so many fish that his net broke (Luke 5:2–7). The little boy who gave his lunch to Jesus was himself filled, along with the rest of the five thousand (John 6:9–12). So too, if you've ever given anything to God, you know from experience that it's impossible to out-give Him.

> And I will rebuke the devourer for your sakes, and he shall not destroy the fruits of your ground; neither shall your vine cast her fruit before the time in the field, saith the LORD of hosts.
>
> Malachi 3:11

"I will rebuke your foe." Some people are perpetually plagued with problems. The money they make goes through their pockets; the labor of their hands never comes to fruition. It is especially to them that God says, "If you tithe, I will rebuke the world's hold on you, which devours your happiness and eats away at your possessions."

> And all nations shall call you blessed: for ye shall be a delightsome land, saith the LORD of hosts.
>
> Malachi 3:12

"I will renew your fruit. Put your trust in Me, and I will make you a fruitful land," declares the Lord. He who tithes will experience renewal and revival.

I would rather teach on any other subject. But the Bible has much to say about tithing because it shows where a person's heart is. Therefore, I would be shirking my responsibility to declare to you "all the counsel of God" (Acts 20:27) if I were to ignore it. The tithe is the Lord's. It's not yours. Whether it's ten cents or ten thousand dollars, the first tenth is the Lord's and is to be brought into the storehouse—the place where the Word is proclaimed and worship ascends.

Heaven is right around the bend, gang. And I don't want a single one of us to regret the stuff we've accumulated with God's tithe or the ways we've indulged ourselves with His offerings.

Maybe you have been robbing God (Malachi 3:8). Maybe you have been wasting your time and treasure and talents. The good news is: It's not too late! Today you can say, "As I race toward heaven, I understand the wisdom of God's way, the rightness of His Word. Therefore, I am going to give Him the tithe. And I am going to see, even as He asked me, what He will do in blessing, in rebuking, and in renewing."

Precious people, you'll be blessed all of your days if you go God's way. Begin today, then watch and see what He will do.

FEBRUARY 20

The word of the LORD came unto Abram in a vision, saying, Fear not, Abram.

Genesis 15:1

That God said, "Fear not" to Abram indicates Abram was fearful. This is not surprising. After his spiritual victory in resisting the material temptation of the riches offered him by the king of Sodom, as well as his military victory in rescuing Lot, Abram hit an emotional slump. This happens. Challenge often follows victory. Think of Jesus. When He was baptized in the Jordan, He heard a voice from heaven, saying, "This is my beloved Son, in whom I am well pleased." Then, the Holy Spirit came upon Him and empowered Him for ministry (Matthew 3:16–17). It was a great day. But immediately following this, He was driven into the wilderness to be tempted of Satan, to wrestle against the Enemy for forty days (Matthew 4). Therefore, don't be surprised if after you experience victory spiritually, like Abram you face a time of discouragement emotionally.

"Fear not." This is the first time this glorious command appears in Scripture. But it is certainly not the last . . .

"Fear not," the angel said to a bunch of frightened shepherds (Luke 2:10).

"Fear not," Jesus said to a crew of seasick disciples (see Mark 4:40).

"Fear not," the angel said to a disheartened Paul (Acts 27:24).

"Fear not, little flock," Jesus says to us (Luke 12:32).

FEBRUARY 21

I am thy shield, and thy exceeding great reward.

Genesis 15:1

Perhaps it suddenly hit Abram that he and his rag-tag army of servants had made enemies of four powerful kings with four huge armies. "*I* am your shield," God told him. "Yes, you came home empty-handed materially, but *I* am your reward."

In this, I am reminded that what every person ultimately desires is not something *from* the Lord, but simply more *of* the Lord.

"I'm not going to show you the way," Jesus declared, "I *am* the Way" (see John 14:6).

"I'm not going to give you bread; I *am* the Bread" (see John 6:35).

"I'm not going to share with you truth; I *am* the truth" (see John 14:6).

Those who come to the Lord not looking for something *from* Him, but simply to cling *to* Him, find all kinds of blessings in all sorts of areas they never expected. Are you disappointed with God because you asked Him for something you have yet to receive? Maybe it's because you're looking for some thing. God loves you too much to toss a boxed little package your way. The issue is bigger; and He wants you to discover today that *He* will satisfy your need, *He* will be your reward.

FEBRUARY 22

And he brought him forth abroad, and said, Look now toward heaven, and tell the stars, if thou be able to number them: and he said unto him, So shall thy seed be.

Genesis 15:5

With his naked eye, Abram would have been able to see at most twelve hundred stars. "I'm going to have a family of *twelve hundred?*" Abram must have thought. But wait. God is able to do exceeding abundantly above all that we can ask or think (Ephesians 3:20). Abram could see approximately twelve hundred stars. But how many stars are there? Far beyond anything Abram could even begin to ask for or imagine in his wildest dreams.

How many stars are there? Scientists tell us that there are as many stars in the sky as there are grains of sand on the seashores of the world. This should not surprise the student of Scripture, for God made the same correlation when He told Abram that his family would number as the stars and as the sand on the shores (Genesis 22:17).

According to the psalmist, the only other thing as innumerable as the grains of sand are the thoughts of God toward us (Psalm 139:17–18). This fascinates me because the Pentium computer chips made of silicon (sand) perform 1 trillion calculations per second. Clear back in antiquity, God measured His thoughts with the substance that would come to epitomize our own computer age.

FEBRUARY 23

And he said unto him, I am the Lord *that brought thee out of Ur of the Chaldees, to give thee this land to inherit it. And he said, Lord GOD, whereby shall I know that I shall inherit it? And he said unto him, Take me an heifer of three years old, and a she goat of three years old, and a ram of three years old, and a turtledove, and a young pigeon. And he took unto him all these, and divided them in the midst, and laid each piece one against another: but the birds divided he not.*

Genesis 15:7–10

Like the one who said, "Lord, I believe; help thou my unbelief" (Mark 9:24), Abram says, "I believe, but how will I know the land is mine?"

I would think that at this point, the Lord would tire of Abram. I mean, God had told him He would be his reward, only to have Abram ask what He would give him. The Lord promised Abram a grand family and a glorious land, only to have Abram ask for proof.

In answer to Abram's request for proof that God would give him an inheritance, God instructs Abram to draw up the equivalent of a modern-day contract. You see, in Abram's day, when two people entered into a legal agreement, they did so by splitting an animal in two, standing in the midst of the carcass, and clasping each other's wrist to show that they were deadly serious about keeping their end of the bargain.

If I were God, I'd say, "So long, Abram." But that's not what our Father does, and I'm oh, so glad. If God continues to be patient with the struggles and doubts of Abram, one of the giants of the faith who should know better, I know He'll be patient with me.

FEBRUARY 24

And when the fowls came down upon the carcases, Abram drove them away. And when the sun was going down, a deep sleep fell upon Abram; and, lo, an horror of great darkness fell upon him. And he said unto Abram, Know of a surety that thy seed shall be a stranger in a land that is not theirs, and shall serve them; and they shall afflict them four hundred years; and also that nation, whom they shall serve, will I judge: and afterward shall they come out with great substance. And thou shalt go to thy fathers in peace; thou shalt be buried in a good old age. But in the fourth generation they shall come hither again: for the iniquity of the Amorites is not yet full.

Genesis 15:11–16

Throughout Scripture, birds almost always symbolize evil. The picture here is that while Abram waited for God to meet him, he did his best to keep evil at bay, shooing away the birds of doubt and unbelief. Exhausted by his own efforts, Abram fell asleep. As he slept, God told Abram that, although He would indeed give Abram's descendants a grand and glorious land, they would first spend four hundred years as slaves in a foreign land, which, of course, was Egypt.

"The Amorites"—a generic term for all of the people living in the land of Canaan—refers to a culture so diseased, defiled, and depraved that it was doomed. Nonetheless, God gave them four hundred years—the period in which the Jews were held captive in Egypt—to repent.

While it may be popular to construct the false image of an angry Old Testament God who needed Jesus to come and calm Him down, nothing could be further from the truth. God waited four hundred years for the Amorites to turn to Him. It would take four centuries before their iniquity demanded that He order their extermination at the hand of Joshua.

The patience of God is incomprehensible. Because God is love, no wonder that the first attribute in Paul's classic definition of love is patience (1 Corinthians 13:4). God was patient with Abram. He was patient with the Canaanites. And He will be patient with you. If you really grasp this, rather than taking advantage of it, His patience will make you long to please Him all the more.

FEBRUARY 25

And it came to pass, that, when the sun went down, and it was dark, behold a smoking furnace, and a burning lamp that passed between those pieces.

Genesis 15:17

When Abram awoke, he saw that the meat on either side of him was barbecued. God had been there, not meeting Abram halfway as was the custom, but walking the entire length alone.

This is still the way of God. Oh, we try and chase away the birds of evil which threaten our families and our country. We hold rallies and sign pledges; we make vows and make promises. But, because "in our flesh dwells no good thing" (see Romans 7:18), like Abram, we eventually become exhausted in trying.

Although numbering over 1 million in attendance, a Promise Keepers' rally in Washington, D.C., was not the biggest Promise Keepers convention in history. One three times as big took place at the foot of Mount Sinai, when 3 million people heard the voice of God and witnessed a divine pyrotechnic display that so impressed them, they said, "All the words which the LORD hath said, we will do" (Exodus 24:3). Those in attendance at that first Promise Keepers convention weren't playing a game. They were sincere. They truly meant to keep the Ten Commandments. After all, they had heard God speak and had seen a mountain quake. But when Moses came down the mountain forty days later, he found them worshiping a golden calf.

Times don't change. People with sincere hearts say, "We will keep our promises." The problem with signing contracts, making vows, and keeping promises, however, is that people fail to factor into the equation a huge component: the flesh.

God's aware of this, gang. That's why He says, "I will wait until you're as tired as Abram was. Then I'll come through on My own. I don't want you to sign a contract or make a promise. I know what you're made of. I know your frailty. So I'm not going to meet you halfway. I'm going to do the whole thing."

FEBRUARY 26

Now Sarai Abram's wife bare him no children.

Genesis 16:1

The promise had been given. God said to Abram, "You're going to have a family as numerous as the stars in the heavens." But time passes, and guess what? Abram starts wondering. Abram is now eighty-six, Sarai seventy-six, and they think, "This is not working."

Always remember this, saint: When God gives a promise, there is often a gap of time between the giving of the promise and the fulfillment of the promise. In Abram's case, there was a thirteen-year gap.

Maybe you've been waiting on God for the fulfillment of a certain promise. Is His delay due to procrastination on His part? No. Is it due to preoccupation? Is He just too busy? No. God's delay is due to *preparation*; He is preparing you in the arena of faith. You see, the gaps between God's promise and its fulfillment provide opportunities for our muscle of faith to be exercised. Like a butterfly emerging from its cocoon, if there is no struggle, faith never soars.

FEBRUARY 27

But Abram said unto Sarai, Behold, thy maid is in thy hand; do to her as it pleaseth thee. And when Sarai dealt hardly with her, she fled from her face. And the angel of the LORD found her by a fountain of water in the wilderness, by the fountain in the way to Shur. . . . And she called the name of the LORD that spake unto her, Thou God seest me: for she said, Have I also here looked after him that seeth me?

Genesis 16:6–7, 13

This is the first time the phrase, "the angel of the LORD," appears in Scripture. The word translated as "angel" means "messenger." Throughout Scripture, angels adamantly refuse to be worshiped. Thus, because this angel of the Lord receives worship, we know He is no ordinary angel. Here, the "angel of the LORD" refers to the second person of the Trinity—Jesus Christ.

How like Jesus to appear not to a man, but to a woman; not to one who sought faith, but to one who was running from the family of faith. After all, Jesus is the Good Shepherd who left the ninety-nine to find the single sheep who had gone astray.

So too, the person who is in the greatest need, the person who feels he's blown it the worst is the very one in whom the Lord is most interested. It would seem more logical to stay with the ninety-nine. But that's not the heart of our Shepherd. He goes after the one. He goes after Hagar. He goes after you.

FEBRUARY 28

And when Abram was ninety years old and nine, the LORD appeared to Abram.

Genesis 17:1

Keep in mind that there are great gaps and spans of time between these appearances of the Lord to Abram. This intrigues me. Abraham is called the friend of God (James 2:23). Why then would God wait fifteen years between conversations? Perhaps you're wondering the same thing with regard to your own situation. "Why don't I hear more frequently from the Lord? Why do I go through weeks or months or years when I don't seem to hear direct words from Him in my spiritual ears?" Keep in mind that Abraham was not only called the friend of God, but he is also referred to as the father of faith (Romans 4:11). Here, God is making a man of faith out of Abram—and he's making a man or woman of faith out of you. Faith means we walk not by what we see physically, hear audibly, or know intellectually. Faith means we hang on to what God had said previously. We just hang on.

Think back for a moment to a time in the not too distant past when you thought, "This will never work. Everything's going wrong. I'll never make it." Yet, here you are today. Why did God allow those things to happen in that way? To teach you to be a man or woman of faith, to teach you to quietly and confidently believe that God is on the throne, that He is in control, and that all things work together for good.

FEBRUARY 29

And Abraham said unto God, O that Ishmael might live before thee!

Genesis 17:18

The Hebrew text makes it clear that this is the passionate cry of a father who says, "I already have a son whom I love deeply. Let *him* be the one through whom the covenant and blessings come." In other words, Abraham is saying, "I know I got ahead of You when Ishmael was conceived. I know that was not Your plan. I know I made a mess, but Lord, bless my mess."

Have you ever done that? Maybe your motives were sincere; maybe your intentions were right. But you didn't wait on God or talk things over with Him. Instead, you just plunged into that relationship, that job opportunity, or that ministry. And when it turned out to be a mess, you asked God to bless it anyway.

I used to think prayer was giving God orders. "Bless this, bless that, bless the other," I'd pray, as if I could ring a bell through prayer (the more faith I had, the louder it would ring), and God would grant me my wishes as if He were a genie. I used to think I knew what God should do. Now I know I don't have a clue. I have found that God gives His best to those who leave the choice with Him. Thus, prayer is not giving God orders. Prayer is simply reporting for duty. Prayer is not "Bless my mess." It's "Lord, have *Your* way."

MARCH 1

And the Lord appeared unto him in the plains of Mamre: and he sat in the tent door in the heat of the day.

Genesis 18:1

The heat of the day in Scripture is often a picture of the hard times that come our way. So often in my walk, I've seen the Lord in a fresh way in the heat of the day, in fiery trials. You have too. This is not surprising. After all, it was when Shadrach, Meshach, and Abed-nego were cast into a fiery furnace that they saw the Lord (Daniel 3:25). Consequently, when I hear about believers who are going through fiery trials and hot times, on one hand my heart goes out to them. But on the other hand, in a sense, I'm envious of them because I know the Lord will make Himself known to them in a special way in the heat of the day.

MARCH 2

And the Lord said unto Abraham, Wherefore did Sarah laugh, saying, Shall I of a surety bear a child, which am old? Is any thing too hard for the Lord?

Genesis 18:13–14

Is anything too hard for the Lord? We have a tendency to think of God's ability in relation to degrees of difficulty.

If someone comes to me and says, "I'm struggling with a headache. Would you pray for me?" I say, "Sure." "Bless Bob, Lord. Take away the tension and allow him to experience a healing touch from Your hand."

But if someone comes to me saying, "I just came back from the doctor's office and he told me I have a malignant tumor. Would you pray for me?" I act as if it's a whole different deal! "Pastors, brothers, gather round," I say. And I fervently plead with the Lord as though cancer is harder for Him to heal than a headache.

Oh, there's nothing wrong with praying passionately, but not because there are degrees of difficulty or because we need to get God's attention emotionally. The prophets of Baal slashed their bodies and cried loudly to get his attention, all to no avail. Elijah, on the other hand, simply prayed two sentences, and through them moved the hand of God (1 Kings 18).

MARCH 3

And the men rose up from thence, and looked toward Sodom: and Abraham went with them to bring them on the way. And the LORD said, Shall I hide from Abraham that thing which I do; seeing that Abraham shall surely become a great and mighty nation, and all the nations of the earth shall be blessed in him? For I know him, that he will command his children and his household after him, and they shall keep the way of the LORD, to do justice and judgment; that the LORD may bring upon Abraham that which he hath spoken of him.

Genesis 18:16–19

The Lord would give Abraham information and revelation not based upon the accumulation of his knowledge, but upon the communication to his family. "I will give Abraham understanding of what I'm about to do," said the Lord, "because I know he is a man who will teach his children."

The same is true today. The revelation God wants to give us concerning what He's doing, how He's moving, or where He's going is not based upon our journal entries or our Bible study notes. It's based upon whether or not we will share what He tells us with our children.

People often say to me, "If I could go back and do it all over again, I would not go into the profession I'm in presently. I would go into the ministry." While I have found the ministry to be absolutely delightful and a wonderful calling, the fact is if you have children or grandchildren, you are in the ministry. No clerical collar or pulpit compares to gathering your family around you, giving a simple Bible lesson, singing songs, sharing with each other, and praying together. That is the ministry. And anyone who takes seriously this call will, like Abraham, receive fresh revelation. I know this to be so, for the most wonderful insights and sweetest revelations of God to my heart have not come as I have prepared sermons, but as I have simply shared in worship with my family.

MARCH 4

And there came two angels to Sodom at even.

Genesis 19:1

Although three men had appeared to Abraham in chapter 18, only two go to Sodom because the Lord Himself does not enter into the city. Why? Psalm 66 tells us that if we regard iniquity in our hearts, the Lord will not hear us. That is, if I am purposely, rebelliously, intentionally, and arrogantly holding on to sin, when I pray, the Lord won't hear my prayer; He'll not come into my city; He'll not enter into my situation.

You see, even though the sin to which I so stubbornly cling was paid for completely on the cross of Calvary, the Lord loves me so much, He says, "I love you too much to let you go on your merry way, day after day, as though there's nothing wrong. If I did that, you would continue in that sin, and that sin would destroy you. Consequently, you won't feel My hand. You won't sense My presence, not because I'm not with you—for I will never leave you nor forsake you—but because your spirit senses something is not quite right."

When I feel as though my prayers bounce off the ceiling, it's not because the Lord is angry with me or mad at me, disappointed in me or turning away from me. Rather, it's an indication He's lovingly given, to show me that something's not right.

The angels went into Sodom, but the Lord did not.

MARCH 5

The men laid hold upon his hand, and upon the hand of his wife, and upon the hand of his two daughters; the LORD being merciful unto him: and they brought him forth, and set him without the city.

Genesis 19:16

"Wilt Thou destroy the righteous with the wicked?" Abraham asked the Lord (18:23). The answer, as illustrated here, is "No." Before judgment could be poured out upon Sodom, before fire and brimstone would come down to destroy Gomorrah, God rescued Lot and those of his house. He rescued the righteous.

Lot righteous? A guy who calls perverted people his brothers? A guy who offers his daughters to a homosexual mob? A guy who lingers when angels tell him to leave? Lot *righteous*?

Yes. That is what Peter calls him (2 Peter 2:7). How can Lot possibly be considered righteous? It is because righteousness is imputed solely on the basis of simple faith. I am righteous and so are you if you have confessed with your mouth that Jesus is who He claimed to be, and have believed in your heart that God has raised Him from the dead (Romans 10:9–10).

I love this chapter because there are a lot of people I care about deeply who, like Lot, made a profession of faith but ended up in Sodom, not living the way they know they should. If you're worried about a friend or a family member, take hope. While we don't want anyone to follow Lot's example because sin brings all kinds of pain and problems presently, as well as empty-handedness eternally, know this: If that son of yours confesses with his mouth that Jesus is who He claimed to be, and believes in his heart that God has raised Him from the dead, he will be saved.

The Lord communicated through this powerful picture, "I'm going to rescue people you may have thought were hopelessly lost."

MARCH 6

Look not behind thee, neither stay thou in all the plain; escape to the mountain, lest thou be consumed.

Genesis 19:17

In telling Lot to escape to the mountain, the Lord wanted to turn a city boy into a mountain man. Throughout Scripture, the Lord continually calls His people to the mountains . . .

Through Abraham, who was ready to sacrifice his son in obedience to the Lord's command, He calls us to Mount Moriah, the mount of devotion.

Through the Israelites, who gathered to receive His commandments, the Lord calls us to Mount Sinai, the mount of instruction.

Through Moses, who viewed the Promised Land, He calls us to Mount Pisgah, the mount of vision.

Through Elijah, whose prayer brought down fire from heaven, He calls us to Mount Carmel, the mount of passion.

Through Peter, James, and John, who beheld the glory of the Lord, He calls us to Mount Hermon, the mount of transfiguration.

But the most important mountain God calls us to is Mount Calvary, the mount of crucifixion, where He calls us to die to self.

MARCH 7

Now therefore restore the man his wife; for he is a prophet, and he shall pray for thee, and thou shalt live.

Genesis 20:7

Here is the first time in the Bible where the word "prophet" appears. Now, if there was ever a time God wouldn't want to introduce Abraham as a prophet, I would think it would be right here. I would think God would be embarrassed by, upset with, and ashamed of Abraham for claiming his wife was his sister. But such is not the case, for God says to Abimelech, "That man who told a lie, who misled you, who jeopardized his wife and your nation—he's My man; he's My spokesman; he's My prophet."

Romans 11:29 tells us that "the gifts and calling of God are without repentance." That means when God gives a spiritual gift, a calling, a ministry to a man, woman, or church, He doesn't change His mind. He doesn't take it back. If God has given you a gift, be it ministry, music, prophecy, teaching, or evangelism; or if He's given you a skill, be it carpentry, mechanics, or athletics, it's yours to keep.

Perhaps you've seen people stumble, fall, or drop the ball, and you wonder how God could still use him, her, or them. The answer is that the gifts and calling of God are without repentance. Sin will always bring about its own sadness, depression, defeat, and despair, for the way of the transgressor is hard (Proverbs 13:15). The fact remains, however, that because the gifts and calling of God are without repentance, God will still use sinners.

I say this because I have found that the thing which hobbles so many people in their service for the Lord is thinking, "God can't use me. God wouldn't use me. God won't use me because I've failed so miserably. I've botched it so badly." That's the voice of the Enemy. The voice of the Lord says, "Because you didn't earn the gifts I gave you or the calling I sovereignly placed upon you, there's no way you can lose them."

If you've been on the sidelines because you think you've messed up once too often, remember this story and the mercy of our Master, the grace of our God, and the kindness of our King. Truly, there's no one like Him.

MARCH 8

*So Abraham prayed unto God: and God healed Abimelech,
and his wife, and his maidservants; and they bare children.
For the LORD had fast closed up all the wombs of the house
of Abimelech, because of Sarah Abraham's wife.*

Genesis 20:17–18

Although Abraham would be used in other arenas and would go on to live a life of blessing before Abimelech, at this point Abraham couldn't preach to Abimelech because in his eyes he was a liar and a coward. Yet even though Abraham couldn't preach to or share with Abimelech, he could still pray for him.

So too, because you have fallen short in their eyes or hurt them badly, there are people to whom you may not be able to preach or with whom you may not be able to share. But this story tells me that although I may not be able to preach to them or share with them, I get to effectively bless them through prayer.

When I pray for my enemies, not only does it release blessing upon them, but it keeps me from getting involved in a cycle of bitterness which will only destroy me. You cannot pray a blessing on a person and remain angry with him. It's impossible. That's why Jesus said, "Pray for your enemies" (see Matthew 5:44).

I challenge you to pray for the people toward whom you feel bitterness or hostility, for the people you just don't like. Pray that they'll be healed, that they'll prosper, that they'll do well. God will answer your prayer, and you'll be blessed in the process.

MARCH 9

And Abraham rose up early in the morning, and took bread, and a bottle of water, and gave it unto Hagar, putting it on her shoulder, and the child, and sent her away.

Genesis 21:14

God made the promise to Abraham, and reiterated it several times, that Ishmael would become a mighty nation. Here Abraham wisely decided not to give God a hand in fulfilling what He had promised. After all, that's how Ishmael was conceived in the first place.

Consequently, Abraham shows incredible peace. He gives Ishmael and Hagar a bit of water and a bit of bread, in effect saying, "I trust the Lord is going to do what He said, not because of my provision, but because of His promise."

Mom and Dad, let this be a comfort to you today. The promises of God toward my children are the same as toward yours . . .

"Train up a child in the way he should go: and when he is old, he will not depart from it" (Proverbs 22:6). No matter what desert your child is in, no matter in what dry region he finds himself, even when he is old he won't depart from the way he's been trained.

"For I know whom I have believed," said Paul, "and am persuaded that he is able to keep that which I have committed unto him" (2 Timothy 1:12). Have you committed your kids to the Lord? God is able to keep them. This doesn't mean He's merely capable. It means He's *committed* to keeping that which has been entrusted to Him.

I hate it when I panic. I get worried. I get uptight. And I run around like a chicken with my head cut off, trying to make something happen. Faith is the opposite of panic. I love it when I'm not panicking, when I'm walking in faith. When I walk in faith, I'm not irritated, anxious, or upset. There's a peace deep within me and a serenity that overflows from me. I like it when I walk in faith like Abraham.

Abraham said, "Ishmael, Hagar, here's some water and some bread. God be with you." He is maturing, this mighty man of God. He is growing, this giant of faith. He'll miss Ishmael, but he trusts God completely, knowing God will do exactly what He said He would.

And He'll do the same for you.

MARCH 10

And she departed, and wandered in the wilderness of Beer-sheba.

Genesis 21:14

Paul calls the story of Ishmael and Hagar an allegory (Galatians 4:24) in which Ishmael is a type of the flesh and Isaac a type of the Spirit. We see in this story Ishmael mocking Isaac—something that happens in each of our hearts constantly.

> For the flesh lusteth against the Spirit, and the Spirit against the flesh: and these are contrary the one to the other: so that ye cannot do the things that ye would.
>
> Galatians 5:17

There's a constant battle going on, and here's the question: Who are we going to allow to win? The Bible says the solution is to cast out Ishmael, the flesh.

How do we cast Ishmael out?

By doing what Abraham did: by giving him no provision.

Abraham didn't give Ishmael a Visa card and a Ford Explorer. He gave him nothing more than prisoner's rations—a little bread and water. That is why Paul emphatically tells us to "make no provision for the flesh" (see Romans 13:14).

Every fleshly thing I see or hear is a seed planted in the soil of my soul that will come up eventually. Likewise, every godly thing I take in will also come to fruition. Perhaps the best illustration of this is one I shared recently with a group of junior highers . . .

It's as if there are two dogs inside of you: one black, one white. The white dog is life, the black dog is death. At any given point, you're feeding one of the dogs—through the type of people with whom you associate, through what you choose to listen to, watch, and take in. If you feed the black dog, he gets bigger and stronger. He bares his fangs and starts ripping on the white dog while the white dog gets smaller and smaller. Once the black dog decimates the white dog, he turns on you and begins to sink his jaws into your innermost being, leaving you wondering why you're so down, defeated, depressed, and discontent. On the other hand, if you feed the white dog, the spirit, by doing what's right in God's sight, the white dog grows bigger and stronger as the black dog grows punier and weaker, until he's no bigger than a Chihuahua. At any given moment, you'll feed one of the two dogs. Which will it be?

MARCH 11

And the water was spent in the bottle, and she cast the child under one of the shrubs.

Genesis 21:15

In Galatians 4, Paul says Ishmael is not only a type of the flesh and Isaac a type of the Spirit, but Hagar is a type of the law and Sarah a type of the new covenant. Hagar represents Mount Sinai, where the law was given. Sarah represents the heavenly Mount Zion, from whence grace flows.

My natural tendency is to say, "The best way to deal with the flesh is to lay down the law. I'm going to set up rules and regulations to keep my flesh in check." But whenever I do, I am bound to fail badly because, although the rules and regulations might be wonderful, I cannot keep them. Oh, for a while I might be able to, during which time I'll say, "What's wrong with you? Why is your Ishmael running about wildly? Why can't you deal with the flesh like I have?"

But eventually I will fall under the weight of my own rules, and I will fail miserably. Then I'll say, "I was doing so well for three days, or three months, or three years, but then I blew it. So why even go to Bible study, why even pray? I'm a failure. The Lord will never use me."

This is why the law doesn't work. It makes you either a self-righteous prude or a self-condemned dude. It causes us to say either, "What's wrong with you?" or "What's wrong with me?"

So what's the answer? Do what Abraham did. Send Hagar away and embrace Sarah. Don't put yourself or others under regulations or rules. Rather, hold fast to the new covenant, and walk in grace.

MARCH 12

And she went, and sat her down over against him a good way off, as it were a bowshot: for she said, Let me not see the death of the child. And she sat over against him, and lift up her voice, and wept. And God heard the voice of the lad; and the angel of God called Hagar out of heaven, and said unto her, What aileth thee, Hagar? fear not; for God hath heard the voice of the lad where he is.

Genesis 21:16–17

Who is "the angel of God"? It's Jesus.

"What's wrong, Hagar?" asked Jesus, just as centuries later He would ask His disciples, "Why are ye fearful, O ye of little faith?" (Matthew 8:26). Referring to the Sea of Galilee, He said, "Let us go over to the other side" (see Matthew 8:18). He hadn't said, "Let us sink out in the middle," or "Let us go down in an attempt." No, Jesus had given the word to His disciples that they would indeed make it to the other side. So too, Jesus had already told Hagar that Ishmael would be blessed (Genesis 16). Thus, the Lord here lovingly rebukes Hagar, "Didn't I give you My Word, Hagar? Have you already forgotten?"

What Word has God given to us? He's told us all things work together for good (Romans 8:28), that He will never leave us nor forsake us (Hebrews

13:5), that He will give us the desires of our hearts (Psalm 37:4). He's told us that our sins are forgiven (1 John 1:9), that His love for us is everlasting (Jeremiah 31:3), and that we are more than conquerors (Romans 8:37). Therefore, "what aileth" us?

MARCH 13

And it came to pass at that time, that Abimelech and Phichol the chief captain of his host spake unto Abraham, saying, God is with thee in all that thou doest.

Genesis 21:22

As I read this, I was reminded of a journal entry I made recently during an Alaskan cruise on which I was speaking . . .

So many blessings, so many thoughts while cruising these waters of Alaska's inland passage and seeing the mountains tower above us, the stars shining over us, the unseen but teeming life beneath us. I am deeply impacted. Not only by His majesty, creativity, power, and glory, but especially and surprisingly by His humility; for this majestic, creative-beyond-genius Being tells us that He stretches the heavens out like a curtain (Isaiah 40:22), He sits upon the circle of the earth (Isaiah 40:22), He measures the heavens with the span of His hand (Isaiah 40:12), yet He did not give us the take-your-breath-away data, facts, and figures of the size of other stars, the range of our galaxy, the puniness of our planet in comparison to the billions and trillions of other objects. He simply allows the vastness of space, the mysteries beneath the sea, and the power of the atom that He holds together (Colossians 1:17) to slowly be discovered. As man's technology and ability increases, he only discovers more wonder. And I wonder at His humility. I would have laid it all out, let it be known what I have done, how great I am with facts and figures and data. But God allowed Himself to be discovered, uncovered, in due season. And that season will fill all eternity. Real power, true genius, creative ingenuity, spiritual authority, if indeed real, can wait, indeed should wait to be discovered slowly, quietly. For only what is real can dare to wait. And only what is humble will ultimately be exalted.

God is the epitome of humility. Only true greatness can be humble. And that's what Abraham is showing us as well. He doesn't try to prove he's a great guy. He just goes about his work, and after years of observation, Abimelech says, "I can see that God is with you."

MARCH 14

And Abraham planted a grove in Beer-sheba, and called there on the name of the Lord, *the everlasting God. And Abraham sojourned in the Philistines' land many days.*

Genesis 21:33–34

As your margin notes may indicate, Abraham planted a tamarisk tree—and in so doing, he finds a creative, spontaneous, and innovative way of worshiping.

When my son Benjamin was three years old, he came out of his room one day holding a picture attached to a helium balloon.

"What's that, Benny?" I asked.

"It's a picture of me and Jesus," he said, as he went out into the backyard, let his balloon go, and watched as it soared heavenward.

Such is innovative, creative worship from the heart of one who loves God.

When you love God, it's not enough just to sing the same songs as everyone else. It's not enough to go through the motions during worship sessions.

A lover of God finds a way to plant a tree and say, "Lord, this is for You."

A lover of God finds a way to break the alabaster box and say, "This is my dowry, and I'm giving it to You" (see Mark 14).

A lover of God finds a way to dance in his undergarments before the Lord (2 Samuel 6:14).

A lover of God finds ways of fresh, personal, intimate expressions others may never see.

MARCH 15

And it came to pass after these things, that God did tempt Abraham, and said unto him, Abraham: and he said, Behold, here I am. And he said, Take now thy son, thine only son Isaac, whom thou lovest, and get thee into the land of Moriah.

Genesis 22:1–2

Sitting only a couple hundred feet above the city of Jerusalem, Mount Moriah is technically only a ridge. But when the Lord said to Abraham, "I want you to take your son, your only son, to Mount Moriah," father and son set off on the greatest mountain climbing expedition in world history, second only to the one another Father and Son would make to the very same destination centuries later.

Put yourself in Abraham's sandals and you will see this is an incredible journey, for God had asked him to sacrifice his son—his only son, the promised son, the one of whom he was so proud, the one in whom he saw such potential. How could Abraham have had such a heart to obey such a command? I couldn't have done it. But Abraham did.

How? The reason Abraham could climb Mount Moriah is the same reason Sir Edmund Hillary could climb Mount Everest. You see, prior to Hillary's ascent up Mount Everest, he spent five years acclimating his body to the altitude, five years allowing his lungs to expand to deal with the lack of oxygen he would encounter at that height, five years to get in shape, and five years to make preparations and gather gear.

So too, Abraham would climb an infinitely higher mountain because, like Hillary's team, there had been great preparation.

"It came to pass after these things that God did tempt, or test, Abraham" (see 22:1). After what things? Fifty-seven years of things . . .

> Leaving his home in Ur for a land God would show him was step #1 in training for the Moriah moment.

> Saying goodbye to his nephew as Lot headed for Sodom was step #2.

> Refusing the spoils of battle offered to him by the king of Sodom was step #3.

> Obeying God's command to send his son Ishmael into the desert was step #4.

Nothing in Scripture is accidental or incidental. Thus, when we read, "It came to pass after these things that God did tempt Abraham," it means that the testing didn't take place until *after these things*—each of which prepared Abraham for this moment.

God will never, ever give you a test He has not thoroughly and painstakingly prepared you to navigate successfully. Never.

We look at Abraham's Moriah moment and think, I couldn't do that. And we're right. We couldn't, because God hasn't prepared us for that—yet.

MARCH 16

And he said, Take now thy son, thine only son Isaac, whom thou lovest, and get thee into the land of Moriah; and offer him there for a burnt offering upon one of the mountains which I will tell thee of. And Abraham rose up early in the morning, and saddled his ass, and took two of his young men with him, and Isaac his son, and clave the wood for the burnt offering, and rose up, and went unto the place of which God had told him.

Genesis 22:2–3

Paul tells us there are three great virtues: faith, hope, and love (1 Corinthians 13:13). Abraham's faith was developed first when God called him out of Ur.

By faith Abraham, when he was called to go out into a place which he should after receive for an inheritance, obeyed; and he went out, not knowing whither he went.

Hebrews 11:8

But God didn't stop there, for He proceeded to build hope into Abraham, as Abraham waited for his promised son . . .

Who against hope believed in hope, that he might become the father of many nations; according to that which was spoken, So shall thy seed be.

Romans 4:18

Nor did God stop there, for the greatest of these is love. Our text contains the first use of the word *love* in Scripture. It's as if God is saying, "Let go of the one you love because of greater love for Me. This is a chance for you to take a quantum leap in growth."

If you say, "I don't want faith or hope or love. I want to be frazzled and afraid and frustrated," don't go down the path that leads to Moriah, the path that leads you on a journey of trials and testing. But if you want to be entire and complete, lacking nothing, there's only one way . . .

My brethren, count it all joy when ye fall into divers temptations; knowing this, that the trying of your faith worketh patience. But let patience have her perfect work, that ye may be perfect and entire, wanting nothing.

James 1:2–4

There's no other way to be complete than to say "okay" to tests, temptations, and trials.

MARCH 17

And Isaac spake unto Abraham his father, and said, My father: and he said, Here am I, my son. And he said, Behold the fire and the wood: but where is the lamb for a burnt offering? And Abraham said, My son, God will provide himself a lamb for a burnt offering.

Genesis 22:7–8

It's as if God says to Abraham, "I've prepared you to do something which may seem unbelievably difficult because I want to show people a picture of My Son. Even though it will be difficult for you, Abraham, your trial will touch multiple millions of people throughout history."

Gang, your Christian life will change radically when it finally sinks in that God does not exist for you. Most believers go through a chunk of time believing God does indeed exist for them. "Bless my marriage. Bless my house. Bless my job. Give me abundant life. Give me joyful days," we pray, as if God exists for our pleasure.

With mountains on either side of them, their backs to the Red Sea, and Pharaoh's army barreling down on them, Moses cried to the Lord.

"Know this, Moses," He answered, "I will get me honour upon Pharaoh, and upon all his hosts. . . . And the Egyptians shall know that I am the LORD." In other words, "Moses, this isn't about you or even the people with you. I've got work to do. I want to show the Egyptians who I am. To do that, I'm putting you in a tight spot, a tough place. But word will get back to the Egyptians that there is no God like the God of Israel" (see Exodus 14:17–18).

So too, God says to us:

"I've got a big job for you—to let people around you know who I am. This means the doctor may say, 'It's cancer.' This means the business may go under. This means the relationship may not work out, that people might see how in your pain, in your difficulty, or in your dilemma I come through not to solve your problem, but to be with you in your problem. I will show Myself in the way that can most effectively reach the people I want to reach through your life. That may mean you go through real problems physically or that things don't work out in the way you thought they would in your family. It may even mean death. But it's not about you. I love you deeply, but there's a bigger thing happening than your comfort."

Because we exist for God, gang (not the other way around), our part is to say, "However He wants to direct His drama on the stage of my life, be it a comedy or a tragedy, so be it."

MARCH 18

So they went both of them together. And they came to the place which God had told him of; and Abraham built an altar there, and laid the wood in order, and bound Isaac his son, and laid him on the altar upon the wood.

Genesis 22:8–9

Abraham was the friend of God (James 2:23). Why, then, would God ask Abraham to sacrifice his son? Friends don't let friends have Moriah moments—or do they?

Paul put it this way:

> That I may know him, and the power of his resurrection, and the fellowship of his sufferings, being made conformable unto his death.

Philippians 3:10

Most of us long for the power of Jesus' resurrection, but know little about the fellowship of His sufferings. Yet the power of His resurrection doesn't come without the fellowship of His sufferings.

I love to laugh with people. But the people I'm closest to are not the ones with whom I've only laughed. They are also the ones with whom I've shed tears. The same is true for you. There's a closeness that occurs when people navigate deep waters together.

Thus, God the Father says to Abraham, "I want you to experience something of what I will do because when you do, you and I will be bonded together uniquely."

There they were—walking around in the fiery furnace.

"How many men did we throw in?" asked Nebuchadnezzar.

"Three," said one of his aides.

"Then how is it that I see four, and the fourth is like the Son of God?" asked Nebuchadnezzar.

Shadrach, Meshach, and Abed-nego could have come out anytime they wanted. But they didn't come out until Nebuchadnezzar commanded them to because it was in the fire where they had fellowship with the Lord, a vision of the Lord, and a closeness to the Lord they had never before known (Daniel 3).

You have found this to be true as well. It's when you're in the fire of affliction and adversity that you have real communion. Don't fear, flock. Don't shy away from the Moriahs that loom over you. God will train you. And when you're there, He'll see you through.

MARCH 19

And Abraham came to mourn for Sarah, and to weep for her.

Genesis 23:2

Even though he was a giant of a man, the friend of God, the father of faith, we see Abraham was also a man who mourned and wept. This being the first mention of weeping or tears in the Bible, God waits until chapter 23 to introduce this concept. It's curious to me that there is no record of tears at the fall of man, when the flood came, or when the people were scattered at Babel. The Holy Spirit purposefully waits to record weeping until the time a giant of a spiritual man was separated from a godly woman.

"Put thou my tears into thy bottle," David wrote. "Are they not in thy book?" (Psalm 56:8). Evidently, God keeps scrapbooks in heaven. Malachi 3:16 tells us every time one of His children talks to another person about Him, God hearkens to it and writes it in a book. And here, we see Him keeping another book—a book of our tears.

Concerning hard times, God doesn't say, "Deal with it." He says, "I understand what you're going through. It's precious to Me."

In Jesus' day, women wore tear bottles—little vials which fit against their cheek and caught their tears. A very precious possession, a woman would give this bottle of tears to the one she loved most. It could be this practice to which the account of the woman washing Jesus' feet with her tears refers (Luke 7:38).

Tears are unique. Under a microscope, you'll see the saline crystals in a tear are shaped in the form of a cross. It's as if the Lord is saying, "I understand. I know. I wept too" (see John 11:35).

MARCH 20

And the children of Heth answered Abraham, saying unto him, Hear us, my lord: thou art a mighty prince among us: in the choice of our sepulchres bury thy dead; none of us shall withhold from thee his sepulchre, but that thou mayest bury thy dead.

Genesis 23:5–6

"You're a mighty prince," said the children of Heth to Abraham. This intrigues me because although Abraham lived very simply in a tent, he had a huge impact on the heathen. Abraham's nephew Lot, on the other hand, wanted to be involved in the cultural climate of Sodom. Yet when he tried to correct them, so little did they think of him that the men of Sodom said, "Who are you?" (see Genesis 19:9).

You might hear the saying, "You're so heavenly minded, you're no earthly good." Abraham proves just the opposite—that you're no earthly good *until* you're heavenly minded. If you want to make a difference on earth, your focal point, priority, and passion should be that of one who lives for eternity.

MARCH 21

And the man bowed down his head, and worshipped the LORD. And he said, Blessed be the LORD God of my master Abraham, who hath not left destitute my master of his mercy and his truth: I being in the way, the LORD led me to the house of my master's brethren. And the damsel ran, and told them of her mother's house these things.

Genesis 24:26–28

Often, people wonder how God will lead them. "How will I know whether to take that job, get involved in this relationship, or take on a new ministry?" they ask.

Here, Abraham's servant says, "Being in the way, the Lord led me." I find his phraseology interesting, for centuries later, Jesus would declare, "I am the way" (John 14:6); and the early church itself was called "the way" (see Acts 19:23).

If you are walking in the way, gang, and if you're obeying Jesus, you will end up at the right spot. You don't have to waste your time struggling and striving to find God's will. Simply walk day by day in the way, and as He did with Abraham's servant, the Lord will also lead you.

MARCH 22

And Rebekah arose, and her damsels, and they rode upon the camels, and followed the man: and the servant took Rebekah, and went his way. And Isaac came from the way of the well Lahai-roi; for he dwelt in the south country.

Genesis 24:61–62

Knowing that his father had sent the servant to find a bride for him, Isaac doesn't go and look for her himself. According to Jewish tradition, the father would arrange the marriage of his son. Upon agreement of both fathers, the bride and groom-to-be would then be betrothed at a simple ceremony in which cups of wine were exchanged and a dowry was given. Then the son would return to his father's house to build a dwelling place for his bride either close to or adjoining the house of his father. When the father deemed all had been properly prepared, he would send his son out to call for his bride—and she would run out to join him.

"In my Father's house are many mansions," Jesus, our Bridegroom, said. "I go to prepare a place for you. And if I go and prepare a place for you, I will come again, and receive you unto myself; that where I am, there ye may be also" (John 14:2–3).

When will this day be? "No man knows the day or the hour—not even Me," Jesus answered (see Mark 13:32).

But this much is sure: Like the brides of old, when our Bridegroom calls for us, we will run to meet Him not in the streets, but in the air (1 Thessalonians 4).

Most of us are watching for the Lord. But there is something more important than that. That is, the Lord (as seen in the person of Isaac, being at the well of *Lahai-roi*, or "The Lord sees") is watching for us. The Lord longs for us more than we long for Him. Why? Because while we can only speculate concerning the wonderful things God has prepared for those who love Him (1 Corinthians 2:9), He knows all about them and is eager to share them with us.

MARCH 23

And she bare him Zimran, and Jokshan, and Medan, and Midian, and Ishbak, and Shuah. And Jokshan begat Sheba, and Dedan. And the sons of Dedan were Asshurim, and Letushim, and Leummim. And the sons of Midian; Ephah, and Epher, and Hanoch, and Abida, and Eldaah. All these were the children of Keturah.

Genesis 25:2–4

I believe the names of the sons born to Abraham and Keturah parallel the prophetic picture of the people of Israel. You see, when the church is taken up in the rapture, the veil will be lifted from the eyes of the Jewish people, and all of Israel will be saved at the end of the tribulation. Then, she will play a primary role as God rules and reigns from Jerusalem in the millennial kingdom (Revelation 20). What a glorious time that will be! Nature will be restored to what it was originally meant to be: the mountains shall sing; the trees of the field shall clap their hands; the lion will lie down with the lamb. Not only will nature react, but also a complete disarmament by all nations and people will result in swords being turned into plowshares and spears into pruninghooks (Isaiah 2).

But wait. There's a dark side, as seen in the sons of Keturah. *Zimran* means "Song." *Jokshan* means "Snare." *Medan* means "Strife." *Midian* means

"Contention." Ishbak means "Man will leave." *Shuah* means "From the pit." What begins with a song ends in the pit.

You see, Scripture tells us man will live to be one thousand years old in the millennial kingdom. Consequently, the world's population will mushroom. At the end of the millennial kingdom, multiplied generations that have never known anything but perfect harmony will become bored with peace, love, and prosperity. Thus, perfection will be a snare to them. Strife and contention will follow. Although many of them will want to do their own thing and leave the way of the Lord, they'll not be able to because righteousness will be enforced in the millennial kingdom. But because God will not force His will on anyone, He will allow Satan to be released from the pit for a short season at the end of the millennium. Satan will lead a rebellion before he is cast permanently into the lake of fire, along with those who, bored with perfection, choose to follow him.

Although the names of Abraham and Keturah's sons paint a prophetic portrait, they also point to a very practical principle. That is, we too live in the age of the kingdom of God, not where the lion is lying down with the lamb externally, but internally where righteousness, peace, and joy in the Holy Ghost abound (Romans 14:17). This being the case, like those living in the millennial kingdom, we are at risk of taking the righteousness, peace, and joy of the present kingdom for granted.

Dear brother, precious sister, may we never be those who take lightly the work God has done in our hearts; for if we stop singing the sweet song of salvation, we will become ensnared in strife and contention, and be lured away from the rule of our King by lies from the pit.

MARCH 24

And Abraham gave all that he had unto Isaac.

Genesis 25:5

Here we see Abraham disposing of his wealth to his son Isaac even as the Father in heaven gave all things to His Son (John 17).

Because all things will find their ultimate destination in Christ, anything I do that isn't for Him results in hopelessness, while everything I do for and in Jesus positions me in the center of God's will.

How does this work practically?

Suppose you are a UPS driver. God's will for you is that you be a UPS driver for His glory. As you pull up to every stop, pray that God will bless those inside. And suddenly, your job will not be a matter of how many deliveries you can make in a day, but of how many people God can bless through you in a day. Whether you're a teacher, a realtor, a mechanic, a doctor, or a homemaker, allow God to use you in and through your profession to bring Him glory. To the extent that you do this in any given day is the extent to which you will experience purpose and deep contentment.

MARCH 25

And these are the days of the years of Abraham's life which he lived, an hundred threescore and fifteen years.

Genesis 25:7

"The days of the years" is a Hebrew phrase which speaks of quality of life, which is made up of days—individual, specific days. In his 64,000 days, Abraham, the friend of God, walked with God. The Christian life is not called the Christian leap, the Christian jump, or the Christian bounce. It's called the Christian walk because it takes place one step and one day at a time.

What am I going to do tomorrow? Will I choose to walk with God, or do I expect somehow to bounce, leap, skip, or hop and end up a spiritual man at age fifty? What I do today will affect how I arrive at the end of my life. One of the greatest misconceptions in spiritual life is that when we're old, we'll automatically be spiritual. I need to know God's Word today. I need to know God's ways today. If I don't, the end of my life will find me nothing more than an old fool.

MARCH 26

And his sons Isaac and Ishmael buried him in the cave of Machpelah, in the field of Ephron the son of Zohar the Hittite, which is before Mamre; the field which Abraham purchased of the sons of Heth. . . .

Genesis 25:9–10

We see Ishmael and Isaac brought together at the death of their father Abraham because true reconciliation can only happen through death.

God reconciled us to Himself through His own death (2 Corinthians 5:18–19). Then, once we were reconciled, He gave us the ministry of reconciliation—to reconcile people to God as we share with them the good news of the gospel, and also to reconcile people to each other.

So important is reconciliation to Jesus that He said something quite shocking: "If, while you are at the altar worshiping the Lord, you become aware that something is not quite right with someone you know or once knew, leave the altar and reconcile yourself to the one who is offended" (see Matthew 5:24).

The Greek word translated "reconcile" is *diallasso*—a word used by tailors and garment-makers with regard to alteration. Thus, Jesus was saying, "If, at the altar, you realize a relationship doesn't fit right, get it altered." In other words, the ill-fitting garment is not to be discarded, taken to Goodwill, or stuffed in the back of the closet and forgotten. "If a relationship isn't right," Jesus declared, "I want you to deal with that matter before you continue to worship."

How will reconciliation happen practically? There's only one way: someone has to die. If there's to be reconciliation with your wife, your husband, your daughter-in-law, your boss, your coach, or your neighbor, you have to die.

"I don't want to die," we protest. "How come *she* can't die? It's *his* turn to die. I'm sick and tired of dying. Why does it have to be *me*?"

I recently met with dear friends. He's been a pastor for years; she's a godly woman with a passion for Jesus. But they're on their way to divorce. And it's a tragedy. There's no real issue—just irritations that have grown over the years. Both argued their points, yet as the hours passed, all I could say was, "One of you has to die or there will be no reconciliation."

Their answer? "Why me? It's his turn. It's her turn."

Many couples drive to church in virtually the same situation. As the husband sits behind the wheel, his words are few, but his thoughts are many. "Why is she so cold?" he wonders. Meanwhile, as she sits on her side of the car, hugging the door handle, she thinks, "Why is he so demanding?"

And the silence is deafening, broken only by the sounds of construction on the wall between them, which is growing higher and higher every day. They come to church and lift their hands in worship, but the Lord would say, "If you're bringing your gift to the altar and you remember that he or she has something against you, don't even continue worshiping until you alter the hurtful situation."

Why should you be the one to die? Three reasons . . .

MARCH 27

. . . There was Abraham buried.

Genesis 25:10

1. Reconciliation delights our Father.

Every parent knows the delight of reconciliation. When I hear one of my kids say to another, "It's your turn. You go first," all I can say is, "Glory hallelujah! The age of miracles is not over! These kids are working it out. They're dying to self. They're letting the other have their way!"

If you are fortunate enough to have a child who goes out of his way to be a peacemaker, you know the place he has in your heart. So too, any one of us who says, "I'm going to die so that there can be reconciliation," brings a great deal of joy to the heart of the Father.

2. Reconciliation defeats our foe.

Satan has one tactic he's used from the very beginning: division. As the worship leader of the angelic chorus, Lucifer persuaded one-third of the angels to see things his way. They joined his rebellion and are now demons, destined for eternal damnation. Because Satan's strategy remains the same, he who says, "I will die before I allow separation between me and another" deals a deathblow to Satan. The person who binds Satan is not the one who loudly declares, "I bind you, Satan." The person who binds Satan is the one who dies to self and reconciles with another person. The binding of Satan comes about not through a statement we make verbally, but through a choice we make actively.

3. Reconciliation destroys our flesh.

The reason we're depressed, the reason for the gnawing ache within us is found in one word: flesh. We think if we could indulge or pamper our flesh, we'd be happier. The opposite, however, is true. Jesus taught that the one who loses his life will find it (Matthew 10:39); that the one who follows Him must deny himself and take up his cross (Matthew 16:24).

The cross you are to bear is not getting the flu or losing your job. It's not even divorce or death in your family—as tragic as those events are. The cross is not something that comes uninvited. Rather, it's something we choose to do which causes pain and agony to our flesh. The cross is what Jesus endured when He prayed, "Not My will, but Thine be done."

"I'm tired of being married to her," or "I'm tired of my dad treating me this way," or "I'm tired of my in-laws. Nevertheless, Lord, not my will but Thine be done. And Your will is that there be reconciliation, which means I must die." *That's* the cross.

The Roman soldier knew Jesus had died when he struck a spear in His side and there was no reaction other than the blood and water that flowed forth. So too, when that person with whom you've had a hard time pokes you yet again and you don't respond, you don't react, and you don't retaliate, you'll know you've died to your flesh.

Designed to be the most torturous death possible, crucified victims would often hang on a cross for two or three days before they died. Jesus hung on the cross for six hours. He was in a hurry because He knew the sooner

He died and completed the work of redemption, the sooner Easter Sunday would come! What if He had decided to struggle hour after hour, day after day? Easter couldn't happen until He died. That's why He said, "If you deny yourself, you'll have life. But if you seek to hang on to your life, you'll only prolong your misery."

Precious people, it's not that we *have* to die. It's that we *get* to. Will you be the one today who loves God so much that you will delight Him by dying to your rights, your way, your self?

If so, reconciliation is sure to follow as you race toward resurrection day.

MARCH 28

And Isaac's servants digged in the valley, and found there a well of springing water.

Genesis 26:19

The term "springing water" is correctly rendered "living water" in some translations. "If any man thirst," Jesus said, "let him come unto Me, and drink, and out of his innermost being shall gush forth torrents of living water. This spake He of the Holy Ghost" (see John 7:37–39). When did Isaac find living water? When he was in the valley. That's often the way it is. At least it was for me . . .

As a twenty-year-old teaching the book of Jonah at a junior-high retreat, it hit me in the middle of my teaching that I didn't care at all about the kids sitting before me. It was as if the Lord held up a mirror and I saw the ugliness of my soul. I saw that I wanted to teach, but that I didn't care about those whom I was teaching. I realized, much to my dismay, that they were just a means for me to do what I wanted to do. Here I was, studying for the ministry, involved in teaching and serving, and yet I knew my heart was calloused and hard. At the end of the weekend, in deep despair, I hopped in my van and drove for a couple of days. I finally pulled into the parking lot of the church I was attending—Calvary Chapel in Costa Mesa. As I did, I saw a pastor I recognized from the Saturday night concerts there. His name was Tom Stipe.

"You need the Holy Spirit," he said. He laid hands on me, prayed for me, and something happened. I felt a warm sensation in my inner being, and I began to worship the Lord in a way I had never done before.

That was a huge watershed for me. I understood that, although previously I had the Holy Spirit inside of me, I lacked the overflow of the Spirit through me. And so I say to you, if you are in a valley spiritually, you're in the perfect place to find the living water because it's there in the valley where you recognize your own inadequacy. Jesus said, "Blessed are those who hunger and thirst after righteousness—those who realize their need—for they shall be filled" (see Matthew 5:6).

When, like Isaac, you say, "I want to be used to water the flock around me," be it your family, your friends, your neighbors, or a Sunday school class, the Lord will truly empower you in a fresh and dynamic way (Acts 1:8).

MARCH 29

And the herdmen of Gerar did strive with Isaac's herdmen, saying, The water is ours: and he called the name of the well Esek; because they strove with him. And they digged another well, and strove for that also: and he called the name of it Sitnah. And he removed from thence, and digged another well; and for that they strove not: and he called the name of it Rehoboth; and he said, For now the LORD hath made room for us, and we shall be fruitful in the land.

Genesis 26:20–22

Now that Isaac had found living water in the valley, was everything smooth sailing for him from that point on? No, *Esek* means "Contention." It was immediately after Jesus' baptism in the Jordan River—where He was filled with the power and presence of the Holy Spirit—that He was led to the desert to be tempted and challenged by Satan. So too, when we are filled with the living water of the Spirit, we must understand that challenges are sure to follow.

Again, Isaac found water, and again he was challenged—thus the name *Sitnah*, or "Hated."

With the exception of Moses, there is not a man in the Old Testament meeker than Isaac. After all, when Ishmael taunted and teased him, did Isaac fight back? No. When his dad laid him on the altar to sacrifice him, did thirty-year-old Isaac try to escape? No. When his father's servant selected a bride for him, did Isaac question his choice? No. When Abimelech rebuked him, did he rationalize his cowardice? No. When his water rights were challenged, did he stand his ground? No.

"Blessed are the meek," Jesus said, "for they shall inherit the earth" (Matthew 5:5). And here we see that happening. Isaac is a man of remarkable meekness. And he will indeed inherit earthly blessings.

As I look back, I see my own life as a series of digging wells and moving on, until finally I found my Rehoboth, for *Rehoboth* means "Room." Over the years, I've watched lots of talented men and women who had an anointing, a calling, and a gifting miss great opportunities because they dug a well and there was strife. When they dug a second one, there was contention. Yet, instead of digging a third well, they gave up, thinking, "What's the use? I won't be used. Why go on?" God's plan is that we keep digging, keep digging, keep digging until we find our Rehoboth, where there's room.

Every one of you, without exception, has a Rehoboth awaiting you. But the Enemy will try to discourage you through contention and strife. Why does God allow this to happen? Because He has a twofold task: not only to prepare a place for you, but to prepare you for the place. This means you'll go through some trying times, some stretching points, and some questions, but you must not throw in the towel, or the trowel. You keep digging, move down the road, dig again, move down the road, dig again, and eventually you'll find your Rehoboth. I promise.

MARCH 30

And Rebekah heard when Isaac spake to Esau his son. And Esau went to the field to hunt for venison, and to bring it. And Rebekah spake unto Jacob her son, saying, Behold, I heard thy father speak unto Esau thy brother, saying, Bring me venison, and make me savoury meat, that I may eat, and bless thee before the LORD before my death. Now therefore, my son, obey my voice according to that which I command thee. Go now to the flock, and fetch me from thence two good kids of the goats; and I will make them savoury meat for thy father, such as he loveth: and thou shalt bring it to thy father, that he may eat, and that he may bless thee before his death.

Genesis 27:5–10

It was clear that Jacob was to be the blessed one (Genesis 25:23). Because Rebekah knew this, when she heard Isaac was about to bless Esau, we see her doing what you and I can fall into oh, so easily: knowing God's Word and doing God's work, but not in God's way. You might have a sincere heart and pure motives in wanting to see God's work done in the ministry or in your family, but God's work must be done God's way. Ask Moses . . .

> Wanting to see his Israelite brothers set free from the tyranny of the Egyptians, one day when Moses saw an Egyptian beating one of the Hebrew children, he rescued his Hebrew brother and killed the Egyptian, thinking he would be a hero in the eyes of the Hebrew people. But because God didn't direct Moses to do this, the end result was the rejection of Moses by the very people he was trying to help (Exodus 2:11–14).

God's work must be done God's way. Ask David . . .

> He knew the people would be blessed, and the glory of God would be experienced if the ark of the covenant was brought into the capital city of Jerusalem. To transport the ark from where it was, six miles outside of Jerusalem, David built a cart and stationed a man named Uzzah, or "Strong," upon it. In front of the ark, leading the

way was a man named Ahio, or "Friendly." It was a great set-up. Mr. Strong controlled the cart; Mr. Friendly led the way. It seemed like such a wonderful way to bring in the glory of God. But you know the story. On the way, the cart hit a rut in the road, and the ark began to wobble. Thinking he had better give God a hand, Uzzah reached out to stabilize the ark. But when his hand touched it, God killed him (2 Samuel 6:7).

Completely disheartened, David pouted for several months. But when he got back in the Word again, he discovered that the ark of the covenant was to be carried on the shoulders of priests rather than on a cart. Why? Because carts are nothing more than boards and big wheels, whereas priests are people who praise and pray. All too often, people call board meetings and bring in big wheels to make God's work happen. But such is the Philistine mentality. God's way is to work through people who praise and pray.

MARCH 31

And Isaac said unto Jacob, Come near, I pray thee, that I may feel thee, my son, whether thou be my very son Esau or not. And Jacob went near unto Isaac his father; and he felt him, and said, The voice is Jacob's voice, but the hands are the hands of Esau. And he discerned him not, because his hands were hairy, as his brother Esau's hands: so he blessed him.

Genesis 27:21–23

Although Jacob didn't sound like Esau, he felt like Esau. Therefore he must be Esau, thought Isaac, trusting his senses rather than the word that he heard.

Joshua made the same mistake when, rather than asking "counsel at the mouth of the LORD" (Joshua 9:14), he decided to sign a peace treaty with the Gibeonites based solely on the fact that he could see that their sandals were worn and that their bread was moldy.

Whenever we make decisions based upon what we feel, what we smell, or what we see rather than upon what we hear in the Word, we will be deceived. If an experience, trend, or phenomenon isn't seen in the New Testament record of the life of Christ and of His church, it's Jacob parading as Esau, and we will be as deceived as Isaac was if we choose to follow our senses rather than the Word.

APRIL 1

And Isaac called Jacob, and blessed him, and charged him, and said unto him, Thou shalt not take a wife of the daughters of Canaan. Arise, go to Padan-aram, to the house of Bethuel thy mother's father; and take thee a wife from thence of the daughters of Laban thy mother's brother.

Genesis 28:1–2

Abraham sent a servant to find a bride for his son, Isaac. Isaac, however, sent his son Jacob to find his own bride. So too, Paul would write, "work out your *own* salvation with fear and trembling, for it is God which worketh in you both to will and to do of his good pleasure" (Philippians 2:12–13, italics added).

Your salvation is going to be worked out or exercised a little bit differently than the salvation of the person sitting next to you or of the generation that went before you. Oh, we're all saved by grace through faith in Jesus Christ. But it's all going to work out a little bit differently in each of us.

This allows me to give freedom to people whose salvation is being worked out a little differently than mine might be. We can give each other lots of space because, within the parameters of grace and faith, God deals with each of us uniquely.

APRIL 2

And Jacob awaked out of his sleep, and he said, Surely the Lord is in this place; and I knew it not.

Genesis 28:16

"God is here, and I didn't know it." Why wouldn't Jacob know this? Because of his circumstances. He knew he was nothing but a conniver, hiding out in a seemingly God-forsaken, rocky region.

That may be your story today. You may feel like you're stuck in a rocky situation, a rocky marriage, rocky finances, or on a rocky road. But God would say to you today, "I'm with you in this place, even though you may not know it."

What can separate us from the love of God? Neither death, nor life, nor angels, nor principalities, nor powers, nor things present, nor things to come, nor height, nor depth, nor any other creature (Romans 8:38–39). Why? Because there is no condemnation to them who are in Christ Jesus (Romans 8:1). There is no separation because there is no condemnation. Why is there no condemnation? Because Jesus Christ—our hero, our Lord—took all of the sin that would separate us from the Father—the sins we committed last year, the sins we're committing now, and the sins we'll commit tomorrow—and paid for them *all*.

If you find yourself in a rocky situation, you have a choice: you can either say, "God is nowhere," or like Jacob, you can look at your surroundings, add the space of grace, and with new eyes say, "God is now here."

APRIL 3

Then Jacob went on his journey, and came into the land of the people of the east.

Genesis 29:1

If your Bible has margin notes, perhaps you see the phrase "went on his journey" rendered as "lifted up his feet." In Hebrew, the literal idea is that of "happy feet." In Genesis 28, God appeared to Jacob, reiterating His promise, presence, and plan for Jacob. As a result, as Jacob heads to Padan-aram, he does so with "happy feet." He does so with enthusiasm.

Enthusiasm, or *en theos*, simply means "full of God." An encounter with God—the giver of joy, the source of all true happiness—manifests itself in a changed walk. And such was Jacob's case.

How I love to be around people who are enthusiastic, who are full of God.

Their faces seem to radiate His joy and I find myself more joyful in their presence, able to continue my own journey with "happy feet."

APRIL 4

And when Rachel saw that she bare Jacob no children, Rachel envied her sister; and said unto Jacob, Give me children, or else I die.

Genesis 30:1

Maybe you have been looking to your husband, wife, friend, or pastor to meet the barrenness, emptiness, or lack of productivity in your life. "Meet this need," you cry, "or I'll die." But the reality is, they can't.

When asked who he was, John the Baptist identified himself by who he was *not*. "I am not the Christ," he said. "I'm not the answer. I'm not the Savior. I'm not the solution. My whole role is to point to the One who *is* the Christ" (see John 1:20).

> For the creature was made subject to vanity, not willingly, but by reason of him who hath subjected the same in hope.

Romans 8:20

For the creature—

    You and me

Was made subject to vanity—

    Or emptiness

Not willingly—

    We don't want to feel empty

But by reason of Him—

    By God's divine design

Who hath subjected the same in hope—

In order that we would look to Him.

The only way you'll be truly satisfied is to be extremely close *to* God, totally dependent *on* God, and passionately in love *with* God. Sunday morning Christianity will never fill the hole in your soul. The hunger in your heart can only be filled through intimacy, dependence, and an ever-deepening relationship with the One who created you for His own pleasure (Revelation 4:11).

APRIL 5

And Jacob's anger was kindled against Rachel: and he said,
Am I in God's stead, who hath withheld from thee the fruit
of the womb?

Genesis 30:2

"Give me children, or else I die. I demand that you give me kids." Such are the prayers of those who say, "We need to speak the Word and demand from God that we not be barren, but that we be rich, healthy, and successful."

Wait a minute. When Rachel finally had a son, she named him Joseph. Why? Because Joseph means, "May God add." In other words, Joseph wasn't enough. Rachel wanted more.

That's always the way it is. When you're looking to something or someone to meet the need of your soul, it's never enough. And here's the real irony: as a result of having another son, Rachel did in fact die.

As she was dying in childbirth, what did she say? Not, "Oh, praise God, another son"; not, "Oh Lord, You're awesome to give this barren women two children." No, as she was dying in childbirth, Rachel named her son *Ben-oni*, or "Son of my sorrow." The last word on beautiful Rachel's lips was "sorrow" (Genesis 35:18).

Rachel demanded her way and it killed her.

Why did Rachel's life end this way? Because she looked to the wrong person and asked in the wrong fashion. So too, a husband, wife, friend, pastor, or parent cannot fill the hole in your soul, because you were created for a deep yet humble relationship with God.

A broken Rachel named her son Ben-oni, "Son of my sorrow." But a wiser Jacob renamed him Benjamin, "Son of my right hand." So too, as the Son of Man, Jesus was called the "Man of sorrows" (Isaiah 53:3). But as the Son of God, He sits at the Father's right hand (Colossians 3:1).

Rachel said, "Give me children, or I die."

The Father says, "For My children, I will die."

God says, "I am so in love with you, I'm not demanding something *from* you, but I'm dying *for* you. I love you to death. And the sins and mistakes you've made so foolishly, I will wash away completely so that you can live with Me eternally."

APRIL 6

And it came to pass, when Rachel had born Joseph, that Jacob said unto Laban, Send me away, that I may go unto mine own place, and to my country. Give me my wives and my children, for whom I have served thee, and let me go: for thou knowest my service which I have done thee. And Laban said unto him, I pray thee, if I have found favour in thine eyes, tarry: for I have learned by experience that the LORD *hath blessed me for thy sake.*

Genesis 30:25–27

As we'll see in chapter 31, Laban isn't a believer, yet even he recognizes he has been blessed by God because of Jacob. The number of his herds, flocks, and grandsons had multiplied radically. Everything was going well for Laban. And in a rare moment of honesty, he says to Jacob, "You have brought the Lord's blessing to my household."

No wonder Laban wanted Jacob to stay. In addition to being supernaturally blessed, Jacob was industrious—which isn't surprising since throughout Scripture God often called men who were already hard at work. When they were called to ministry,

Moses was watching his father-in-law's sheep (Exodus 3:1).

Elisha was plowing behind the oxen (1 Kings 19:19).

Peter was casting his net into the sea (Matthew 4:18).

Matthew was collecting taxes (Matthew 9:9).

"Whatsoever ye do in word or deed, do all in the name of the Lord Jesus" (Colossians 3:17). "Ye have not chosen me, but I have chosen you," Jesus said, "and *ordained you*" (John 15:16, italics added). We're *all* in the ministry, gang. Christians must be, can be, get to be the very best workers in whatever field the Lord places them, for then even the Labans will be drawn to the One we serve.

APRIL 7

And Jacob beheld the countenance of Laban, and, behold, it was not toward him as before. And the LORD said unto Jacob, Return unto the land of thy fathers, and to thy kindred; and I will be with thee.

Genesis 31:2–3

Many times, we're in a place where we wonder if God is trying to get us to make a move—geographically, professionally, or in ministry. I believe Jacob's story provides key clues to this question.

First, notice that the situation around Jacob soured. Jacob could see that Laban was no longer looking kindly upon him. So too, the Lord can speak through our circumstances to begin to nudge those who have eyes to see and ears to hear His leading.

Second, the Word of the Lord within Jacob sweetened. As Jacob's situation soured, the Word within him stirred. The same thing happens today. When the Lord wants to move us, the Scriptures we read day after day all seem to point in that direction.

APRIL 8

And Jacob sent and called Rachel and Leah to the field unto his flock, And said unto them, I see your father's countenance, that it is not toward me as before; but the God of my father hath been with me. And ye know that with all my power I have served your father. And your father hath deceived me, and changed my wages ten times; but God suffered him not to hurt me.

Genesis 31:4–7

While Jacob was right in his assessment of Laban's deceitful ways, he failed to see the most obvious truth about Laban: that is, Laban was in actuality a full-length mirror, a life-size reflection of his own flawed character.

I have discovered that the flaws and faults I see most clearly in others are my own. The more flawed a person is, the more he will see others' flaws. Jacob will point out over and over that Laban is a deceiver, because it was Jacob's own tendency to be a deceiver, a conniver, and a cheater. My prayer is that, before I die, God will deliver me from a Jacob mentality and will work in me the agape love that doesn't even notice when others do wrong (1 Corinthians 13:5).

APRIL 9

And Jacob said, O God of my father Abraham, and God of my father Isaac, the LORD which saidst unto me, Return unto thy country, and to thy kindred, and I will deal well with thee.

Genesis 32:9

Both at the beginning and at the conclusion of his prayer (verse 12), Jacob is insistent in that he says, "Lord, You are the One who told me to go back home. You are the One who promised You would save my life." In so doing, Jacob takes the promises given to him and lifts them back to the Lord in prayer.

This is a great, great key to praying effectively. "Concerning the work of my hands command ye me," the Lord declares (Isaiah 45:11).

"Command Him?" you say. "That sounds an awful lot like the 'name-it-and-claim-it' mentality."

However, contextually you will see God is talking about the promises and prophecies He had *already* made to the people. Listen to what Jesus would say along the same line: "If ye abide in me, and my words abide in you, ye shall ask what ye will, and it shall be done unto you" (John 15:7). In other words, "If you're abiding in Me, hanging around Me, and clinging to Me, you can ask anything of Me because within you will be My Word."

What word? "Exceeding great and precious promises" (2 Peter 1:4).

It has been said that there are between three and five thousand promises given to us in the Word. Therefore, it is as if God says, "I want you to take these exceedingly great and precious promises, and I want you to command Me."

Too often, we live like spiritual paupers. We don't see our families, our friends, or our country being blessed. Why? Because we have not asked (James 4:2). It is only as we pray the promises of God that we are able to draw from the inexhaustible resources the Lord has provided. Jacob understood this. That is why he was insistent in prayer.

APRIL 10

*And he said, Let me go, for the day breaketh. And he said, I
will not let thee go, except thou bless me.*

Genesis 32:26

Why did God wrestle Jacob? Why does He want to wrestle with you and
me? For the same reason I used to wrestle with my sons. It's something
called intimacy. God likes to wrestle things through with me and you because He enjoys us. It's as if He says to us, "Let's wrestle this thing through
hour after hour, day after day, even month after month because not only
will you find that I'll come through eventually, but in the process, we will
develop a wonderful intimacy."

That's why the original Greek text makes it clear that we are to "*keep* asking,
keep seeking, *keep* knocking" (see Matthew 7:7), for that is how intimacy is
developed; that is how prayer is answered.

Wrestling provides unique opportunities for discovery. As you measure
your strength against that of your opponent, as you assume various positions and are held in numerous holds, you discover things about yourself
and your opponent you couldn't have known otherwise. So too, God invites
us to wrestle with Him in order that we might discover things about Him
and ourselves we could learn in no other way. As you wrestle in prayer, you
might find that what God gives to you and does for you is entirely different than what you had expected. Jacob asked to be blessed, instead he was
broken, but the answer was better, because our Father knows best.

Keep on wrestling, gang. You'll have intimacy with the Lord. You'll make
discoveries about the Lord. And you'll be changed radically by the Lord in
the very process of praying.

APRIL 11

And he said unto him, What is thy name? And he said, Jacob. And he said, Thy name shall be called no more Jacob, but Israel: for as a prince hast thou power with God and with men, and hast prevailed.

Genesis 32:27–28

Does this mean the Lord didn't know with whom He was wrestling? No. The Lord knew Jacob's name, and now He's giving Jacob an opportunity to be reminded of it as well. You see, years earlier his dad had asked him, "Who are you?"

"I am Esau," Jacob had answered (Genesis 27:19).

It's as if the Lord is saying, "Let's try it again, Jacob. What is your name?"

Perhaps the great majority of people wish they were someone else. Jacob certainly did. "I want to be firstborn. I want the blessing. I want to be Esau," he said. So too, you can go through life trying to be someone you're not. You can copy the way she dresses or the way he talks, but it will lead to nothing but frustration until you have come to the moment when, in total honesty, you say, "I've tried to be this guy, tried to do that thing, but now I admit who I am. I'm Jacob."

No sooner does Jacob confess and come clean regarding his true identity than the Lord changes his name entirely—from Jacob to Israel, from "Heel snatcher" to "Governed by God."

"When did I prevail?" Jacob must have wondered.

And God would answer, "It was when you were broken, when you were pinned by Me, when you were weeping, but wouldn't let go of Me, when you said, 'I can't go through another day without You,' *that's* when you prevailed."

And that's when we'll prevail as well.

APRIL 12

Therefore the children of Israel eat not of the sinew which shrank, which is upon the hollow of the thigh, unto this day . . .

Genesis 32:32

To this day, the Orthodox Jews don't eat the thigh meat of an animal in honor of their great-great-great-great-great-great-great grandfather Jacob. Thus, down the tunnel of time, Jacob's descendants commemorate not his cleverness, intelligence, or charisma. They commemorate his pain.

A can-do kind of guy, Jacob was clever, charming, skilled, intelligent—a man any smart CEO would want to hire. God, on the other hand, said, "I have big plans for you, Jacob. You are going to have a huge impact on the history of the world, for from you will come an entire nation. And from that nation will come Messiah. I have big plans for you, but you're too smart, too self-confident, too clever. Therefore I'm going to break you."

Dear sister and brother, you must understand that no matter how charming, intelligent, or clever you are, or how good you may be in any given area, your skill is puny, your intelligence is nothing, and your strength is scrawny in comparison to God's. So God says, "I'm going to allow this pain in your life because then, and only then, will you lean on Me every step of the way, knowing that if you don't, you'll fall flat on your face. And as you lean on Me, you'll draw strength from Me and you'll be governed by Me instead of trying to make things happen in your own energy."

"Okay, Lord," we say. "I understand I have to be broken that I might learn to lean on You. But once I'm broken, can't You heal me? Once I've wrestled with You about a certain issue, can't You make me like new again?"

I am reminded of the story of another man who was lame . . .

> He had laid on the deck of a pool in Jerusalem day after day for thirty-eight years, hoping against hope that somehow, according to tradition, when an angel stirred the waters, he would be the first one in the pool and would be healed. Then, one day a young Rabbi came his way and asked him, "Wilt thou be made whole?"

"I can't," he answered, "because I don't have anyone to help me into the water."

And then something amazing happened—when the Rabbi told him to take up his bed and walk, the once-lame man was able to do just that.

"Whee!" he said. "I can walk! I can run! I can leap!"

"Hold on," said some Pharisees who had observed the scene. "It's the Sabbath day. You're not supposed to carry your bed on the Sabbath day. Who told you to do this? Who is this One who healed you?"

"Hmm," said the newly-healed man. "I don't know. I'm just so happy to be walking. I don't know who it was" (see John 5:2–13).

That's the issue, gang. We all would like to be healed, to have the pain go away, to have the hurt be gone. The fact, however, is if that were to happen, like the lame man, we would say, "Whee!" but we wouldn't know Who. Therefore, the pain stays; the limp continues day after day, year after year, that we might lean on Him, talk to Him, and draw strength and insight from Him, which we would never have received if we were just saying, "Whee!"

APRIL 13

. . . because he touched the hollow of Jacob's thigh in the sinew that shrank.

Genesis 32:32

Mom and Dad, Grandma and Grandpa, the degree to which your kids and grandchildren see you limp through life, leaning on God and drawing from Him strength, character, and depth is the degree to which they will value your legacy. They won't remember how successful you were in climbing the corporate ladder, how big your bank account was, how skilled you were mechanically, or how gifted you were musically. They will remember what they learned as they watched you limp.

"I know I have to lean on Him," you might be saying, "but sometimes I lose my way. Sometimes I forget. What do I do then?"

"Do this in remembrance of Me," Jesus would say to you. "It wasn't just My hip that was dislocated. My entire body was broken for you."

Thus, it is at the cross that I am reminded, in light of what Jesus did for me, that the pain He's allowing in my life is because He wants my very best. Communion is essential because we can get mixed up; we can get confused by pain and sadness and sorrow. But when we come to the Lord's Table and are reminded once again of His inexpressible love for us, we gladly exchange the leap of the lame man for the limp of Jacob because it is in limping that we remain close to Him all the days of our lives.

APRIL 14

Then the handmaidens came near, they and their children, and they bowed themselves. And Leah also with her children came near, and bowed themselves: and after came Joseph near and Rachel, and they bowed themselves. And he said, What meanest thou by all this drove which I met? And he said, These are to find grace in the sight of my lord. And Esau said, I have enough, my brother; keep that thou hast unto thyself.

Genesis 33:6–9

When, at last, Jacob and Esau met again, Esau asked the reason for the gifts Jacob had sent him.

"I sent them to you in order that I might find grace in your sight," Jacob answered.

And in Jacob we see an illustration of our tendency to think we have to give something to the Lord in order to receive grace from the Lord. Why is it so difficult for us to receive grace graciously? It's because we've been so convinced that "there's no free lunch." But guess what? There *is* a free lunch, and breakfast and dinner too! "Come and dine," says the Lord (John 21:12). "Ho, every one that thirsteth, come ye to the waters, and he that hath no money; come ye, buy, and eat" (Isaiah 55:1).

Now if Esau, who is a type of the flesh, says, "That's not the way it works," how much more our Lord, who is the epitome of grace and goodness, would say, "You don't have to do this, do that, or give up the other before you come into My presence." "Let us therefore come *boldly* unto the throne of grace, that we may obtain mercy, and find grace to help in time of need" (Hebrews 4:16, italics added).

If you're in need today, know this: There's nothing keeping you from going boldly to the throne and saying, "Father, I'm stuck," or "Father, I don't understand," or "Father, I need help."

This is the genius of true spirituality, the uniqueness of biblical Christianity. Every other philosophy and religion is based upon responsibility—the responsibility of its adherents to fast, to chant, to give, or to work. Christianity isn't based on responsibility. It's based on response—the response to unconditional love, unrestrained mercy, and undeserved grace.

For many years, I thought my salvation was based on my responsibility to pray, my responsibility to tithe, or my responsibility to be at church. But then I began to understand that God blesses, God gives, and God avails Himself not on the basis of what I do or don't do, but on the basis of what *He* did in sending His Son to die on the cross in order to pay the price for my sin. And when that pressure was taken off me, I wanted to study the Word. I wanted to be in church. I wanted to pray, not to earn blessing, but because I had already been so blessed.

APRIL 15

So Esau returned that day on his way unto Seir.

Genesis 33:16

Although he had reason to be angry, Esau did not hold a grudge against

Jacob. Furthermore, he only accepted Jacob's gift when pressed. Finally, he offered to accompany Jacob on his way as a means of protection for Jacob and his family. Thus, Esau would be considered refined and polished in our society. Yet the Bible says he was an uncouth man spiritually.

> . . . lest there be any fornicator, or profane person, as Esau, who for one morsel of meat sold his birthright. For ye know how that afterward, when he would have inherited the blessing, he was rejected: for he found no place of repentance, though he sought it carefully with tears.
>
> Hebrews 12:16–17

Esau is a picture of the flesh—a doomed and damned man for whom there was found no place to repent.

"But my unsaved neighbor or co-worker or uncle is so nice, so generous, so kind, so giving" we say. They may be. They may be gems, real diamonds. In comparison, the Christian you're sitting next to may be a cabbage. But there's a big difference. A diamond is brilliant, polished, and highly esteemed, but dead. A cabbage is common, lowly, and ugly, but alive.

People get mixed up about this. They say, "I see Christians and they're rude and mean." The real issue, however, is this: we may be cabbage heads, but we're alive.

> But God, who is rich in mercy, for his great love wherewith he loved us, even when we were dead in sins, hath quickened us together with Christ, (by grace ye are saved;) and hath raised us up together, and made us sit together in heavenly places in Christ Jesus.
>
> Ephesians 2:4–6

Diamond-like as we may have been, we were nonetheless dead, but God made us alive. And now, cabbage-like as we may be, we're nonetheless growing. We're not what we should be, but we're not what we used to be, and we're not what we're going to be, for when we see Him, we shall be like Him (1 John 3:2). Oh, glorious day!

APRIL 16

And God said unto Jacob, Arise, go up to Bethel, and dwell there: and make there an altar unto God, that appeared unto thee when thou fleddest from the face of Esau thy brother.

Genesis 35:1

With his daughter raped and his sons being mass murderers, Jacob's family is falling apart (Genesis 34). Therefore, in light of his situation, what God says to Jacob amazes me. He doesn't say, "Sit down. You're benched," or "Back off. You're done," or "That's it. You're through." He says, "Arise. Go up," because our God is a God of unbelievable grace.

Bethel—previously called Luz until the night Jacob had an encounter with God—was the place where Jacob was saved. Now the Lord says, "Go back to the place you met Me."

How I appreciate our Lord, because that's what He says to you and me. We tend to think God is mad at us, is angry with us, and has had enough of us. But our brother Paul would come on the scene and say, "Where sin abounds, grace abounds more" (see Romans 5:20).

Jacob and his clan are neck-deep in sin, and yet God says, "Rise up. Let's get going again. I want to 'alter' you once more."

APRIL 17

Then Jacob said unto his household, and to all that were with him, Put away the strange gods that are among you, and be clean, and change your garments: and let us arise, and go up to Bethel; and I will make there an altar unto God, who answered me in the day of my distress, and was with me in the way which I went. And they gave unto Jacob all the strange gods which were in their hand, and all their earrings which were in their ears.

Genesis 35:2–4

Evidently, Jacob's family had added pagan gods and trinkets to the idols Rachel had stolen from her father. Here, Jacob says, "We're going to Bethel. We're going to the house of God. So give me all of those earrings and bracelets and stuff you picked up from the heathens."

Notice God didn't say to Jacob, "If you deal with the pagan gods in your family, then I might give you a second chance." No, God simply said, "Rise and let us go to Bethel."

Perhaps it was because Jacob was so amazed by this that he said, "It's time to clean up, not *so* God will call us, but because He *has* called us."

That's what grace does. When I realize how kind and good and benevolent and merciful God is to me day after day after day, it causes me to want to put away my trinkets and toys that are not of Him. Too often, we think, I've got to get my life cleaned up and maybe then I can hear God's voice; maybe then He'll lead me again. No. God is ready to lead us today right where we are, and because of that we say, "Lord, You're so good. I don't want the things of the world anymore."

APRIL 18

And Jacob hid them under the oak which was by Shechem.

Genesis 35:4

In Scripture the tree, of course, speaks of the cross. In other words, the picture is that Jacob left his sin at Calvary. When Jesus died on the cross, not only was the penalty of sin paid for completely, but power over sin was provided for fully. So too, this very day you can say, "Lord, truly You are good in allowing me to go to Bethel once more. I'm tired of my sin, and I want my way to be free and unencumbered from the junk that entangles me."

Practically, how does this happen? You reckon the old man dead. You say, "Lord, on the basis of Your Word, I no longer have to do that, go there, be involved with the other, not because of positive thinking, but because of what You did on Calvary's tree." Just as by faith you receive forgiveness, so too, by faith you gain victory.

Thus, I can truly say to that Double Quarter Pounder® with Cheese, "I no longer have to submit to the demand you are placing on me. I reckon the old man dead to that sin." And I truly, honestly, absolutely, and unequivocally can turn away from that Quarter Pounder® and walk free, if I choose to! If you haven't spent time in Romans 6 lately, I encourage you to marvel at it and say, "Thank You, Lord, that, because on the cross You not only removed the penalty of sin but broke the power of sin, I don't have to give in. I can walk away a free man."

Gang, I am simple-minded enough to believe this applies to a heroin addict, to a gossiper, to a person who's hooked on pornography, or to a person with a negative attitude. *Whatever* the sin might be, its power was shattered on the cross.

"Give me that stuff," Jacob said to his family.

"No, it's too strong. No, it can't be done. No, it's too important," they could have said. Instead, they responded to the command given to them by Jacob, just as you can respond to the Word given to you by the Lord.

APRIL 19

So Jacob came to Luz, which is in the land of Canaan, that is, Bethel, he and all the people that were with him. And he built there an altar, and called the place El-beth-el: because there God appeared unto him, when he fled from the face of his brother.

Genesis 35:6–7

Jacob has his problems, indeed. Jacob has all kinds of baggage, without question. But through it all, he's growing because when he comes to Bethel the second time, he no longer calls it Bethel, "The house of God," but El Bethel, or "The God of the house of God." This shows monumental maturity, for Jacob understands that it's not the house of God that is important, but the God who dwells in it. So too, it's not church attendance that's important, but the God whom we meet there. It's not worship that's important, but the God whom we worship. It's not the Bible that's important, but the God of the Bible. You see, the Word is not an end in itself. The goal of Bible study is not to try and gain more intellectual or theological understanding. It's much more than that. The Word of God is simply a door I go through many times a day to meet the God of the Word.

"That's obvious," you say.

Not always. A lot of people initially delight in church or Bible study or worship, but will eventually lose interest in them because those things are not God. Be like Jacob. Keep your focus on God, and view everything else in light of Him.

APRIL 20

And Jacob called the name of the place where God spake with him, Bethel. And they journeyed from Bethel.

Genesis 35:15–16

To this man who experienced devastation in his family, God said, "Go to Bethel and dwell there. Go to Bethel and stay put." *Bethel* literally means "house of God." Jacob went to Bethel and found refuge and renewal, revival and refreshment, and then he left! Why? Why do people leave Bethel? Why do people leave the house of God? Let me give you the only answer we see in the text: After talking about Jacob's revival in Bethel in verse 7, verse 8 says, "Now Deborah, Rebekah's nurse, died." In other words, although he had met God, heard the promises of God, and fellowshipped with God at Bethel, Jacob evidently couldn't deal with the fact that his nanny was no longer there.

Both Abraham and Jacob would leave the house of God because of changes. Abraham left Bethel because of famine. His grandson left Bethel because of family. Abraham left because things were changing financially. Jacob left because he couldn't handle it emotionally.

Why did Jacob's nanny die? Why do things change? Because God is not static. Spiritual life will always be in motion. Therefore, it is the unwise man or the foolish woman who says, "If nanny's not here anymore, I'm not coming either." Precious fellow pilgrim, on our spiritual journey, we must build our altar, offer our praise, receive instruction, and *remain* in Bethel—in the place of fellowship with God.

APRIL 21

Now Israel loved Joseph more than all his children, because he was the son of his old age: and he made him a coat of many colours.

Genesis 37:3

In the book of Acts, Stephen refers to the text before us, saying that Joseph's brothers were moved with envy against him (Acts 7:9). Of what were they envious? Joseph's coat. Although your King James Bible describes this coat as being "of many colours," a better rendering is that it was a coat of "many pieces," or literally, a coat of "big sleeves."

You see, in Joseph's day most coats were actually vests because most men were workingmen and sleeves would only hinder their movement. However, those who held the position of boss or foreman would be given garments with sleeves. A coat with sleeves was not only a symbol of authority, but it was also a matter of practicality. In those days, before briefcases and hand-held computers, documents, and writing instruments, supplies would be kept in the sleeves secured by drawstrings at the wrists. Consequently, a man on the job site with sleeves was equivalent to a man carrying a briefcase and talking on a cell phone. In other words, the man with sleeves was clearly the boss.

And that's the issue in the story before us. Joseph's ten older brothers said, "Hey, what's the big idea? Why did Dad give the coat with big sleeves to little Joey? Why should *he* be the boss, the big cheese, the big shot? It's not right. It's not fair. It's not acceptable!" And so envious were they that they threw Joseph in a pit and sold him as a slave.

"Why can't I be the manager at McDonald's?" we say. "Why do I have to work the drive-thru year after year?"

"Why can't I be the boss at the company? I've been there longer than he has."

"How come I didn't get the contract? My bid was lower; my work is better. I don't understand."

In other words, we are prone to say, "I should have the big sleeves."

Whether it's on the job, at school, or in church, there will always be opportunity for you and me to say, "How come I'm not noticed or acknowledged, elevated or rewarded?" Yet I believe the real question is: Are you sure you want to be?

We think we know what we want. But the fact is, the coat of big sleeves caused Joseph big headaches. Therefore, it is the wise person who says, "Lord, I think I want that. I think I deserve that. I think I should be that. But, Lord, I understand that inherent in that position there may be headaches, problems, and pressures of which I am completely unaware. So have Your way, and I know it will be best."

APRIL 22

And Joseph was a goodly person, and well favoured.

Genesis 39:6

If I were in Joseph's sandals, would I give myself wholeheartedly, enthusiastically, and energetically to serving an Egyptian taskmaster, or would I say, "Lord, You've given me dreams and talents and abilities, but they're all being wasted because I'm just a slave"? One of the many things that impresses me about Joseph is that he didn't focus on what he lacked, but instead threw himself into the task at hand.

One Arizona dad, watching the tears on the faces of the boys who were too slow, too small, and too clumsy to get on the roster of one of the five north Phoenix Little League teams, asked if he could form a sixth team from the kids who were cut.

"Sure," said the officials, "if you'll coach them and pay for their uniforms."

So the dad did, naming his team the Phoenix Diamondbacks.

Last Friday, the Phoenix Diamondbacks won their last game by a score of 19–0.

It was the League Championship game.

Some say, "I could have really been used if I had made the team," or "I'll really be used as soon as my situation changes." Others, however, join Joseph in saying, "So what if I'm a slave? It's a great opportunity to work hard for the glory of God and see what He'll do."

APRIL 23

And Jacob their father said unto them, Me have ye bereaved of my children: Joseph is not, and Simeon is not, and ye will take Benjamin away: all these things are against me.

Genesis 42:36

Here's the question: How will I react to difficulty? Will I be like Jacob and say, "All things are working against me"—even though I know in my heart such is not the case? Or will I be like Joseph and say, "Man may have meant this for evil, but God meant it for good" (see Genesis 50:20)?

Unfortunately, all too often, I choose the sniveling of Jacob over the security of Joseph. Why? To elicit sympathy. What is it about our flesh that wants people to think we have it hard? While this may seem an insignificant quirk, in reality, it borders on blasphemy. In getting you to feel sorry for me, I get you to question God's goodness, provision, and protection in my life. Thus, your pity for me is at God's expense.

Who will I be? I can be self-indulgent and allow God to be cast in a bad light, even though I know in my heart the promise given to me, the price paid for me, and the peace available within me. I can deny all of this and say, "I want you to feel sorry for me. Listen to my tragedy."

Or, I can say, "I will not dishonor this good, gracious, loving God, who has been so kind to me, so good to me. He's my Creator and my Father. Therefore, I will not bring shame to His name in seeking sympathy from anyone." That is called the fear of the Lord. It's saying, "Father, I care more about Your reputation than I do about getting sympathy from the congregation. I don't want them to think questioningly, negatively, or blasphemously of You."

Where are the men and women who say, "We fear God. We will not snivel. God is good and we know deep within our hearts that He is working all things together for good"?

Here's the question: In the name of compassion, are you one who constantly weeps with others? Perhaps what we need in the Christian community during this time of self-centered Christianity are men and women who say, "I fear God. So, dear brother, precious sister, even if you don't understand, even if you think this is cold-hearted or lacking compassion, you *know* that this difficulty or tragedy will work for good. Stand on that knowledge. Cling to it. I will weep for you if you don't get it. But I'm not going to weep with you as you question God. He's too good for that."

May God give us wisdom. May God give us peace. May God give us understanding. All things work together for good to them that love God, to them who are the called according to His purpose (Romans 8:28). I *know* it. And so do you.

APRIL 24

And the man did as Joseph bade; and the man brought the men into Joseph's house. And the men were afraid, because they were brought into Joseph's house; and they said, Because of the money that was returned in our sacks at the first time are we brought in; that he may seek occasion against us, and fall upon us, and take us for bondmen.

Genesis 43:17–18

After selling him into slavery, no wonder Joseph's brothers were afraid when he called for them. "Oh, no!" they said. "He's calling us to his table because he wants to send us away as prisoners."

People still have this view of the greater than Joseph, Jesus Christ. People still say, "I've blown it so badly; I've erred so greatly; I know the Lord will yell at me and imprison me if I even come near His house."

Not true! Even though these guys had sinned greatly, they will discover incredible grace and unbelievable mercy because Joseph is a picture of Jesus. And where sin abounds, His grace abounds much more (Romans 5:20). When you are aware of your failings, your weaknesses, your inconsistencies, your stubbornness, rebellion, and sin, there's a tendency to say, "I can't go to church because I know Jesus is mad at me. If I go, I'll be bound with rules and regulations; I'll be sent away to the prison of condemnation."

> For my thoughts are not your thoughts, neither are your ways my ways, saith the LORD. For as the heavens are higher than the earth, so are my ways higher than your ways, and my thoughts than your thoughts.
>
> Isaiah 55:8–9

Through Isaiah, God says, "When someone offends you, is mean or nasty to you, I know that your ways and your thoughts center on one thing: revenge. But I don't think like you do. Therefore, I don't work like you do."

We need to realize how much different the Lord is from how we are in our fallen condition, in our depraved nature. "God is good," declares the psalmist (Psalm 73:1). He's just flat out, plain old good. He looks for ways not to blast, but to bless.

APRIL 25

And he entered into his chamber, and wept there.

Genesis 43:30

Joseph's heart was pounding, his stomach was churning, and his eyes were weeping, yet he didn't reveal himself to his brothers. Why? Because there was still work to do. There was still testing to take place.

So too, Jesus passionately wants to be with you and me, His bride. But He hasn't yet come for us because there's still work to do in us. It is true that Jesus is in heaven preparing a place for us (John 14:2), but He's also preparing us for the place. And when we're ready, He'll take us home, either through the rapture or through death. When the time is right, when the work He wants to do has come to completion, He'll take us home one way or the other. Therefore, if we're still here, it means there's still work to do, not just through us, but in us.

APRIL 26

And he took and sent messes unto them from before him: but Benjamin's mess was five times so much as any of theirs.

Genesis 43:34

Benjamin was given five times as much food as the others. Why did Joseph do this? I suggest it was in order to observe the reaction of his brothers. When Joseph was given the coat with the big sleeves, what was their response? Envy, jealousy, hostility, and anger. Therefore, Joseph wanted to see if his brothers would deal with Benjamin the same way they had dealt with him years earlier.

So too, the Lord measures the changes that have taken place in my life by how I react to my brothers, not just when they're hurting, but when they, like Benjamin, succeed. It's easy to weep with those who weep. It's harder to rejoice with those who rejoice. If someone undergoes a tragedy, a catastrophe, or a problem, most of us feel a certain amount of sympathy rather easily. But it's a little tougher for us to rejoice with the one who has everything going his way.

You'll know a deep work has taken place in your life when you not only weep with those who weep, but rejoice with those who rejoice (Romans 12:15), without being jealous or envious, hostile or cynical.

"All men will know you are My disciples," said Jesus, "by your love one for another" (see John 13:35). And "one another" includes the happy as well as the hurting.

APRIL 27

And Joseph said unto his brethren, Come near to me, I pray you. And they came near. And he said, I am Joseph your brother, whom ye sold into Egypt. Now therefore be not grieved, nor angry with yourselves, that ye sold me hither: for God did send me before you to preserve life.

Genesis 45:4–5

"Don't be upset with yourselves," he said to his brothers. "Your selling me into this foreign land as a slave was all part of God's plan."

I love these words of Joseph because they express the heart of Jesus. "Father, forgive them," He prayed from the cross, "for they don't know what they're doing" (see Luke 23:34). Those who crucified Jesus were indeed forgiven. The price was paid. And Peter would go on to declare that it was all part of a divine design, a grand plan, that Jesus would die for the sins of every man (Acts 2:22–24). "I know you are aware of your flaws and failings," Jesus would say to us, "but don't be grieved. I've forgiven you."

Christianity is unique in that it is not a matter of us cleaning ourselves up and getting our acts together. It is a matter of constantly rejoicing in the fact that the blood of Jesus cleanses us continually, that our sin is washed away constantly by what He did for us on the cross of Calvary. Thus, Christianity is celebration of what He's done, not condemnation for what we have or haven't done.

"Don't be angry with yourselves," Joseph said to his brothers. "God had a plan in all of this."

And God has a plan in everything you're involved in as well. That is, to make you appreciate what He's done for you, not so you can boast in your own righteousness, your own purity, or your own holiness, but to say, "Lord, Your forgiveness and kindness, Your goodness and mercy are awesome."

APRIL 28

And the children of Israel did so: and Joseph gave them wagons, according to the commandment of Pharaoh, and gave them provision for the way. To all of them he gave each man changes of raiment; but to Benjamin he gave three hundred pieces of silver, and five changes of raiment.

Genesis 45:21–22

The brothers didn't seem to notice that Benjamin had three hundred more pieces of silver and four more suits than they did. So blown away were they by Joseph's forgiveness that there was no room for envy or jealousy. I am so looking forward to that time when our greater than Joseph is revealed, when we are living with Jesus, for one of the heavenly things about heaven is that everyone will be 1,000 percent thrilled for everyone else. Our competition-based society places a high premium on getting ahead. But this is not the way of the kingdom . . .

When the water stirred, the first one into the pool of Siloam would, according to tradition, be the one who would be healed. So what did Jesus do? He didn't go to the ones close to the pool. He went to the guy in the back, the one who had been there for thirty-eight years, and took him away from the competitive scene altogether (John 5:8).

The reason Joseph's brothers didn't even notice that Benjamin was three hundred pieces of silver richer and four suits ahead of them was because they had been forgiven, and earthly riches no longer mattered.

APRIL 29

And to his father he sent after this manner; ten asses laden with the good things of Egypt, and ten she asses laden with corn and bread and meat for his father by the way. So he sent his brethren away, and they departed: and he said unto them, See that ye fall not out by the way.

Genesis 45:23–24

Here Joseph says, "I'm giving you everything you need to make the journey from where you are to where I am. Just see to it that you don't fall out by the way."

It's easy to fall out by the way. It's easy to say, "My body is hurting. My stocks are dropping. My head is spinning. And it's time to kick back a bit." But our greater than Joseph would say to us, "Don't do it. Don't fall back. Don't give up." In this regard, it's sobering to realize that Jesus told us only one-fourth of the seeds scattered would go on to bear significant fruit . . .

> In some people, the seed of the Word falls in soil and springs up quickly. But then comes the heat—tragedies, setbacks, and difficulties—that causes it to shrivel. In others, the cares of this world, the lust for riches, and the desire for other things are like weeds that choke out the Word. In others, the Word doesn't take root at all.

But some falls on soil where its roots grow deep and where it goes on to bring forth much fruit (Matthew 13).

Over the years, I've known those whose roots have gone deep into the soil of the Word, whose lives have borne much fruit, who despite setbacks and shortcomings, have not fallen out of the way. May we be those kinds of people.

APRIL 30

And Israel took his journey with all that he had, and came to Beer-sheba, and offered sacrifices unto the God of his father Isaac.

Genesis 46:1

I admire Jacob here because, although accepting this invitation to live among royalty and to be with his son Joseph again seems like the right thing to do, he stops and offers a sacrifice to God to ensure that what he is doing is truly acceptable in the Lord's sight.

Appearances can be deceiving. I'm learning that, aren't you? Jacob stops and says, "I want to make sure I'm going to Egypt with God's blessing." Why would he be so reticent? Perhaps it was because his grandfather had also gone down to Egypt in a time of famine, returned with a servant girl named Hagar, and set in motion a series of events for which the Middle East is paying the price to this day.

MAY 1

And God spake unto Israel in the visions of the night, and said, Jacob, Jacob. And he said, Here am I. And he said, I am God, the God of thy father: fear not to go down into Egypt; for I will there make of thee a great nation: I will go down with thee into Egypt; and I will also surely bring thee up again: and Joseph shall put his hand upon thine eyes.

Genesis 46:2–4

God says, "Jacob, I want you to go to Egypt. I'm not going to hold something from you that would be good for you. Your son will touch your eyes; you'll be in fellowship with him once again."

Romans 12 says this about God's will: It's good and acceptable and perfect. So often we think, "I hate the heat and can't stand snakes. Therefore, I know God will send me as a missionary to Africa." But that's not the way the Father works! His will for you is good, acceptable, and *perfect*. Understand this, precious people: whatever God tells you to do will be good, *really good* for you.

In a 1998 newspaper article, I read the following . . .

> Attending religious services lowers blood pressure more than tuning into religious TV or radio, a new study says. People who attended a religious service once a week and prayed or studied the Bible once a day were 40% less likely to have high blood pressure than those who don't go to church every week or pray and study the Bible less. "If they relied on TV or radio for their religious service," said David B. Larson, head of the National Institute for Healthcare Research, "it wasn't as beneficial. It shows that church attendance is better for your health than even watching religious TV." The link between religious activity and blood pressure is surprisingly strong. Previous studies show other health benefits from prayer. A 1988 study found that patients who were prayed for needed fewer antibiotics and had fewer complications in surgery. Last year, researchers found monthly church visits improved the mental health of the elderly. And researchers found earlier this year that adults who attend

church once a week were more likely to have high levels of an immune system protein associated with age-related diseases. The new findings, part of a National Institute of Health initiative, came from a study of 2,391 people.[1]

I like that! The will of the Father is indeed perfect.

MAY 2

And Jacob rose up from Beer-sheba: and the sons of Israel carried Jacob their father, and their little ones, and their wives, in the wagons which Pharaoh had sent to carry him. And they took their cattle, and their goods, which they had gotten in the land of Canaan, and came into Egypt, Jacob, and all his seed with him: His sons, and his sons' sons with him, his daughters, and his sons' daughters, and all his seed brought he with him into Egypt.

Genesis 46:5–7

The whole family is saved from the famished condition of where they were previously and has been called to live with Joseph in a land of luxury. I personally believe the Lord wants to save entire families. "Believe on the Lord Jesus Christ," Paul said to the Philippian jailor, "and you will be saved—and your house" (see Acts 16:31). This doesn't mean the whole family is automatically saved if the parent is a believer. But it does mean that a believing father or mother can expect the Lord to work in the rest of the family as he or she is obedient to the Word.

I'm simple enough to expect that my kids and grandchildren, should the Lord tarry, will travel with me, to be with the greater than Joseph—Jesus Christ—in the mansion He is preparing for us.

This note was left on my windshield yesterday . . .

I was so glad to see your car here, Brother Jon. I have the opportunity to share with you some wonderful news. While visiting my mother a few months ago, I accidentally left a set of tapes at her house. The tapes were of services I had missed from our current Genesis study. Now my mother thought I had left them there with hopes of converting her. But it truly was a mistake. I had really wanted to listen to them myself. But God is so faithful. For whatever reason, Mom started listening to the tapes, and she accepted Jesus as her Savior and is going to be baptized this Sunday in a church in Kennewick, Washington. My mother is saved. She's saved, she's saved! God used this chain of events just for her, and I couldn't be happier.

That's not coincidence. That's providence! Grandpa, believe it. Mom, don't doubt it. Parents, lay hold of it. Believe that the Lord will work in your family.

MAY 3

And Jacob blessed Pharaoh, and went out from before Pharaoh.

Genesis 47:10

According to Hebrews 7:7, the greater blesses the lesser. Although Jacob couldn't hold a candle to Pharaoh politically, financially, or militarily, he was unequivocally the greater spiritually because he was linked to the God of the universe.

The privilege of bestowing blessing—of proclaiming prosperity, happiness, and success—was reserved for patriarchs. Thus, Jacob was perfectly justified in pronouncing blessing, for he was a patriarch. But guess what? It is equally proper for us to pronounce blessing, for it was also a privilege for priests and kings, and according to 1 Peter 2:9, we are a chosen generation, a royal priesthood.

Wherever we go, we hear people mock, dishonor, and trivialize God. But you and I get to be those who say, "The Lord *bless* you." We get to be those who speak the Lord's name upon someone's life, into someone's day.

"But I'm old," you say.

So was Jacob.

"But I'm poor," you say.

So was he.

"But I'm nothing," you say.

In the eyes of men, neither was Jacob.

"But I'm not godly," you say.

Neither was Jacob.

Yet he walked into the palace of Pharaoh and blessed him. And that's what you can do. It just takes a moment or two, but you can bless people by speaking God's name in their ear, by adding God's presence to their day.

MAY 4

And Jacob said unto Joseph, God Almighty appeared unto me at Luz in the land of Canaan, and blessed me, and said unto me, Behold, I will make thee fruitful, and multiply thee, and I will make of thee a multitude of people; and will give this land to thy seed after thee for an everlasting possession.

Genesis 48:3–4

As Joseph enters with his sons Ephraim and Manasseh in tow, they who had blessed Jacob in coming are about to be blessed themselves.

Haven't you discovered that when you share with someone in need, you might set out, saying, "I don't know if I'll be able to help, say the right thing, or do enough," only to find that when you get there, *you* are the one who is blessed?

Jesus wants us to minister to each other because He taught that whatever measure a man gives out, it will be given back to him (see Matthew 7:2). It's in giving that we get. It's in praying for the sick that we become healthier. It's in cheering the discouraged that our own emotions begin to soar. It's in explaining truth to others that we begin to see things more clearly.

MAY 5

And Joseph said unto his father, Not so, my father: for this is the firstborn; put thy right hand upon his head. And his father refused, and said, I know it, my son, I know it: he also shall become a people, and he also shall be great: but truly his younger brother shall be greater than he, and his seed shall become a multitude of nations.

Genesis 48:18–19

"The Spirit of God has revealed to me that the younger son will be the greater," insisted Jacob. "Manasseh will be blessed, too, but there's a greater plan for Ephraim."

And that's exactly what happened. Ephraim became the greater tribe by far. The ten northern tribes of Israel are called Israel, but they're also referred to as Ephraim because Ephraim was predominant within the ten northern tribes.

Culturally and traditionally, the elder son, the firstborn, was to receive all of the benefits and assume the greater position. Quite often, however, the Lord seems to tweak this . . .

Cain was the firstborn, but it was Abel who was blessed.

Ishmael was the firstborn, but it was Isaac who was blessed.

Esau was the firstborn, but it was Jacob who was blessed.

Reuben was the firstborn, but it was Joseph who was blessed.

Aaron was the firstborn, but it was Moses who was blessed.

Throughout the Word, the Lord often makes the lesser the greater, and uses the younger to rule the older. Why? I think the basic message is simply this: What is coming is always better than what has been. We tend to wax eloquent about the good old days. The Lord, however, says, "The best is yet to come. I'm going to take you from glory to *greater* glory" (see 2 Corinthians 3:18).

This gives me real hope because I truly believe for our churches, for our families, and for us personally the best is yet to come. It just seems to be the way of the Lord if we choose to believe on Him and walk with Him.

MAY 6

Joseph is a fruitful bough . . .

Genesis 49:22

The Bible defines fruit in five specific areas . . .

In Romans 1:13, Paul tells us that the winning of souls is fruit unto God. Did Joseph win souls? Indeed! He saved his whole family from famine and drought. So too, when you share with your family, neighbors, or friends the good news of the gospel, saving them from the drought in their own souls and from the fires of hell, you bear fruit that pleases God.

Romans 6:22 identifies holiness as fruit. Perhaps best epitomized by his flight from the advances of Potiphar's wife, Joseph lived a holy life. In fact, he is one of only two major Old Testament characters of whom there is no recorded sin.

Philippians 4:17 identifies tithes and offerings as fruit. Joseph gave more than money in Egypt. He gave his life.

Colossians 1:10 says good works are a fruit unto God. Did Joseph do good works? Yes. He saved an entire nation from starvation by storing up goods to distribute when there was need.

Hebrews 13:15 names praise as fruit. When Joseph came to Pharaoh with the interpretation of Pharaoh's dream, he directed all praise to God (Genesis 41:16).

These five areas, so evident in Joseph's life, are summed up in a sixth New Testament reference to fruit:

> But the fruit of the Spirit is love, joy, peace, longsuffering, gentleness, goodness, faith, meekness, temperance: against such there is no law.
>
> Galatians 5:22–23

The fruit of the Spirit is love as defined by joy, peace, longsuffering, gentleness, goodness, faith, meekness, and self-control. The fruit of the Spirit is love. That's why we give of our time and money. That's why we lift our hands in praise. That's why we share with others.

With all of these qualities flowing through his life, no wonder Jacob said to Joseph, "You are a fruitful bough."

"Good for Joseph," you might be saying. "But why should I be fruitful?"

Because if we don't satisfy Jesus, not only will we not satisfy anyone else, but we won't satisfy even ourselves. Listen, gang, if you are not living to please God, then your life will dry up from the roots, from below the surface, from deep within, and you will experience emptiness, frustration, depression, and a lack of satisfaction. Live to please God, on the other hand, and your life will be marked by love.

MAY 7

. . . even a fruitful bough by a well; whose branches run over the wall.

Genesis 49:22

Like Joseph whose roots went into the well, so too, if the Word abides in you, you'll bring forth much fruit.

If I went out to my backyard, cut off a limb from the apple tree and said, "I have great news, kids: You no longer need to go outside to pick apples. Here's a branch we're going to keep right in the kitchen," they would wonder about me!

"You can't cut off a branch and have it bear fruit," they'd say. "It has to be connected to the tree."

So too, it's as if Jesus says, "The sap of the Scriptures must flow from Me to you in order for there to be fruit in your life."

As I have observed the apple tree in my backyard bring forth apples, never once have I seen the branches connected to the trunk struggling to bear fruit. The branches just hang there. They abide, and the fruit is produced naturally. So too, you might decide to be loving, to do good works, or to praise the Lord in your own energy. And you might be able to fake it for an hour or two, for a day or three, but ultimately you'll come up empty. The only way to produce genuine fruit morning by morning and day by day is to hang in there, abide in Christ, and allow the Spirit to flow to you and through you. Fruit cannot be faked for very long. You've got to have the Word in your life.

MAY 8

The archers have sorely grieved him, and shot at him, and hated him: But his bow abode in strength, and the arms of his hands were made strong by the hands of the mighty God of Jacob.

Genesis 49:23–24

Throughout his life, there was no shortage of archers who took potshots at Joseph . . .

He was shot at by his brothers because they were envious.

He was shot at by Potiphar's wife because he was righteous.

He was shot at by the butler who was thankless.

Joseph's brothers fired the arrows of envy; Potiphar's wife, the arrow of fury; and the butler, the arrow of apathy. Wherever Joseph went, there would be those who would view him as a target and let their arrows fly.

But what did Joseph do when he was shot at?

When he came into power, he could have nailed them all. He could have pinned his brothers to the wall, put Mrs. Potiphar in her place, and done in the butler. He had the power, the opportunity, and the legal right, but he didn't fire back. He didn't defend himself. His bow abode in strength. His bow remained silent.

Why didn't Joseph fire back?

According to our text, Joseph's God kept him from grabbing his bow and letting the arrows fly. Joseph's God kept Joseph's hand in His.

I can't control the tendency to want to defend myself, to retaliate, or to get revenge. When I hear or see things I feel are unfair or untrue, everything within me says, "Fire back. Clear the record. Straighten it out."

The only way to refrain from this tendency is to say, "Father, I want to stand up for my reputation, my right, my point of view. Restrain me, Lord."

Why shouldn't you clear the air and fire back for what you think is right?

Because those who find fault with you, those who come against you, those who shoot at you from a distance are ultimately instruments of God for your growth and for your good. You see, it was his brothers, Potiphar's wife, and the butler who were used by the Lord to create in Joseph character, strength, and a depth he would not have had if he hadn't been shot at, or if he had fired back.

The secret of strength is to refrain from using the power you have, to keep from trying to outmaneuver your enemy intellectually or retaliating physically, and to let the Lord fight for you and do a work within you.

MAY 9

And when Jacob had made an end of commanding his sons, he gathered up his feet into the bed, and yielded up the ghost, and was gathered unto his people.

Genesis 49:33

Jacob let go of his spirit, and was gathered unto his people. We will all be gathered unto our people. The only question is: Who are your people? Who are the people with whom you're most comfortable? They're the ones with whom you'll spend eternity.

Sometimes people say, "Hell won't be so bad. At least all my friends will be there." But nothing could be further from the truth. No one will be playing poker with his buddies and listening to country music in hell. No, hell is completely dark and totally hot. In hell, everyone is isolated.

Why would a loving God send anyone to a place like that?

He doesn't.

God is Light. Therefore, he who doesn't want God in his life gets darkness. God is Love. Therefore, he who doesn't want God in his life gets hate. God is a Father. Therefore, he who doesn't want God in his life will be an orphan—alone for all eternity. God is the wellspring of joy and source of happiness. Therefore, he who doesn't want God in his life will experience nothing but drought and depression. The person in hell isn't there because God wants to torture him. He's there because he doesn't want God in his life.

"Please reconsider," God says. "If you choose to turn your back on Me, I will give you that option. But the only way I'll let you go is over My dead body, for you'll have to walk over the body of My Son."

MAY 10

And Joseph wept when they spake unto him.

Genesis 50:17

Joseph cries. The word translated "wept" isn't the word for sobbing. It's the word for quiet weeping. Tears just rolled down his cheeks. His brothers didn't get it. They thought he was holding a grudge against them. They thought he was simply waiting for the right time to pounce on them. They thought he was angry with them, bitter toward them.

So too, we often think of our Lord Jesus as keeping a record of our previous failures; that He must be getting tired of us, exhausted by us. But we are told that, like Joseph, Jesus wept . . .

> "If you had only been here, our brother would not have died," cried Martha and Mary. "We told You he was sick. We sent You word, but You didn't come. And now he's dead." And Jesus wept. He knew what He would do. He knew He would bring Lazarus back to life. So it wasn't for Lazarus He wept. It was for the unbelief of Martha and Mary (John 11).

> Jesus wept a second time when He said, "O Jerusalem, Jerusalem, I would gather you under My wing and nestle You close to My heart, but you wouldn't let Me" (see Matthew 23:37).

If you think you've botched it so many times that the Lord must be just about ready to throw in the towel with you, you don't understand the heart of our Lord. It was for the man most in need, upon the man who couldn't handle things all that well, toward the man with the paralyzed hand that Jesus had compassion (Mark 3:1–5). So too, if you are struggling and are barely able to hold things together, you are the very one for whom Jesus has the most compassion. The person who's not reaching out, not doing well, unable to handle life is the one for whom Jesus has special affection and on whom He has a laser-like focus.

Each of us is struggling with one thing or another. Thus, Jesus would say to all of us, "No matter how withered it might be, stretch out your hand. Grab hold of Me. Receive from Me that which I long to give you."

No matter what pit you've dug, or what brother you've sold, our greater than Joseph has washed away your sin with His own blood.

MAY 11

So Joseph died, being an hundred and ten years old: and they embalmed him, and he was put in a coffin in Egypt.

Genesis 50:26

Thus ends the book of Genesis. The book that began with creation ends with a coffin. The book that began in glory ends in a grave. The book that began with the living God ends with a dead man. The book that began with the brightness of heaven ends with bones in Egypt.

Why?

It's the Holy Spirit's commentary on the condition of man, the repercussions of sin, and the need for a Savior.

Joseph is the most Christlike man in the Bible, and yet we see him in a coffin. Although Satan said otherwise, God had said, "In the day you eat of the forbidden fruit, thou shalt surely die" (see Genesis 2:17). Joseph was a very good man, but the fact is that *all* have sinned and come short of the glory of God, and that the wages of sin is death (Romans 3:23; 6:23).

Is there any way out? Is there any hope? Is there any plan?

Yes! We'll see God's redemptive plan unfold in Exodus. We'll not stay in a coffin in Egypt indefinitely, gang. We're going to heaven. We're on our way home!

MAY 12

But the more they afflicted them, the more they multiplied and grew.

Exodus 1:12

The book of Exodus is the book of redemption, wherein we see that God's heart is for us and that He has a plan to set us free. Exodus is a picture book of God's redemptive character, of His desire to set at liberty those who were enslaved by sin and stuck in a coffin in Egypt.

Between Genesis 50 and Exodus 1 is a time gap of approximately four hundred years, a time gap during which something quite amazing happened. You see, the seventy souls who originally entered the land of Egypt in Genesis 50 numbered approximately 3 million in Exodus 1. Worried that they would one day be outnumbered, the Egyptians tried to slow down the population growth of God's people. But, as always, God had a plan even in this.

God allows His people to be afflicted because He knows the same thing my high school football coach knew. Coach Dominguez told us that the only way to increase our strength was to break down our muscles. And he was right. The foundational premise of weight training is that hard exercise allows a muscle to break down, eventually repairing itself stronger than it was before.

The same thing holds true spiritually. Because faith is a muscle that needs to be worked, if I am to grow in depth, in strength, or in maturity, there's no other way than to go through testing, trial, and affliction. Therefore, when I feel like I'm breaking down, falling apart, or caving in, if I listen, I'll hear the voice of the ultimate coach, Jesus, saying, "Trust Me. I know what I'm doing. These hard times are necessary to build your strength, to give you victory."

MAY 13

And the king of Egypt called for the midwives, and said unto them, Why have ye done this thing, and have saved the men children alive? And the midwives said unto Pharaoh, Because the Hebrew women are not as the Egyptian women; for they are lively, and are delivered ere the midwives come in unto them. Therefore God dealt well with the midwives: and the people multiplied, and waxed very mighty. And it came to pass, because the midwives feared God, that he made them houses.

Exodus 1:18–21

Midwives were midwives because they were barren. But God blessed these midwives and gave them children of their own.

"Wait a minute," you protest. "Hadn't these women lied?"

Yes, but God blessed them anyway. It isn't that God approves of lying. Rather than focusing on the fault of these women, however, He sees that they feared Him, that they disobeyed Pharaoh and risked their own lives to do what was right in His sight.

God the Father has a way, not only with Egyptian midwives, but with you and me, of finding what is good and celebrating that. Aren't you glad that God doesn't focus on our failings and shortcomings, but rather has a way of looking at us and approving the things which are excellent, just as Paul tells us we all should do (Philippians 1:10)? This doesn't mean God doesn't convict us of sin and call us to repent and change direction. But it does mean that our God is exceedingly kind. We might judge these women for lying. God, however, declares, "They did something good in My sight and I'm going to honor them."

MAY 14

And there went a man of the house of Levi, and took to wife a daughter of Levi. And the woman conceived, and bare a son: and when she saw him that he was a goodly child, she hid him three months. And when she could not longer hide him, she took for him an ark of bulrushes, and daubed it with slime and with pitch, and put the child therein; and she laid it in the flags by the river's brink.

Exodus 2:1–3

Jochebed, Moses' mother, was a woman of vision, for she saw that her son was "a goodly child." Not only was she a woman of vision, but she was a woman of the Word, for what else would explain her decision to place her son in the very river in which all other male babies his age were being drowned? My tendency would be to stay as far from the river as possible. But not Jochebed. Why? I suggest it was because she knew the story of another "goodly" man who was saved in a time of destruction and judgment. I suggest it was because she knew the story of Noah. You see, the Hebrew word translated "ark" in verse 3 is used only one other place in all of Scripture: in reference to Noah. Thus, I believe it was not mere coincidence that prodded Jochebed to fashion an ark and to line it with pitch, just as Noah had done (Genesis 6:14).

How I encourage you who are parents to follow the pattern of Jochebed. Ask God to give you a vision for your child. Even if others think he is ordinary or not all that special, in God's sight that child of yours has a wonderful, huge, important, and unique calling. Ask God to show a portion of it to you. Second, immerse yourself in the Word. Believe in it, act on it in faith, and don't be surprised if, in so doing, like Jochebed, you raise a hero of the faith.

MAY 15

And Moses was content to dwell with the man: and he gave Moses Zipporah his daughter. And she bare him a son, and he called his name Gershom: for he said, I have been a stranger in a strange land.

Exodus 2:21–22

In Acts 7, we read that not only was Moses "mighty in works," which means he was a military hero, but that he was "full of the wisdom of Egypt." In other words, he was schooled in philosophy and astronomy, in science and history, in language and botany. And yet here he is in a desert with one man and his seven daughters. From Genesis 46:34 we know that in the eyes of the Egyptian, shepherds were an abomination. Therefore, the man who had been most respected was now utterly rejected.

And yet he was content.

According to Paul, contentment is precisely what you and I are to study (Philippians 4:11). "Learn to be content," he tells us, understanding that if we're not content where we are today, we'll not be content wherever we plan on going tomorrow.

If asked whether we're content right here, right now, most of us would answer, "Not yet, but I'm going to be tomorrow, next month, real soon, around the corner, coming up. Any day now, things will be perfect." Moses, however, wouldn't have answered this way, for he had learned the hugely important lesson of contentment.

"I know I'm supposed to learn to be content," people say. "But how?"

I believe verse 21 tells us how: Be a Gershom. You see, *Gershom* means "stranger." Therefore, in naming his son Gershom, Moses in essence said, "I'm just passing through. This world is not my home."

Contentment is not hard to learn if you realize what you really long for is heaven. Once I understand that I'm just a stranger here, that I won't ever fit in, that I'm just passing through, I enjoy life because I'm not expecting the job, the car, the house, the relationship, or the bank account to do what those things can never do. If I am truly Gershom, I'll take a whole lot more things a whole lot less seriously, and as a result, my life will be characterized by joy and contentment.

MAY 16

Now Moses kept the flock of Jethro his father in law, the priest of Midian: and he led the flock to the backside of the desert.

Exodus 3:1

It seems God often plants His people in the desert before He uses them.

Elijah was a man of the desert.

John the Baptist grew up in the desert regions of the Dead Sea.

Paul spent the three years following his conversion in the deserts of Arabia.

John the revelator was banished to the desert isle of Patmos.

Like you, I have gone through desert times, dry seasons when I have wondered, "Lord, where's Your presence and where's Your power?" But, as the years have gone by, I have come to understand that those desert times are imperative if I am to be one who is not dependent upon my feelings or my emotions. Desert seasons are essential for me to come to a place where I can say, "Lord, You promised You would be with me. You promised You would never leave me no matter how dry the times might be or how solitary the setting might seem. The fact of the matter is, Your Word has been given and You're teaching me to stand upon it rather than sink in my own emotions."

Over the years, I have seen lots of talented people in all sorts of ministries fall away because their emotions, rather than the Word, dictated their walk. Emotions go up and down. Emotions are fickle. Emotions are affected by how our job is going, how our family is doing, or how much pizza we had the previous evening. But because God wants us to be stable and solid, to walk by faith and not by feelings, He will put us into a desert place where we, like Moses, must learn to be content and say, "Lord, You've given me the promise of Your Word. And that is all I need."

MAY 17

And the angel of the LORD appeared unto him in a flame of fire out of the midst of a bush: and he looked, and, behold, the bush burned with fire, and the bush was not consumed.

Exodus 3:2

To speak to Moses, I would have thought the Lord would use a mighty oak tree, strong and sturdy; or a majestic pine tree, tall and stately; or a fragrant cedar, smelling sweetly. But the Lord didn't use any of those. He used a bush. The Hebrew word translated "bush" is *cenah*, and literally refers to a thorny bush. According to botanists, thorns are basically aborted branches. That is, they should have been branches, but just didn't get that far. So here's this bush. It's common; it's prickly; and even its attempts at growing branches were too weak to amount to anything. In other words, it's just like me.

The Lord loves to use bushes like you and me . . .

> For ye see your calling, brethren, how that not many wise men af-
> ter the flesh, not many mighty, not many noble, are called: but God
> hath chosen the foolish things of the world to confound the wise; and
> God hath chosen the weak things of the world to confound the things
> which are mighty; and base things of the world, and things which are
> despised, hath God chosen, yea, and things which are not, to bring to
> nought things that are: that no flesh should glory in his presence.
>
> 1 Corinthians 1:26–29

God chooses those who are bushes, those who are bush-league, those who feel bushed, because when He uses a bush all of the glory goes to Him.

So great a violinist was Niccolò Paganini that a legend arose wherein he walked onto the stage of a Viennese concert hall one evening, violin in hand, and broke a string. He followed this by breaking a second string, then a third. With only one string remaining, Paganini nestled the violin under his chin and, for the next eighteen minutes, played magnificently. As the crowd rose to its feet in ovation, Paganini said, "One string and Paganini." And, realizing they had heard a true master, the crowd erupted in applause.

I might feel like I only have one string. I might feel strung-out, strung-along, or third-string. But the reality is, the Lord loves to use that which is weak, unimportant, and unimpressive because then He, the Master Musician, gets the ovation, the glory, and the adoration.

Why does God reserve all glory for Himself? Because He knows that if He shares His glory with us, if people look up to you, lean on me, or become impressed with us, every one of us will ultimately disappoint them. Therefore, He says, "I alone will receive glory because I alone will never disappoint anyone who looks to Me, who trusts in Me, who leans on Me." Only God is solid and stable enough to see us through day after year after decade on through eternity. So He uses bushes, one-stringed violins, common people like you and me in order that He alone might receive the praise.

MAY 18

And Moses said, I will now turn aside, and see this great sight, why the bush is not burnt.

Exodus 3:3

Would Moses have turned aside to study this situation—this interesting phenomenon of a bush burning but not being consumed—if he had been in the city, if he had been engaged in lots of activity, if he had been in the palace of Pharaoh as he was forty years previously? I don't think so.

And now I see that the Lord places me in desert regions because it's only then that I have eyes to see and ears to hear that which He desires to tell me. When things are humming, active, and hectic, I believe I miss many of the key indicators God sends my way. So if you're in a desert place, a desert job, a desert marriage, rejoice, for it will give you opportunity to see and sense the Lord in ways that, if you were more active, more engaged, or even more fulfilled, you would miss.

MAY 19

And when the LORD *saw that he turned aside to see, God called unto him out of the midst of the bush, and said, Moses, Moses. And he said, Here am I.*

Exodus 3:4

Here's Moses on the backside of the desert day after week after month after year. Decades go by. And then something happens. Among the many bushes in the wilderness, one burns brightly without being consumed, causing Moses to eventually realize that the Lord was with him.

Where is God today?

He's in the bush sitting next to you.

"That prickly person?" you ask.

Yes. God is here in the person sitting next to you, in the person you're married to, in the person you work with.

"Wait a minute," you protest. "The Lord certainly can't speak through my husband, my parents, or my boss. They're not on fire."

Oh, but there's what you need to see. The bush was not on fire. The fire was in the bush. You might think people around you aren't on fire. That may be true. But if they're believers, the fire is in them . . .

Although Jesus did mighty works in Capernaum, there were those who scoffed and said, "We know Him. He's the son of the carpenter. Aren't His brothers and sisters among us?" (Matthew 13). They thought He was the son of a carpenter, failing to realize He is the Son of the Creator.

In Mark 6, the disciples are toiling; the waves are mounting; the wind is howling. And in the middle of the night, they see someone walking toward them. A legend of their day said that right before fishermen drowned, they saw a spirit coming toward them. No wonder their fear was rising. "It's a ghost!" the disciples cried, until Jesus said, "Be of good cheer. It is I."

As two disciples walked toward Emmaus, they were joined by One who asked them why they were so sad. "Are you a stranger here?" they asked incredulously, not recognizing it was Jesus Himself who walked beside them (Luke 24).

Finding the tomb empty that Easter morning, Mary Magdalene wept. Seeing a man she supposed to be the gardener, she said, "Sir, if you have moved the body, tell me where you have taken Him." But when the "gardener" answered and spoke her name, she recognized Him for who He was (John 20).

Jesus dwells with us in the carpenters' sons, in those we think we know. He speaks to us through people who may frighten us as they dare to rattle the bars of our beliefs. He reaches out to us through strangers walking alongside us. He speaks to us through gardeners, through plumbers, through those who work beside and for us. Oh, they might not be on fire. But the fire is in them; and the Lord can use them as easily, as powerfully, and as surprisingly as He can use a common, everyday bush like you.

MAY 20

And Moses said unto God, Behold, when I come unto the children of Israel, and shall say unto them, The God of your fathers hath sent me unto you; and they shall say to me, What is his name? what shall I say unto them?

Exodus 3:13

At the ripe old age of eighty, Moses was given a massive, monumental task. He was called by God to lead the children of Israel out of the bondage of Egypt into the Land of Promise. For the previous forty years, he had been on the backside of the desert, seemingly forsaken and forgotten. No wonder he said, "Lord, who am I? I'm eighty years old. I've been out of the loop for forty years. I've been out here in the desert for four decades. Lord, who am I?"

"Certainly I will be with thee," God answered. In other words, the question isn't who you are, but "Who is with you?" And the answer is "I AM."

Like Moses, we might say, "Who are we?"

And, as He said to Moses, the Lord would say to us, "The issue isn't who you are, but 'Who is with you?'"

Fifteen hundred years later, Jesus said to His disciples, "Go into the world and preach the gospel. Make disciples and baptize them in the name of the Father, Son, and Holy Spirit" (see Matthew 28:19). Jesus commissioned His disciples to see people set free.

"Who are we to do this massive, monumental task?" they must have wondered.

But Jesus went on to say, "And lo, I am with you alway, even unto the end of the world" (Matthew 28:20). "It's not who you are, but who's with you. *That's* the key."

After hearing that the Lord is with him, Moses asks, "What shall I say Your name is?" Moses asks this question not for the sake of identification. He already knows God is talking to him. God had already identified Himself in verse 6. So it wasn't a matter of identification. Nor was it a matter of conversation. Moses wasn't trying to make small talk, not with the lives of 3 million people at stake.

Moses' question was neither for identification nor for idle conversation. It was for the purpose of communication.

"I know You are the God of Abraham, Isaac, and Jacob. I know You are the Supreme Entity. Those are Your titles. But what's Your *name*?" Moses asked God. It's as if he's saying, "Lord, if I'm going to lead 3 million people across the wilderness, I need to be able to reach You."

"That I may *know* him," Paul declared, "and the power of his resurrection"

(Philippians 3:10, italics added). You may not have to lead 3 million people across the wilderness today, but even to navigate whatever is on your schedule, there is not a more joyful or needful goal than that of knowing God.

MAY 21

And God said unto Moses, I AM THAT I AM: and he said,
Thus shalt thou say unto the children of Israel, I AM hath
sent me unto you.

Exodus 3:14

In Bible days, a person's name was an indication of his nature. That's why we're told to pray in Jesus' name. "If you ask anything in My name," He said, "I will do it" (see John 14:14).

"In Jesus' name" is not merely a phrase to tack on to the end of your prayers, like "over and out." No, praying in Jesus' name means praying according to His nature, praying in harmony with His heart, praying as He would pray if He were in our situation. So in asking God's name, Moses in essence is saying, "What's Your nature?" And God, for the first time, here in Exodus 3, identifies His name as literally, I AM THAT I AM.

"I AM . . . what?" Moses may have wondered.

"I AM whatever you have need of," God must have intimated. "Moses, you're on a journey. The task before you is huge and you want to know who I am. I AM whatever you need. Not I USED TO BE, not WILL BE, but I AM presently. Immutable. Unchangeable. The same yesterday, today, and forever. Rock solid. I AM. That's My name; I AM whatever you need."

Fifteen hundred years later, Jesus would shed further light on God's name by declaring,

I AM the Bread.

I AM the Way.

I AM the Truth.

I AM the Life.

I AM the Light of the World.

I AM the Good Shepherd.

I AM the Door.

I AM the Vine.

Jesus took the name of God and filled in the blank.

"Show us the Father," said Philip.

"He that has seen Me has seen the Father," Jesus answered (see John 14:9). No wonder two hundred armed soldiers seeking to arrest Jesus fell down backwards upon hearing His irrefutable declaration of deity, upon hearing Him say, "I am He," or literally, "I AM."

For many years, I didn't fully understand this, and thought Jesus was not I AM but I GIVE, as in "I give bread, deliverance, strength, and healing." Now I understand that He's infinitely more than that. We think we need bread, healing, deliverance, and companionship. In actuality, however, we're craving Jesus. It's not something He gives us, but who He will be for us step by step, day by day.

MAY 22

And the LORD said unto him, What is that in thine hand? And he said, A rod.

Exodus 4:2

Often people say, "I can't be used. If I try to serve in some way, the people won't respond. If I try to be used at work or in Sunday school, in my neighborhood or in my family, no one will listen. If I try to pray with my wife, she won't receive from me; that's for other guys, not me." But before you fall prey to that kind of thinking, take a look at what is in your hand.

"What's in your hand?" God asked Moses.

"A shepherd's rod," Moses answered.

"That's what I'll use," said God.

"What's in your hand, Paul?"

"A pen. I'm a scholar."

"I'll use that," said God. "You will write a great portion of My Word."

"What's in your hand, Peter?"

"A net. I'm a fisherman."

"I'll use that," said God. "You will be a fisher of men and haul people into the kingdom."

If you wonder how you can serve God, how you can be used by Him, take a look at what's in your hand. When you were born, God gave you gifts that are simply waiting to be activated when you become born again. You're already doing that which He will energize and empower for ministry. What's in your hand? A computer? A hammer? A basketball? That's what He will use for His glory.

MAY 23

And he said, Cast it on the ground. And he cast it on the ground, and it became a serpent; and Moses fled from before it. And the LORD said unto Moses, Put forth thine hand, and take it by the tail. And he put forth his hand, and caught it, and it became a rod in his hand: that they may believe that the LORD God of their fathers, the God of Abraham, the God of Isaac, and the God of Jacob, hath appeared unto thee.

Exodus 4:3–5

You may be an accountant, a carpenter, or a surgeon. God says, "Throw down your occupation, your profession and see what it is in and of itself: it's a snake. If you're living for it, if you're all caught up in it, if you're depending on it, you will be bitten by it." The same holds true—maybe *especially* true—with regard to ministry. Moses had been a faithful shepherd for forty years. Here, God makes it clear that nothing could compare to an empty hand lifted and open to Him. It's as if, at the outset of the monumental ministry to which He was calling Moses, God said, "I must be your passion, not your service for Me, not your talents or abilities, not your spiritual gifts. Nothing must take the place of an open hand, an open heart to embrace Me personally."

Maybe you've been forced to throw down some skill, some calling, some position you were good at or gifted for. Don't despise this, for now you can say, "Lord, now that I don't have that in my hand anymore, I'm rediscovering it's not doing something for You that I crave, but it is simply You. I'm not looking for an opportunity to exercise my gift or to be used in ministry. I'm just looking for more intimacy with You. No wonder it had to be pried out of my hand. I get it. It's a snake." And once you understand this, you're in a position to pick it up once again.

To avoid getting bit, the wisest thing to do is to grab a snake by the back of the head. God, however, tells Moses to grab it by the tail as if to say, "Now that you see that ministry is not the priority, pick it up again, only this time by the tail. It's not going to have priority in your life. It's not going to be the thing that drives you." There is no stopping the man or woman who puts ministry in its rightful position—as the tail—thus allowing God to take His rightful position as head.

MAY 24

And the Lord *said furthermore unto him, Put now thine hand into thy bosom. And he put his hand into his bosom: and when he took it out, behold, his hand was leprous as snow. And he said, Put thine hand into thy bosom again. And he put his hand into his bosom again; and plucked it out of his bosom, and, behold, it was turned again as his other flesh. And it shall come to pass, if they will not believe thee, neither hearken to the voice of the first sign, that they will believe the voice of the latter sign. And it shall come to pass, if they will not believe also these two signs, neither hearken unto thy voice, that thou shalt take of the water of the river, and pour it upon the dry land: and the water which thou takest out of the river shall become blood upon the dry land.*

Exodus 4:6–9

God had given Moses the ability to herd sheep. In addition to this ability, here we see God gave him a testimony. Leprosy is a picture of sin in Scripture. Therefore, the illustration of a leprous hand made whole is one of being born again. What God has done in each of our lives is a powerful tool in ministry. Share your story. Share your testimony. It's powerful and cannot be denied.

In addition to ability and a testimony, the third tool God gave Moses was authority. He was to pour water from the Nile River—the river that sustained the entire Egyptian Empire—on the ground, where it would become blood. And in so doing, the people would see that no matter how refreshing their surroundings might be, apart from God, even their best efforts at life were doomed to die.

With regard to ministry, never underestimate the power of telling the truth directly, of saying, "The path you're on will lead to death. But here's what God has done: He died on the cross that you might live. The water you're drinking will lead to death. But if you drink of Jesus, the Water of Life, you will never thirst again."

Regarding ministry, a lot of people have gifts, callings, and good intentions. But they never get to the root issue. They never directly say to a family member, neighbor, relative, or friend, "What you're drinking will kill you. You need to be born again." When is the last time you truly shared the message of the cross with a non-believer? As good as simply being nice to people, helping them out, making them feel loved, welcomed, or affirmed might be, these things can't hold a candle to the power of the cross. There is nothing more powerful than a clear, simple presentation of the cross.

MAY 25

And it came to pass by the way in the inn, that the LORD met him, and sought to kill him.

Exodus 4:24

"Let My son go," God said to Pharaoh, "or your son will die" (see Exodus 4:23). Two sons are being talked about, but there are three sons in the story, for Moses had a son as well. And Moses couldn't pronounce judgment on Pharaoh's house while his own house was in error (1 Peter 4:17). You see, in Genesis 17:11, God instituted circumcision as an outward sign of an inward belief, its counterpart seen in the New Testament ordinance of baptism (Colossians 2:11–12). Circumcision was given to the Jewish nation as a mark of differentiation between them and every other culture round about them. Yet, Moses never circumcised his son. As a descendant of Abraham, Moses certainly knew the significance of this act. Why, then, wouldn't he have circumcised Gershom?

It could be that he was preoccupied with his occupation. It could be that he was so into watching sheep that he forgot about the spiritual needs of his son. And before we wonder how watching sheep in the desert could be that consuming, we would do well to ask ourselves why we expend so much time and energy simply to make another sale, to get another client, to climb another step, to make another dollar. When we get to heaven, on the other side of eternity, we will surely say, "What was I thinking? Why did I take my career so seriously? Why wasn't I there for my son, helping him to grow in his walk with the Lord?"

Or perhaps the reason Moses didn't circumcise his son was a little more subtle. Perhaps it was because he was caught up in ministry. Listen carefully, Mom and Dad: there is no ministry in which you will ever be engaged that is more important, more fulfilling, more satisfying, gratifying, or thrilling than discipling your own children. God tapping you on the shoulder and saying 3 million people will listen to you would be incomparable to seeing your son or daughter discipled and trained. And lest you think your family isn't a big enough ministry for a man of your skills and abilities, consider this: Jesus, the perfect Man, the ultimate minister, chose only twelve disciples into whom to pour His life. Therefore, one, two, or three kids is more than enough for even the best of us. From day one you get to pray for them, love them, and model God to them. It's an incredible opportunity.

MAY 26

*And Pharaoh said, Who is the L*ORD*, that I should obey his voice to let Israel go? I know not the L*ORD*, neither will I let Israel go.*

Exodus 5:2

Revelation is directly linked to obedience. Pharaoh didn't know the Lord solely because he had no intention to obey Him.

Do you desire to be obedient to the Lord? If so, He will give revelation to you and will provide direction for you. But our God is so good that He will not give further revelation to us or further direction to us if we have not been obedient to that which He has already told us to do. Often, people say,

"I just don't know what the Lord's plan or will for me is." And frequently, it's an issue of whether or not they've obeyed the last thing He told them to do.

The desk in my study is piled high with papers. My in box is overflowing. The Lord, however, is so good to us that He doesn't keep stacking up our spiritual in boxes. He gives us one thing to do, one assignment, one memo, one piece of information, one directive. And then He waits until we do it before giving us another. "My burden is easy," He declared. "My load is light" (see Matthew 11:30). He gives us one thing to do. He doesn't overwhelm or overwork us.

MAY 27

Let there more work be laid upon the men, that they may labour therein; and let them not regard vain words.

Exodus 5:9

Pharaoh referred to Moses' request to worship as "vain words," or a waste of time. And Pharaoh's mentality prevails to this day. "You don't have time for Communion. You don't have time for worship. You don't have time for devotions. There's work to do," our society barks.

Nowhere is this mindset seen more clearly than in Judas who, observing Mary anoint Jesus with ointment costing a year's salary, said, "That's a waste. That money could have been spent on the poor. That money could have been used to do some good work" (see John 12:4–6). Yet Jesus would later refer to Judas himself as "the son of perdition," or literally, "the son of waste," because the biggest waste is that of wasting the opportunity to worship.

> The moles in my backyard drive me crazy. To rid my yard of them, I've stuck a hose down their holes and flooded them for an hour at a time. I've tossed in little smoke bombs. I've stood vigilantly over their holes with shovel in hand—all to no avail. Then I read

that in one night, a single mole will often dig three hundred feet of tunnel. And, as my experience proves, the moles' efforts are not in vain, for even though they're digging under the surface where no one can see them, when the smoke bombs are thrown in or the water is turned on, they can escape to any number of tunnels and bomb shelters.

That's exactly what the devotional life does for you and me. "What a waste of time it is staying up late or getting up early to study the Word. What a waste of time it is to go to church on a Thursday night," some might mutter. But they fail to understand that those things are tunnels and bomb shelters that will protect you from the inevitable attacks of the Enemy.

"Why couldn't we cast this demon out?" the disciples asked Jesus.

"This kind does not come out but by prayer and fasting," Jesus answered (see Matthew 17:21). In other words, we are to live a life of prayer and fasting, for if we wait to lay the spiritual groundwork until the challenge is before us, it will be too late. We won't be able to do what we could have done, or to be who we might have been because there were no tunnels dug under the surface early in the morning and late at night.

MAY 28

Then the officers of the children of Israel came and cried unto Pharaoh, saying, Wherefore dealest thou thus with thy servants?

Exodus 5:15

Although we sympathize with the children of Israel, we must make note of their mistake in crying to Pharaoh instead of calling out to God. Are you having a hard time at work? Is your boss cracking the whip? Is your supervisor loading you down? Are your co-workers demanding more of you than you think reasonable? Don't cry to your boss. Cry to the Lord first. Get direction from Him, for as the old hymn rightly declares, "O what peace we often forfeit, O what needless pain we bear, all because we do not carry everything to God in prayer."²

This is so simple and we know it to be true. But I must be reminded of it over and over again. Maybe you do too. It's so easy to cry to Pharaoh—to cry to a husband or wife, brother or sister, pastor or elder. It's easy to seek out people, when in reality God would say, "Woe to the rebellious people who take counsel but not of Me" (see Isaiah 30:1). Is the whip cracking? Is your back aching? Cry to the Lord.

MAY 29

And I will bring you in unto the land, concerning the which I did swear to give it to Abraham, to Isaac, and to Jacob; and I will give it you for an heritage: I am the LORD.

Exodus 6:8

"I will give you salvation, liberation, redemption, adoption, revelation, direction, and provision." In Exodus 6:6–8, we see seven "I wills," seven statements of promise made by God. The one thing we don't see is a single, "If you . . ." because such is the nature of the gospel. The gospel is the expression of God's fervent love toward us. It's all about what He has done and nothing about what we must do. The gospel is nothing short of the best news the world has ever heard: Our sin is forgiven. The price is paid. The work is done.

Although he was about to be beheaded, when Paul wrote to his protégé Timothy, he didn't say, "Be strong in righteousness," or "Be strong in your understanding of theology." No, as good as those things may be, Paul's final word to Timothy was, "Be strong in *grace*" (see 2 Timothy 2:1). So too, the degree to which we understand that grace is not the beginning point, but the only point. As grace does its work in our hearts day by day, we will want to study, will desire to pray, and will be eager to worship.

MAY 30

And the LORD said unto Moses, See, I have made thee a god to Pharaoh: and Aaron thy brother shall be thy prophet. Thou shalt speak all that I command thee: and Aaron thy brother shall speak unto Pharaoh, that he send the children of Israel out of his land. And I will harden Pharaoh's heart, and multiply my signs and my wonders in the land of Egypt. But Pharaoh shall not hearken unto you, that I may lay my hand upon Egypt, and bring forth mine armies, and my people the children of Israel, out of the land of Egypt by great judgments. And the Egyptians shall know that I am the LORD, when I stretch forth mine hand upon Egypt, and bring out the children of Israel from among them.

Exodus 7:1–5

"Go speak to Pharaoh," God instructed Moses. "He won't listen to you, but that will give Me the opportunity to stretch out My hand upon the land of Egypt. As a result, the entire nation will know that I am the Lord and there is none like Me." Yes, there would be problems. Yes, there would be tribulation. Yes, there would be difficulty, all of which would affect God's people. But it was all part of God's purpose and plan not only to provide liberation for His children, but to give revelation to the Egyptians.

"Lord, liberate me," we cry. "Set me free from the snap of the whips of the Egyptian oppressors. Set me free from the bondage of baking bricks under the desert sun."

"Gladly, for that's My intention," the Lord says. "But I am also doing something else simultaneously. You see, I want the Egyptians, the unsaved, the lost souls to see My power, to understand My reality. And for that to happen, there will be a series of problems which will affect you too."

"But why do I have to endure this trial, Lord? Why can't You take this cancer away immediately? Don't You have that ability? Why can't You solve the problem today? Why can't You work now?"

And the Lord answers, "I've got two things I'm doing simultaneously. Yes, I'm bringing you into the Land of Promise. But at the same time, there are

Egyptians watching carefully to see how you handle the same trials they face. I want them to see My power. I want them to see what I can do. I want to show them that I can see you through."

Seeing you win the Publisher's Clearinghouse Sweepstakes doesn't cause the Egyptian to scratch his head and say, "Wow." No, the Egyptian scratches his head when he sees you facing problems on the job, difficulties in the family, setbacks financially, difficulties physically, and yet walking through them victoriously. God never promised to protect us from problems. He promised to see us through them. And as He does, the neighbor, the co-worker, brother, sister-in-law, or father will say, "There's something about the way you navigate through life that I don't understand."

And then you can say, "It's the power and reality, the grace and goodness of God. And He's available for you too."

MAY 31

And Moses and Aaron went in unto Pharaoh, and they did so as the LORD had commanded: and Aaron cast down his rod before Pharaoh, and before his servants, and it became a serpent. Then Pharaoh also called the wise men and the sorcerers: now the magicians of Egypt, they also did in like manner with their enchantments. For they cast down every man his rod, and they became serpents: but Aaron's rod swallowed up their rods.

Exodus 7:10–12

I like that, don't you? Aaron's snake just got bigger and bigger as the magicians' snakes were scarfed up. "Go into all the world and preach the gospel," Jesus said. "And if you come across any serpents, they will not hurt you" (see Mark 16:18). As Paul put wood on a fire, when a snake in the sticks felt the heat, it fastened its fangs into his hand. Observing this, the natives decided Paul must be a murderer to deserve such a fate. But when they saw him shake the snake into the fire and feel no harm, they changed their minds about him and he was able to give a grand and powerful witness for Jesus Christ (Acts 28:1–10).

As believers, we are not free from attack, but we are immune to its effect. Snakes show up and they strike. But, like Paul, we can shake them off. Even though the Enemy was able to produce snakes, Aaron's rod ate them up.

> Joshua and Caleb were among the group of twelve who spied out the Land of Promise. "The land is a glorious place," they said to the children of Israel upon their return.
>
> "But there are giants there. And we're like grasshoppers in their sight," argued the other ten.
>
> "No. God is with us, and these guys will be bread for us. We can eat them up," countered Joshua and Caleb (see Numbers 14:9).
>
> But the people listened to the ten instead of the two and wandered for forty years.
>
> After their entire generation died, Joshua and Caleb were at last allowed to enter the Land of Promise. When they arrived, a now eighty-five-year-old Caleb said, "Joshua, for my inheritance, give me the land where the giants are" (see Joshua 14:12).
>
> Why would Caleb make such a request? Because he knew something about giants. He knew they were bread. And he was hungry. "Give me the challenges which challenge others," he said. "Give me the giants—and pass the butter."

Don't run away from challenges or obstacles, gang. Instead, say, "This is a chance for me, like Aaron's rod, to grow bigger and bigger. It's a way for me, like Caleb, to grow spiritually strong."

JUNE 1

*Then Pharaoh called for Moses and Aaron, and said, Intreat
the Lord, that he may take away the frogs from me, and
from my people; and I will let the people go, that they may
do sacrifice unto the Lord. And Moses said unto Pharaoh,
Glory over me: when shall I intreat for thee, and for thy servants, and for thy people, to destroy the frogs from thee and
thy houses, that they may remain in the river only? And he
said, Tomorrow.*

Exodus 8:8–10

"Ask your God to take the frogs away," Pharaoh begged Moses and Aaron.

"When do you want this to happen?" asked Moses.

In what is arguably the most amazing answer ever given in all of Scripture,
Pharaoh didn't say "Immediately!" or "Right away!" He said, "Tomorrow."
Why? He wanted one more night with the frogs. Oh, he knew they had to
go—but not quite yet. Not right now.

So too, there are activities, people, or places in our lives about which the
Lord says, "You thought you had that under control, all hemmed in. But
now it has hopped its banks and is taking over."

And we say, "You're right, Lord. It has. What I'm doing with my computer
is out of control. What I'm watching on TV is out of control. What I'm
reading, where I'm going, the way I'm living is out of control." But when
the Lord asks us when we want to be set free, all too often our answer is the
same as Pharaoh's: tomorrow.

The problem is, by saying "tomorrow," Pharaoh's heart grew harder and
harder still. You see, he could have gotten off relatively easy had he been serious and said, "I want the frogs to go right now. I repent of what I've been
doing. I'm changing my way of life. Moses, you and your people are free to
go." Had he done so, Pharaoh would have spared himself, his family, and his
country the unbelievable horrors that awaited them.

The Bible says, "Today if you hear His voice, harden not your hearts" (see

Hebrews 4:7) because although there is pleasure in sin for a season, the end result is always destruction (Hebrews 11:25).

I find it amazing that Pharaoh would say, "Tomorrow," until I analyze my own life and see the same tendency within me. I can hear a truth and say, "That's right. That's gotta go. That's gotta be corrected, adjusted, changed, repented of. And I'm going to get right on it . . . tomorrow." How I desire to be one who says, "This is the time—right here, right now."

You who have heard God's Word, you who have heard His heart, don't be like Pharaoh and wait for your own heart to harden. Instead, say, "I'm going to go Your way, Lord, not tomorrow, not Tuesday, but today."

JUNE 2

And in very deed for this cause have I raised thee up, for to shew in thee my power; and that my name may be declared throughout all the earth.

Exodus 9:16

God raised up Pharaoh to show all people throughout history that He is singular, that He is omnipotent, that He is sovereign. And to those who would protest that it was unfair for God to use Pharaoh in such a way, Paul would say, "Who are you to question God? Can the clay say to the potter, 'Why did you make me thus?' The potter has the right to do whatever he chooses with the lump of clay. And God has the right to do whatever He wants with us" (see Romans 9:21).

How arrogantly foolish of us to think that we can figure out God. Truly our God is an awesome God. Yes, He's a loving Father, our Abba, our Papa. But He is also the One who, without any explanation, told His friend to sacrifice his son (Genesis 22:2); He is the One who struck a king with leprosy, a man who served him well, for offering a sacrifice in the temple (2 Chronicles 26:20). I can't read my Bible without realizing that my Father is loving and kind, compassionate and tender; but He is also awesome and huge, powerful and "other." Yes, we rejoice in our Father. Yes, we understand His nature as we look at Jesus. But along with that, we must also understand that the fear of the Lord is the beginning of wisdom (Proverbs 9:10). We think we have God all figured out. But one can't read the Scriptures without coming to the conclusion that He doesn't fit into any box very easily.

Stand in awe of God. Be amazed by His greatness, by His size, by His sovereignty. And then marvel that He's allowed us to be brought into His family, that He's made Himself known to us through Jesus personally, that He placed us at a time in history where the gospel message surrounds us constantly. Sometimes I lift my hands in love and adoration to the Lord. Other times, I fall on my face on my living room floor, speechless in His presence. He raised up Pharaoh simply to show His power. And He stooped to save us to do the same.

JUNE 3

And the LORD said unto Moses, Go in unto Pharaoh: for I have hardened his heart, and the heart of his servants, that I might shew these my signs before him: and that thou mayest tell in the ears of thy son, and of thy son's son, what things I have wrought in Egypt, and my signs which I have done among them; that ye may know how that I am the LORD.

Exodus 10:1–2

God's intent in baring His arm and raining plagues upon Egypt was not only so the Egyptians would see His power and superiority, but so His own people would know that He is indeed who He claims to be. Then they could pass this knowledge on to their children and grandchildren. They could learn a portion of this lesson by *observing* God's dealings with the Egyptians, as the hail fell upon them and the flies tormented them. But the other part of the lesson could only be learned firsthand as they *experienced* the effects of water turned to blood, of frogs swarming their houses, and of lice covering their bodies.

There's no "test-imony" without tests. A vibrant, passionate, and authentic walk with the Lord does not come from secondhand theology. It only comes through the things we experience personally.

JUNE 4

And Pharaoh called unto Moses, and said, Go ye, serve the
LORD; only let your flocks and your herds be stayed: let your
little ones also go with you. And Moses said, Thou must give
us also sacrifices and burnt offerings, that we may sacrifice
unto the LORD our God. Our cattle also shall go with us;
there shall not an hoof be left behind; for thereof must we
take to serve the LORD our God; and we know not with what
we must serve the LORD, until we come thither.

Exodus 10:24–26

Moses and Pharaoh had been duking it out, mixing it up, and sparring round after round . . .

Round 1:

After being punched with the plagues of blood, frogs, lice, and flies, Pharaoh said to Moses, "I'll let you and your people serve the Lord—but you must remain in Egypt" (see 8:25).

"We'll be stoned if we stay here," said Moses. And both returned to their corners.

Round 2:

"I'll let you leave the country—but don't go very far" (see 8:28).

"We must go where God directs," said Moses. And both returned to their corners.

Round 3:

Having been struck with boils and hail, Pharaoh said, "You and your men can go as far as you want. But your women and children must stay here" (see 10:11).

"We're taking our families," Moses countered. And both returned to their corners.

Round 4:

Following the double punch of locusts and darkness, Pharaoh said, "You and your families can go. But your livestock must stay."

"No," said Moses. "We're going to take our families and flocks. We're going to take our kids and our cattle. We're going to take everything."

Satan seeks to make people compromise in this same way today . . .

"Stay in the world," he says. "Sure, you might have to bake a brick or two, but at least you're familiar with the system. Why take a risk on what you can't see? Why leave the known for the unknown? Why set your sights on a kingdom that claims to be eternal, but still invisible?"

And when we choose to listen to God instead, Satan changes his tactic, "All right, go ahead and believe in Jesus. But don't go too far. Don't get too radical."

And when we ignore him again, Satan says, "Be radical in your faith if you want. But don't rope your kids into it. When they're older, let them make their own decision about whether or not to follow Jesus. Until then, leave them in Egypt where they can play soccer and take ballet lessons."

And when we decide, like Moses, that we will worship as families, Satan comes up with a final compromise: "Go ahead. Throw in your lot with God. You and your family can even be radical in your faith. But don't spend money on it. Don't tithe. Don't give God His due. Don't invest in eternity."

"Where your treasure is, there will your heart be also," Jesus said (Matthew 6:21). Had Moses left the livelihood of his people in Egypt, their hearts would have remained there too. And to the degree that we sink our hearts into the soil of this world, ours remain here as well.

JUNE 5

In one house shall it be eaten; thou shalt not carry forth ought of the flesh abroad out of the house; neither shall ye break a bone thereof.

Exodus 12:46

Why was no bone to be broken? I suggest three reasons . . .

Restoration. David—a shepherd by trade and a sheep by nature—speaks of restoration when he writes, "Make me to hear joy and gladness; that the bones which thou hast broken may rejoice" (Psalm 51:8). You see, in Bible days if a lamb continually placed its life in jeopardy by wandering away, the shepherd would break its legs, set the bones, and carry it on his shoulders for the following six to eight weeks until the bones were healed. During that period, the lamb would develop such a deep affection for the shepherd, that when its legs were healed, it would remain by the shepherd's side all the days of its life. Jesus, being the sinless Lamb of God, however, had no need to be broken.

Redemption. "Where sin abounds, grace abounds more," Paul declares (see Romans 5:20). What is the basis of grace? The blood of Calvary. Where is blood produced? In the bone. Therefore, in insisting that not a bone be broken, it's as though God is saying, "I don't want any suggestion that there is a limitation to the blood. I want people to understand that where sin abounds, grace always abounds *more.*"

Reconciliation. To hasten death, soldiers would break the legs of those being crucified. However, when they came to do this to Jesus, they were so surprised that He had died in only six hours that they poked a spear in His side to make sure (John 19:34).

If you are estranged from, or at odds with someone with whom you were once close, the only way there can be reconciliation is if someone dies. Jesus models that for you and me. He died to reconcile us to the Father, but He died quickly. It was not unusual for victims of crucifixion to prolong their lives eighteen hours or more as they hung on the cross. Not Jesus. With the work of reconciliation complete, He released His spirit relatively quickly in order that He might race to Easter, to resurrection day. That's the key: the sooner we die, the sooner we'll be at Easter Sunday.

JUNE 6

And it shall be when the LORD shall bring thee into the land of the Canaanites, as he sware unto thee and to thy fathers, and shall give it thee, that thou shalt set apart unto the LORD all that openeth the matrix, and every firstling that cometh of a beast which thou hast; the males shall be the LORD's. And every firstling of an ass thou shalt redeem with a lamb; and if thou wilt not redeem it, then thou shalt break his neck.

Exodus 13:11–13

The only way a donkey could live was if a lamb was slain for it. I like this analogy. Because we know the lamb speaks of Jesus, it's not too difficult to figure out who the donkey represents.

The donkey is mentioned twenty-five times in the Old Testament, among which are the following:

In Genesis 22, when Abraham took Isaac up to Mount Moriah, a donkey was saddled for them, which speaks of a loss of liberty.

Later in the same chapter, the donkey was to be tied up while Abraham and Isaac ascended the mountain, which speaks of an inability to worship.

As Jacob pronounces blessing on his sons in Genesis 49, he likens Issachar to a donkey that is heavily laden.

In Deuteronomy 22, we read that the ox and donkey were not to plow together, the implication being that the donkey would only slow the ox down.

In 1 Samuel 9, we see Saul trying to locate his father's donkeys that had wandered away.

Jeremiah 22 speaks of a donkey left for dead and tossed outside the city gates.

Taken together, these references speak of you and me: laden down, tied up, lacking an ability to serve or worship the Lord, lost, left for dead, tossed out—not a very flattering picture. But the final mention of a donkey in the Old Testament is a glorious one indeed . . .

> Rejoice greatly, O daughter of Zion; shout, O daughter of Jerusalem: behold, thy King cometh unto thee: he is just, and having salvation; lowly, and riding upon an ass, and upon a colt the foal of an ass.
>
> Zechariah 9:9

A week before He would go to Calvary, Jesus said to His disciples, "Go into the village and you'll see a donkey. Untie it and bring it to Me. And if anyone asks why you are untying it, tell him the Lord has need of it" (see Matthew 21:3).

"I choose a donkey," Jesus said. "Let Alexander the Great ride on the back of his mighty black stallion. Let the Romans ride their dazzling white horses. I'll use a donkey."

Jesus wants to enter your city, your workplace, and your family. And He chooses to use you as a means of getting there.

"How can He use me?" you ask. "I'm nothing but a donkey."

That's right. And He loves using donkeys—the foolish things of the world to confound the wise (1 Corinthians 1:27). But before He can use you, you first must be untied and released because you can't be used if you're bound up with guilt, sin, and worry. So He sends disciples to untie you, maybe through a Bible study, maybe over the radio, or maybe with a word from the Lord just for you. Before the donkey was ridden, he was released. But before he was released, he had to be redeemed. The donkey would die unless a lamb died in its place. And that's exactly what the Lamb of God did when He died for us.

JUNE 7

And they took their journey from Succoth, and encamped in Etham, in the edge of the wilderness.

Exodus 13:20

When the Israelites left Succoth, they didn't go to the Land of Promise. They went to Etham, a town on the brink of disaster, a town on the edge of the wilderness. In the Bible, the word "wilderness" does not refer to a land of pine trees, mountain streams, rainbow trout, and wildflowers, but to the bleak, brutal, and blistering desert.

"You brought us to the desert, Lord? There's nothing but nothing before us," the Israelites must have cried.

Oh, but the place is called *Etham*, or literally, "with them."

"I'm with you," the Lord declares. "I know it looks like you're on the brink of disaster, like there's nothing good ahead. But I'm with you to see you through."

How can the Lord teach us He is truly with us except to take us to the desert? When everything is fine, we go on our merry way as if His presence in our lives is optional. It's only when we're on the brink of disaster that we realize how much we need Him.

JUNE 8

And the Lord went before them by day in a pillar of a cloud, to lead them the way; and by night in a pillar of fire, to give them light; to go by day and night.

Exodus 13:21

When I heard this story in Sunday school, saw it on the flannelgraph board, or watched it in the movies, it seemed to me that the cloud was always in front of the congregation. That is, the Israelites would see the cloud off in the distance and simply follow wherever it lead. But I don't think this was what really took place. In Psalm 105:39, we read that the cloud wasn't ahead of the congregation, but above it, covering the congregation.

This means that when God wanted His people to move, He got them to move in a very simple, practical way. With daytime temperatures reaching 125 degrees in the desert, God put a cloud over the entire congregation to shade them. And when He wanted them to move, He would simply move the cloud, knowing His people would move as well simply to stay in the shade.

And that's the way the Lord directs us. "My burden is easy, My load is light," Jesus declared (see Matthew 11:30)—a New Testament principle pictured in the Old Testament priesthood . . .

> And it shall come to pass, that when they enter in at the gates of the inner court, they shall be clothed with linen garments; and no wool shall come upon them, whiles they minister in the gates of the inner court, and within. They shall have linen bonnets upon their heads, and shall have linen breeches upon their loins; they shall not gird them-selves with any thing that causeth sweat.
>
> Ezekiel 44:17–18

When you want to know what God's will for you is, first ask yourself, Is it cool, or is it wool? Will it cause inspiration, or perspiration? "Delight thyself also in the LORD," the psalmist declared, "and he shall give thee the desires of thine heart" (Psalm 37:4). In other words, if you delight in, love, and enjoy the Lord, He will give you that which your heart desires. How can that be? Because He has already written His will on the table of your heart (Jeremiah 31:33). The desire of the heart in fellowship with Him is His desire.

It has been rightly said that there are lots of cheap imitations of price-less masterpieces in the church today. "Look at him. Look at her. Look at them," we say. "I'm going to be just like him or her or them." But when we try to imitate or duplicate someone else's calling or ministry, the best we can be is only a cheap imitation. You are a masterpiece because the Master has pieced you together to do exactly what He intended you to do since before the world began (Ephesians 1:4).

"You are His workmanship," Paul wrote to the Ephesians (see 2:10). *Poiema*, the Greek word translated "workmanship," is the word from which we get our word "poem." You are God's poetry. He has created you specifically and uniquely to do that which He knows will satisfy you most completely. Therefore, when you get to heaven, the Lord is not going to say, "Why weren't you more like Moses? Why weren't you more like Abraham? Why weren't you more like Paul or Billy Graham?" No. He's going to say, "Why weren't you more like *you?* Why weren't you simply the person I made you to be—My masterpiece, My poetry?"

Don't strive, dear saint. Don't sweat, fellow priest. Stay in the shade and be whom the Lord intended you to be—His unique masterpiece, His inimitable poetry.

JUNE 9

And I, behold, I will harden the hearts of the Egyptians, and they shall follow them: and I will get me honour upon Pharaoh, and upon all his host, upon his chariots, and upon his horsemen. And the Egyptians shall know that I am the LORD, when I have gotten me honour upon Pharaoh, upon his chariots, and upon his horsemen.

Exodus 14:17–18

God boxed His people in between the mountains and the Red Sea as a demonstration of His preeminence. Even more fundamental than our experiencing His power and His presence is the world's understanding of His sovereignty. "I'm going to put you in this horrible predicament, this tough spot, this brutal place," He says, "because I want to make Myself known to the Egyptians."

"I'm stuck in this marriage. I'm stuck with that parent. I'm stuck in a financial crunch," we cry, failing to understand that sometimes He can touch people who don't know Him by putting us in uncomfortable, difficult, heartbreaking, and challenging situations.

God doesn't exist for us. We exist for Him.

So scandalized was the church that for decades she refused to acknowledge Copernicus' discovery. After all, how could the sun be the center of the planetary system? Surely the planets revolved around the earth, around man.

And it remains equally shocking today to discover that it is the Son rather than our own worlds, our own concerns, or our own comforts who is at the center of God's creation. But it is not until we finally understand that we exist for God rather than He for us that the rotation of our worlds, our situations, and our lives makes sense. If the pain doesn't go away, if the business doesn't work out, if the marriage isn't great, God says, "I love you. But it's not about you. I have a bigger plan. The Egyptians are watching, and when the people you work with see you continue to praise Me, when your neighbors see you worshiping Me, when your family sees you thanking Me, I will be glorified."

You can fight it until the day you die, or you can finally come to the place in your life where you say, "The Son is the center of everything. Come what may, the Son is the center of my universe."

And although life might not seem fair right now, it will eventually. The waters will part, and you will be ushered into eternity where you will hear, "Well done, good and faithful servant. I had you boxed in. But you stood still. You didn't fall away. You didn't turn back. You didn't walk out. Enter into the joy of the Lord" (see Matthew 25:21).

Perhaps special teams football players have the best grasp of this idea. "Special teams" is suicide. Special teams charge down the field full steam ahead, throwing their bodies directly at men who are also running full steam ahead in their direction. They crack heads. They take hits. They endure pain. Why? So that the one carrying the ball can gain yards.

It's such a simple concept, but it sometimes takes decades to understand that we're not the sun, that we're not the ball carrier, but that we exist for the One who is. And the degree to which we allow Him to do what He wants to do through our lives is the degree to which we will be rewarded immensely, immeasurably, and eternally.

JUNE 10

The LORD is a man of war: the LORD is his name. Pharaoh's chariots and his host hath he cast into the sea: his chosen captains also are drowned in the Red sea. The depths have covered them: they sank into the bottom as a stone. Thy right hand, O LORD, is become glorious in power: thy right hand, O LORD, hath dashed in pieces the enemy. And in the greatness of thine excellency thou hast overthrown them that rose up against thee: thou sentest forth thy wrath, which consumed them as stubble. And with the blast of thy nostrils the waters were gathered together, the floods stood upright as an heap, and the depths were congealed in the heart of the sea. The enemy said, I will pursue, I will overtake, I will divide the spoil; my lust shall be satisfied upon them; I will draw my sword, my hand shall destroy them. Thou didst blow with thy wind, the sea covered them: they sank as lead in the mighty waters.

Exodus 15:3–10

"God is love," John tells us (1 John 4:8).

"The Lord is a man of war," Moses says.

Is this a contradiction?

No, because although God is indeed love, there are forces all around us which are anything but lovely or loveable. And God wages war against these forces as surely as He waged war against Pharaoh. That is why when you study the Old Testament, you'll see violence in virtually every book. And because the Old Testament is a picture book illustrating physically what we're to do spiritually, we're to be violent as well (Matthew 11:12).

How?

We're to do battle violently in prayer against the spiritual forces that seek to deceive, defile, and destroy those around us. Wife, did you do battle in prayer for your husband today? Did you pray passionately that the forces of the Enemy would not gain a toehold in his life? Dad, did you do what Job did, who energetically sacrificed for each of his children before the break of day lest they sin against the Lord? (Job 1:5). Did you pray earnestly lest they fall prey to the Enemy who seeks to derail and destroy them spiritually?

"The effectual *fervent* prayer of a righteous man availeth much," James tells us (5:16, italics added). Praying, "Lord, help everyone to be nice," is neither effective nor fervent, and it doesn't make much of an impact. God is a man of war, but He's a gentleman nonetheless, and therefore, won't force His way into any situation. He will wait for an invitation (Revelation 3:20). The question is, are we actively, fervently, and passionately opening the door to Him and bidding Him to come in?

JUNE 11

And Miriam answered them, Sing ye to the LORD, for he hath triumphed gloriously; the horse and his rider hath he thrown into the sea.

Exodus 15:21

As good as this song is, how much better it would have been had it been sung *before* the Red Sea parted, had it been sung by the children of Israel *before* they were rescued.

To you who are boxed in, with your back to the Red Sea, this is your moment; now is your opportunity for greatness. You see, once the Red Sea parts—once the financial crisis is over, the relationship is restored, the disease is healed—you will no longer have before you the opportunity for greatness. Then you can be grateful, but only now you can be great.

When the hour was dark, when nothing was externally right, there in the middle of a black, bleak night, what did Paul and Silas do? They sang songs of praise. And so intriguing was this to their fellow prisoners that when an earthquake caused the prison doors to open, they chose to stay in the dungeon with Paul and Silas rather than to flee, to remain imprisoned physically in order that their souls might be set free (Acts 16).

So too, you who are in a dungeon financially, relationally, or physiologically have a unique opportunity to show us greatness. And once this experience is over, you'll never have the same opportunity again.

"I want to be like David," we say. "I'd like to grab some stones and nail Goliath." You can. There's a huge giant before you, a giant headache, a giant heartache, a giant problem. Are you going to be like Saul and his men, murmuring and complaining, depressed and discouraged? Or are you going to praise the Lord in the face of the giant who seems to stomp up and down the valley of your life day after day? Ninety-nine percent of people will choose to be like Saul. This is your chance, however, to be a David.

The difficulties in the lives of any great man or woman in Scripture weren't pleasant, weren't easy. We know how their stories end—Joshua, Deborah, Gideon, Jeremiah, David, and Paul—but when they were living out their stories, their trials were every bit as brutal as your situation. Yet, they chose by God's grace to be great, to be heroic. And we are the richer for it.

When there's an ugly giant before you, or prison bars all around you, it's your chance to be great. Don't miss it, because, although opportunities for greatness come to everyone, they usually only come once or twice in a lifetime. Will your story be one of mediocrity, or one of greatness? It all depends on what you do this side of the Red Sea.

JUNE 12

And when they came to Marah, they could not drink of the waters of Marah, for they were bitter: therefore the name of it was called Marah. And the people murmured against Moses, saying, What shall we drink? And he cried unto the Lord*; and the* Lord *shewed him a tree, which when he had cast into the waters, the waters were made sweet.*

Exodus 15:23–25

Feeling as though death were breathing down upon them, the Israelites' need for water was immediate and great, when suddenly the report must have filtered through the congregation that water lay ahead. I can see in my mind's eye the people stampeding in the direction of the report, finding a pool, and diving in, only to come up sputtering and spitting out bitter water.

The same thing happens to us. We come to our own Marah—a situation, a relationship, an occupation, or even a ministry we think will be cool and refreshing—only to find it bitter, not what we thought it would be. Why did the Lord choose Marah as a stop for His people? I believe it was to teach them three lessons, the first being that life is a mixture of sweetness and bitterness—for were it only sweet, we would have no desire for heaven.

I believe a second lesson God wanted to teach His people at Marah was that trials are the X-rays that allow us to see what's going on in our hearts. You see, although the children of Israel murmured against Moses, in reality, they were murmuring against God for bringing them to Marah in the first place. And the same is true of us. I will never know what's in my heart until I dive into a pool expectantly and find it isn't what I thought it would be. People do not make us bitter. Situations do not make us bitter. They simply show us what is already within. I know this because, when I look at Jesus, I see that, although He was spat upon, cursed at, and nailed to a cross, He said, "Father forgive them. They don't know what they're doing" (see Luke 23:34). No bitterness came out of Him because there was no bitterness within Him.

Third, notice that God didn't create this tree on the spot; it was there all along. The tree in Scripture is emblematic of the cross (1 Peter 2:24; Galatians 3), and it is the cross of Calvary that still transforms bitter experiences, bitter people, and bitter circumstances. How? By realizing that the wrongs done to us, the offenses against us, and the disappointments registered by us have all been paid for, dealt with, and washed clean by the blood of Calvary.

JUNE 13

And they came to Elim, where were twelve wells of water, and threescore and ten palm trees: and they encamped there by the waters.

Exodus 15:27

Following their time at Marah, God led the children of Israel to Elim, or "mighty ones." With twelve wells of water and seventy palm trees, God had led them to a wonderful oasis indeed. I'm so glad that the Lord not only takes us to the bitter water of Marah, but to the cool wells of Elim! It's interesting to note that the palm tree is the only tree in the world which bears more fruit as it gets older. Another fascinating reminder is that there were twelve disciples and seventy more later whom Jesus sent out to minister. I believe this little vignette is the Holy Spirit's way of saying that the only place we will find true refreshment is when we are "mighty ones" in ministry.

"Whatever measure you give out will be the measure you'll get back," Jesus told us (see Luke 6:38). At Elim, there's no murmuring, nothing negative, nothing but refreshment in the place of service. Today, serve someone and bless someone, share your faith, intercede for someone, and be blessed and refreshed yourself in the process.

JUNE 14

And the children of Israel did eat manna forty years, until they came to a land inhabited; they did eat manna, until they came unto the borders of the land of Canaan. Now an omer is the tenth part of an ephah.

Exodus 16:35–36

It was in the wilderness that God gave manna to His people. And it is in our wilderness here on earth that He daily provides the Bread of His Word, the Bread of Himself. If I don't feast on the Scriptures daily, I become disillusioned, disoriented, and confused. I get mixed up on days when I don't get away with the Lord in a quiet spot at a quiet time and enjoy the truths and promises of His Word. I think about fleshpots and the bread of Egypt; I become restless and troubled. But when I take in the Word, I find what Jeremiah said to be oh, so true. I find it to be the very joy and rejoicing of my heart (Jeremiah 15:16).

So too, like manna, Jesus Christ, the Word made flesh, came to this wilderness—to murmurers, sinners, and complainers—and dwelt among us (John 1:14). God didn't wait for the children of Israel in the Promised Land. He joined them in the wilderness. And He does the same for us. You don't have to climb a mountain or clean up your act to find Him. You don't have to ascend into heaven or descend into the depths of hell and depression. He's already as close as the word in your mouth, as close as your confession (Romans 10:8–10).

It was hunger that inevitably drove the Prodigal Son home (Luke 15:17). And it is hunger—a hole in your heart, a longing in your soul—that will drive you home as well. All you must do is humble yourself, bow your knee, and stoop to pick up the manna of the Word, the manna of the Son, which God has provided so lavishly and lovingly, so freely and faithfully.

JUNE 15

And the LORD said unto Moses, Go on before the people, and take with thee of the elders of Israel; and thy rod, wherewith thou smotest the river, take in thine hand, and go. Behold, I will stand before thee there upon the rock in Horeb; and thou shalt smite the rock, and there shall come water out of it, that the people may drink. And Moses did so in the sight of the elders of Israel. And he called the name of the place Massah, and Meribah, because of the chiding of the children of Israel, and because they tempted the LORD, saying, Is the LORD among us, or not? Then came Amalek, and fought with Israel in Rephidim.

Exodus 17:5–8

Massah and *Meribah* mean "temptation" and "chiding." It was hot. The people were thirsty. And God said to Moses, "Here's what to do: Take the rod which had become a snake before Pharaoh, smite the rock, and out will come water." Paul gives the interpretation of this account in 1 Corinthians 10:4, where he tells us the Rock was Jesus Christ. This means that Jesus, the Rock of our salvation, was smitten by the "serpent" of Moses' rod—perfectly portraying the prophecy given in the garden of Eden when God said to Satan, "You shall bruise His heel, but He will crush your head" (see Genesis 3:15). Was the heel of Jesus bruised? Yes. A spike was driven through it on the cross of Calvary. But Satan was crushed, for the power he held over us was obliterated, washed away by the blood Jesus shed that day. What happened when Jesus was pierced with the spear? Blood and water flowed from His side (John 19:34). So too, here at Rephidim, the rock, smitten by the rod that was once a serpent, pours forth water. The analogy is perfect. This passage points to Jesus.

Why would God lead His people from a place where they were being satisfied with manna to a rest stop where the drinking fountain was out of order? You might leave a Bible study or a retreat where you've been feasting on the manna of the Word only to find yourself in a place of dryness. "I don't understand," you say. "I was doing so well, but now there is a drought in my soul. Why am I so dry? Is there sin in my life?" Not necessarily. God led His people to Rephidim in order to do something very important. You see, after they ate of the manna, to make them aware of their need for a fresh drenching of water, God brought them to Rephidim to create in them a thirst for more of Him. Why would He do this? Because He knew what was about to happen.

You see, every time the Amalekites are mentioned in the Bible, they portray the ongoing war we wage with our flesh. It's as if God says, "I know you feasted on the bread. You've taken in the manna. But right around the bend, right up ahead, war is about to break out. And if you try to defeat Amalek in your own strength, you'll be trounced." Therefore, He took His people—as He does us—to a place where they were aware of their dryness in order that, after crying out to Him, they would be empowered afresh with the water of His Spirit.

If you are going through a desert season, God has led you there. For what purpose? To create within you a craving for more of Him. "Blessed are they which do hunger and thirst after righteousness," Jesus said, "for they shall be filled" (Matthew 5:6). Who is filled? The one who hungers. The one who thirsts. The one who's at Rephidim, longing for water.

JUNE 16

But Moses' hands were heavy; and they took a stone, and put it under him, and he sat thereon; and Aaron and Hur stayed up his hands, the one on the one side, and the other on the other side; and his hands were steady until the going down of the sun.

Exodus 17:12

In the middle of the battle, were Joshua to look over his shoulder, he would have seen three men on a hill—the one in the middle holding a wooden rod. This makes us think of another Man on a hill, flanked by two others, arms outstretched, not holding a wooden rod, but pinned to a wooden beam. But His arms didn't sag; His soul didn't sag; His spirit didn't sag. No, Jesus our Savior hung in there for you and me. And the Man in the middle not only bled and died for me, but He rose again and ascended into heaven, where He lives to make intercession for me (Hebrews 7:25). Aaron might get busy sometimes. Hur might not always be available. But Jesus ever lives to make intercession for me. He lives to pray for me. Amazing.

"If that's the case," you say, "then why should we pray at all? Why not just let Him do the heavy lifting?" Because, although the victory is won, there are still mop-up operations going on. Do you want to be fruitful, successful, and blessed in the daily skirmishes of life? Do you want to see your kids do well, the church blessed, and the country changed? Jesus won the victory completely at Calvary. All the rest is mop-up stuff. And we have the privilege of taking part. "Seek Me," the Lord says. "Talk to Me. Call on Me with uplifted hands. And watch and see what I will do as you open the door for Me to work."

JUNE 17

And Joshua discomfited Amalek and his people with the edge of the sword. And the LORD said unto Moses, Write this for a memorial in a book, and rehearse it in the ears of Joshua: for I will utterly put out the remembrance of Amalek from under heaven. And Moses built an altar, and called the name of it Jehovah-nissi: For he said, Because the LORD hath sworn that the LORD will have war with Amalek from generation to generation.

Exodus 17:13–16

When the battle was finally won, God instructed Moses to record what had transpired in a book—in order that future generations would know that the battle was won not with the sword in the valley of interaction, but through prayer on the mount of intercession.

Oftentimes, we think that if we were more skilled with the sword of Scripture, if we were better able to dialogue and counsel, if we could love more and do more, we'd see the salvation of our parents or grandchildren, our neighbors or friends. But this story tells us that is not where the battle is won. The battle is won through prayer.

Why is prayer so important? Because the old adage that prayer changes things is only partly true. I think it's more accurate to say, "Faith changes things. Prayer changes *me*."

Yes, God wanted the children of Israel to win the battle. But He also wanted to win the heart of Moses in a deeper way. And He wants to do the same with us. We may think that our situations need to change. God, however, knows that even if they did, we'd still be unhappy, sleepwalking through life unless our hearts were changed. Therefore He says, "Because I want to fill your heart, inflame your soul, and satisfy that ache within you which can be satisfied only by Me, you're going to have to come to Me time after time because when you do, you'll get to know Me in the process. And when you get to know Me, it is only then that you will be content and fulfilled, blessed and happy."

"Behold, I stand at the door, and knock," Jesus said. "If any man hear my voice, and open the door, I will come into him, and sup with him, and he with me." Addressed to the church, Revelation 3:20 tells us Jesus knocks at the door of the church, of the heart of believers. Therefore, when we pray, we are acting as doormen, opening the door and inviting Him in. He doesn't beat the door down. He doesn't bust His way in. He doesn't force His presence or force the issue. But whoever hears the knocking and is wise enough to open the door in prayer will enjoy His presence and company.

By praying, I open the door. That doesn't mean Jesus is obligated to do what I ask or desire. That's up to Him. I have learned, however, that if He doesn't do what I suggest, He'll do something infinitely better. But if I don't open the door, if I don't pray, I'm left on my own with my kids, my marriage, and my ministry—not a good place to be. "You have not because you ask not," James tells us (see 4:2). It's all about prayer.

JUNE 18

Ye have seen what I did unto the Egyptians, and how I bare you on eagles' wings, and brought you unto myself.

Exodus 19:4

With eagles soaring over their heads and eagles' nests perched on the ledges of the Sinai mountain range, this image would be very clear to the children of Israel.

> As an eagle stirreth up her nest, fluttereth over her young, spreadeth abroad her wings, taketh them, beareth them on her wings: So the LORD alone did lead him, and there was no strange god with him.
>
> Deuteronomy 32:11–12

After selecting a site on a high precipice, the mother eagle builds her nest. And as her newly-hatched eaglet grows, he's comfy and cozy, until one day the mother eagle overturns the nest and the young eagle is sent tumbling downward, squawking all the way. Just before he hits the rocks below, however, the mother eagle swoops down and rescues him, bearing him upon her wings. She returns him to the nest, only to overturn it a few days later and bear him on her wings yet again. This process is repeated six or seven times, until one time, the eaglet catches a thermal and starts flying. Higher and higher he goes, set free to experience life in an entirely different dimension with a higher perspective than he ever had previously.

Because faith cannot grow in comfort and security, we'll all be knocked out of our nests of cozy complacency from time to time. What do we do at such times? "They that wait upon the LORD shall renew their strength," Isaiah declares. "They shall mount up with wings as eagles" (40:31). To wait upon the Lord doesn't mean to passively wait, but to wait on Him as a skilled waiter would wait on the guest of honor. To wait upon the Lord means to lavish praise, to minister, to fellowship day by day, moment by moment. And those who do, mount up with wings as eagles.

JUNE 19

And thou shalt set bounds unto the people round about, saying, Take heed to yourselves, that ye go not up into the mount, or touch the border of it: whosoever toucheth the mount shall be surely put to death: There shall not an hand touch it, but he shall surely be stoned, or shot through; whether it be beast or man, it shall not live: when the trumpet soundeth long, they shall come up to the mount.

Exodus 19:12–13

Not only were the people to wash their clothes, but they were to watch their step. They were to stay away from the mountain, for if they got too close to God's "pulpit," they would die.

"That doesn't sound very loving," you might say.

Oh, but any dad who has wrestled with his two-year-old knows that it is.

Dad, when you wrestle with your toddler, you want contact with your kids, but you place limits on yourself because otherwise they'd be wiped out. The same is true of God. His beauty, His glory, His splendor, majesty, and holiness would be so powerful that were the children of Israel to get too close to Him, their hearts would simply stop beating from awe.

So often we trivialize God. Yes, through the person of Jesus Christ, He is our friend, but His grandeur and glory remain undiminished. Therefore, the fear of the Lord—the fear of doing anything that would grieve Him—should cause us to fall at His feet in speechless humility.

JUNE 20

*And God spake all these words, saying, I am the L*ORD *thy God.*

Exodus 20:1–2

God doesn't say, "I am the Lord God." He says, "I am the LORD *thy* God," as if to say, "I made you; I created you; I know what will make you happy." Thus, because of the incredible tenderness embedded in the little word "thy," the Ten Commandments could be called the "Ten-der" Commandments.

For this is the love of God, that we keep his commandments.

1 John 5:3

John doesn't say we'll earn God's love by keeping His commandments. No, he says keeping His commandments is the love of God.

"I'm not experiencing God's love," you say.

Are you keeping His commandments?

"I don't have to. I'm under grace."

Yes, you are. But you'll experience God's love when you keep His commandments because He alone knows how you are made and how you tick, and His commandments constitute His personal instruction book for you, straight from your Manufacturer.

And his commandments are not grievous.

1 John 5:3

God's commandments are not grievous because rules provide liberty.

There is a rule I keep every single day. That is, in the morning—every morning—I brush my teeth. You might call this legalism. But I find it to be exceedingly refreshing. Not only that, it also releases me from philosophical questioning. I never once ask, "To brush, or not to brush? Do I have time? Is this the right day? Does brushing apply to me?" I could waste a great deal of energy debating and wondering if I should brush my teeth, but because brushing my teeth is a non-negotiable rule for me, I am released from all kinds of mental turmoil. And not only does brushing my teeth refresh and release me, but it relieves those around me. Thus, it's a win-win situation. The same is true of God's law. It provides an opportunity to experience His love personally and to express my love practically.

JUNE 21

Thou shalt have no other gods before me.

Exodus 20:3

In this simple phrase, we see a premise and a promise. The premise is that there are indeed other gods . . .

Baal was the god who supposedly hurled lightning down from heaven (1 Kings 18:24). Baal was the god of power. Munching on power bars, listening to power tapes, thinking they're powerful and in control, lots of people still unknowingly worship Baal today.

Ashtoreth was the goddess of sensuality, of pleasure, a goddess worshiped extensively in our society by those with the "if it feels good, do it" mentality.

Mammon was the god of money, the god of prosperity. Because it is the love of money, rather than money itself, which is evil (1 Timothy

6:10), it is not only the wealthy who are prone to worship mammon. Anyone who places a priority on money, worries about money, or strives for money is vulnerable.

Molech was the god of practicality. To earn Molech's blessing upon his new business, the Molech worshiper would place his firstborn in an earthen jar and build the walls of his shop around it, believing that the baby entombed within the wall wasn't really dead, but would reappear in his next child. Many a parent does virtually the same thing today when, in the name of practicality, they ignore their children in the name of advancing their careers, mistakenly thinking that once their business is successful and their place in the company is secure that they can re-connect with their kids. The problem, however, is that kids grow up, time is lost, and opportunity dies on the altar of practicality.

In addition to the premise that there are indeed other gods, this first commandment carries a promise that other gods will not pull on God's people indefinitely.

Having captured the ark of the covenant—the gold-covered box which held the Ten Commandments—the Philistines placed it in the temple of their god, Dagon, a being which was half man and half fish. The next day, when the priests of Dagon went into the temple, they found Dagon knocked down before the ark. The priests returned Dagon to his original position, only to come in the following day to find him on the floor once again, his head and hands severed from the fall (1 Samuel 5).

The same thing happens today. "Let Me into the temple of your heart," God says, "and I'll knock Dagon down; I'll knock Baal out. I'll take care of Mammon. I'll deal with Ashtoreth."

The Ten Commandments is the only law of antiquity that forbids the worship of other gods. All other codes and cultures allowed and even encouraged the worship of other deities. Why? Because all other gods work as a team to bring hell into peoples' lives and to damn them eternally. There will be no other gods before the true and living God because those gods will not come through ultimately. In the last day, every knee shall bow, every tongue will confess that Jesus alone is Lord (Philippians 2:10–11). And what a day that will be!

JUNE 22

Thou shalt not make unto thee any graven image, or any likeness of any thing that is in heaven above, or that is in the earth beneath, or that is in the water under the earth.

Exodus 20:4

To understand what God must look like, man has looked to nature for clues.

Looking to the sky, the Native American saw the eagle soaring majestically overhead and decided God must be an eagle.

Looking at the grassy plain, the Indian saw the powerful yet peaceful cow and decided God must be a cow.

Looking down to the sea, the Pacific Islander saw the massive sea turtle with its impenetrable shell and decided God must be a sea turtle.

Although we know better than this, we as believers can fall prey to the same tendency. You see, there are those who say, "When I get to heaven, I'm going to sit on God's lap and feel His embrace." While I understand their sentiment, the image is faulty, for in the book of Revelation, God is not described as having a long white beard, flowing hair, bulging biceps, and muscular calves, reaching out His finger to touch man as Michelangelo portrayed Him in the Sistine Chapel. He's described primarily by color—the flame of His eyes; the red of His garment (Revelation 19). Jesus simply said, "God is Spirit" (see John 4:24). Therefore, I don't believe we're going to see the Father as having arms, hands, and legs.

"But doesn't Scripture say He spans the universe with His hand?" you ask (Isaiah 40:12).

Yes, but it also says He covers us with His wings (Psalm 91:4). Therefore, I believe it is as much a mistake to think that God the Father has two eyes, a nose, and two ears, as it is to think He has wings or feathers.

God cannot be contained by a body, no matter how great. He's Spirit. He's everywhere. When we get to heaven, with our new bodies, we'll be able to bask in His glory, just as the high priest did in the Holy of Holies on the Day of Atonement. But I don't believe we will "sit on His lap," as we would with our earthly fathers. God is everywhere, all around us. The Holy Spirit dwells within us. Jesus relates to us.

Christianity is not about making an image of God, no matter how noble or grand. It's about looking at Jesus, and allowing Him to conform us into His image.

JUNE 23

Thou shalt not take the name of the LORD thy God in vain; for the LORD will not hold him guiltless that taketh his name in vain.

Exodus 20:7

Because virtually everyone would agree that societies and families work best when there is no murder, stealing, or lying, people have an easy time understanding the commandments that prohibit those activities. But in the minds of most people, the third commandment is a different story. After all, they reason, everyone takes the Lord's name in vain occasionally. God, however, does not agree. And to underscore this, although He prohibited stealing, coveting, killing, lying, and committing adultery with a simple "Thou shalt not," He amplified the prohibition to take His name in vain as if to say "This is exceptionally serious."

Why?

I suggest two reasons . . .

First, when the Lord's name is used in vain, in a manner devoid of meaning, the result is desensitization. This commandment is not about God being offended, but about people being lost, desensitized to the reality of the name that will save them and the reality of where they will spend eternity if they don't receive Him.

In addition to desensitization, when the Lord's name is taken in vain, there are real ramifications. The man who accidentally hits his thumb while pounding a nail and says blasphemously, "God damn it," is actually saying, "God, doom this project I am working on." And because life and death are indeed in the power of the tongue (Proverbs 18:21), his words, in one way or another, will have a negative impact on the task he is engaged in. Rather dumb!

Mock Buddha and you'll hear from the ACLU. Make fun of an Indian religion and you'll be politically incorrect. But use the name of Jesus Christ in any manner whatsoever and no one will even raise an eyebrow. While we may not be able to keep this from happening outside of our homes, we can use it as an opportunity to talk about Jesus to the one who uses His name blasphemously. And in sharing His reality, we can turn the situation around for His glory.

JUNE 24

Remember the sabbath day, to keep it holy. Six days shalt thou labour, and do all thy work: But the seventh day is the sabbath of the LORD thy God: in it thou shalt not do any work, thou, nor thy son, nor thy daughter, thy manservant, nor thy maidservant, nor thy cattle, nor thy stranger that is within thy gates: For in six days the LORD made heaven and earth, the sea, and all that in them is, and rested the seventh day: wherefore the LORD blessed the sabbath day, and hallowed it.

Exodus 20:8–11

Having worked four hundred years as slaves in Egypt, the concept of a day off would have sounded radical indeed to the children of Israel. And not to them only, but to the surrounding civilizations as well, for no other society of antiquity entertained the idea of a Sabbath day—a day of rest.

With the Assyrians bearing down on them, the children of Israel set up an alliance with the Egyptians, failing to realize that it was only in God that their help would be found. Ever feel like financial, relational, or physical problems are waging war against you? Ever feel like you can't get ahead or even catch up? Listen to what God says . . .

> For thus saith the Lord GOD, the Holy One of Israel; In returning and rest shall ye be saved; in quietness and in confidence shall be your strength: and ye would not. And thine ears shall hear a word behind thee, saying, This is the way, walk ye in it, when ye turn to the right hand, and when ye turn to the left.
>
> Isaiah 30:15, 21

The bills are mounting; the pressures are building; the Assyrians are coming. What am I to do? It's only in returning to God and resting in Him that I'll know. If I consistently take one day of every seven and say, "This is Yours, Lord," I am saying, "Lord, I acknowledge that what I have and enjoy is not because of my work ethic, my creativity, my business acumen, my energy. It's all from You. And I'm going to prove that to myself and to my family by stopping one day in seven. In so doing, I am acknowledging that You are the giver of every good gift, the provider of the bread I enjoy, that You are the One who truly holds my life together."

If I keep the Sabbath, I'll know which way to go as I hear a voice in my ear telling me how to walk. I'll experience a fullness in my heart, a richness in my soul. And so will you.

JUNE 25

Honour thy father and thy mother: that thy days may be long upon the land which the LORD thy God giveth thee.

Exodus 20:12

The fifth commandment is unique indeed, for, as Paul reminds us, it is the only one with a promise attached to it (Ephesians 6:1–3). As evidenced by the fact that many saints die at a young age, while many sinners seem to live indefinitely, the long days promised to those who keep this commandment refer not necessarily to quantity but to quality—to a life full of rich and meaningful days. Living until the age of 930, the first Adam lived thirty times longer than the last Adam, Jesus Christ, who died at the age of thirty-three. Yet no one would argue that the first Adam honored his heavenly Father thirty times more than did the last Adam, for Jesus honored His Father perfectly. And the way He related to His heavenly Father provides a picture, a pattern, and an example for how I am to relate to my earthly mother and father . . .

Jesus was a reflection of His Father (John 5:19). So too, because you are a reflection of your parents, if you're down on them, you'll be down on yourself. Therefore, the way to be well emotionally and relationally is to honor your father and mother.

Jesus was dependent upon His Father (John 5:26). So too, we are dependent upon our earthly parents. Given the fact that the chemical components that comprise our bodies are the same as those of a slug, we should be eternally grateful we were born as humans rather than slugs. Therefore, if there's no other reason to honor them, we should honor them because they gave us life, sustained our lives, and saved our lives probably many more times than we could even imagine.

Jesus was submitted to His Father (John 5:30). The two key qualities that will bring fulfillment and success to anyone's life are those of humility and submission. And those qualities are born only in the context of family. You see, if I don't like my job, I can quit; if I don't like my friends, I can avoid them; if I don't like my neighbors, I can move; if I don't like my school, I can drop out. But my relationship to my parents is the one relationship I can't change. And it is precisely when I don't agree with them or understand them that submission and humility are worked into my soul. At the peak of His maturity, Jesus said, "I am in submission to My Father." And so must I be.

JUNE 26

Thou shalt not kill.

Exodus 20:13

There are two Greek words translated "anger" in the New Testament. The first is *thumos,* and refers to the anger one feels that causes his veins to bulge and his face to get red. The word used in Matthew 5:22, however, is *orgizo,* a word that refers to the anger that smolders internally day after week after month after year. Jesus said the person who harbors this kind of anger without a cause is a murderer.

"Oh, but I have a cause. I have a reason to be angry," you say.

Do you?

In Matthew 18, we read the story of the master who forgave his slave's debt of 10 million dollars only to discover that the slave threatened to kill a fellow slave over a debt of two thousand dollars. In telling this story, Jesus' point was that as real as the two thousand dollar debt was, it was nothing in comparison to the debt of which he had been forgiven. In other words, if all of our mixed motives, evil intentions, and sinful imaginations were brought to light, we would see that we owe a debt far greater than any owed to us, that we are worse than the worst offense committed against us.

> Therefore if thou bring thy gift to the altar, and there rememberest that thy brother hath ought against thee; Leave there thy gift before the altar, and go thy way; first be reconciled to thy brother, and then come and offer thy gift. Agree with thine adversary quickly, whiles thou art in the way with him; lest at any time the adversary deliver thee to the judge, and the judge deliver thee to the officer, and thou be cast into prison. Verily I say unto thee, Thou shalt by no means come out thence, till thou hast paid the uttermost farthing.
>
> Matthew 5:23–26

The only way to keep from murdering others is to be reconciled. And the only way to be reconciled is to agree with your enemy. Even if his facts are wrong, you're a bigger sinner than he can even imagine. So you are to go to him and say, "I'm wrong. I'm sorry. Please forgive me." If you don't, you'll end up in court. What court? The court that exists in your mind. You practice law daily. You gather new witnesses and new evidence systematically. You build an airtight case, and every time court convenes, you win. The other guy never wins. Consequently, your relationships dwindle and your life grows smaller. Families divide. Hell breaks out. And although you may be technically, judicially, or legally right, you're oh, so wrong when you fail to reconcile with your adversary.

I know this because Jesus absorbed the blame for us totally. On the cross, He absorbed the full punishment for our sin, paid the entire price for you and me. Even on the cross, He said, "Father forgive them." And as a result, Jesus is free from the chains of death and the grave, just as you will be if you choose to absorb the blame wholly, completely, and unconditionally.

JUNE 27

Thou shalt not commit adultery.

Exodus 20:14

Because the seventh commandment is the least understood, it is the most argued.

> But whoso committeth adultery with a woman lacketh understanding:
> he that doeth it destroyeth his own soul.

Proverbs 6:32

The world thinks sex is about procreation and recreation, failing to understand that it's primarily about unification, about two souls being mystically and miraculously merged into one. The issue is not unwanted pregnancy, disease, or AIDS. God says the issue of intimacy is the soul. That is why, after presiding over the first marriage ceremony, He looked at the couple and called their name Adam, singularly (Genesis 5:2). Sex outside of marriage destroys one's soul irreparably, inevitably. Every time people are involved in sexual activity outside of marriage, there will be destruction as the soul is destroyed a piece, a layer, a step at a time. That is why Jesus was so emphatic when He dealt with the subject of adultery (Matthew 5:27–30). Knowing its danger, He told us to deal with it radically, brutally, and severely—to do whatever it takes to keep it from our lives.

If there was a sign that read:

> Please proceed with great caution because behind these doors there are experiments taking place with chemical components which may be used one day to cause an explosive reaction at some future point.

I'd probably ignore it.

But if the sign said:

> Danger! Explosives!

I would stay away.

"Thou shalt not commit adultery." If you want to read the fine print, you can explore the Scriptures and find the reason why. But here, it is as if God is simply, clearly, and undeniably saying, "Take My Word for it: Adultery is explosive. It is dangerous. It will destroy you."

JUNE 28

Thou shalt not steal.

Exodus 20:15

Although the eighth commandment is straightforward and simple, it is even more so in Hebrew, where it reads simply, "Steal not." As a society, we know that stealing is wrong, so we teach our kids from the earliest age not to take what isn't theirs. And yet, according to the IRS, if no one cheated on his taxes, our national debt would be retired in one year. But make no mistake, stealing is not limited to money or material goods. We can rob our employers through two-hour lunches or leaving early from work.

Following are four prescriptions for the epidemic of thievery that pervades our culture . . .

"Let him that stole steal no more: but rather let him labour, working with his hands the thing which is good" (Ephesians 4:28). We are to work with our hands. When man fell in the garden of Eden, God told Adam that he was to work by the sweat of his brow. This wasn't punishment but protection, for in his sinful state, man needed to work or else he would be vulnerable to stealing, taking shortcuts, or cheating. One of the greatest ways to be free from thievery is to work hard. Why? If you're not working hard, you're a candidate for depression. You'll be down on yourself, disillusioned with yourself, and sad about your situation. I believe depression can be linked to people who no longer work hard.

Jesus said if someone compels you to go a mile, go two (Matthew 5:41). Go twice as far, twice as hard as your boss expects. Satan will tell you that you deserve a break, but Jesus tells us to go twice as far because, His burden being easy, His load light, He knows it's for our benefit.

"...that he may have to give to him that needeth" (Ephesians 4:28). We are to reach out our hands. If we're going the second mile, working harder than others, we'll inevitably experience a certain degree of success, not to accumulate more for ourselves, but to reach out our hands and give to others. In so doing, a dynamic takes place that leads to joy and liberty, happiness and freedom (Luke 19:8).

"Will a man rob God? Yet ye have robbed me. But ye say, Wherein have we robbed thee? In tithes and offerings" (Malachi 3:8). We are to open up our hands. God indicted His people of robbery when they failed to tithe. The whole earth is the Lord's (Psalm 24:1), and we acknowledge that fact by tithing. He who robs God also robs everyone around him in sneaky, subtle ways.

"He that spared not his own Son, but delivered him up for us all, how shall he not with him also freely give us all things?" (Romans 8:32). We are to look at His hands. The holes in Jesus' hands tell me that God loves me, that He cares about Me, that He'll do what's best for me, which obliterates the need for thievery. I look at His hands, and in them I rest.

By working with your hands, reaching out your hands, opening your hands, and looking at *His* hands, you'll not only keep the eighth commandment, but you'll find deep fulfillment.

JUNE 29

Thou shalt not bear false witness against thy neighbour.

Exodus 20:16

The biblical viewpoint of bearing false witness is not confined to the telling of bold-faced lies, but also includes being tricky with the truth. In the one account where the phrase "false witness" is used in Scripture, we see individuals falsely accusing Jesus of threatening to destroy the temple when, in fact, He was speaking of His own death (Matthew 26:59–61).

Because he is the Father of Lies, Satan is the ultimate false witness, accusing us day and night before God's throne as he points out our failings, our shortcomings, and our sins (Revelation 12:10). Jesus, on the other hand, is the faithful and true witness (Revelation 1:5; 3:14), our Advocate, our defense lawyer.

Are you a true witness or a false witness? If the person sitting next to you is a believer, he or she is righteously robed, heaven bound, Spirit-filled, positionally pure. Speaking anything less of them is bearing false witness. Oh, you might give the right information, but in so doing, do you convey the wrong implication? You might say lots of nice things about them, but do you add a "but, . . ." a "however, . . ." an "I don't know if I should share this, but . . ."? If so, you're a false witness because, although you might be telling the truth, you're not telling the whole truth. You're failing to factor in God's estimation of them.

If you're prone to bearing false witness, consider the following remedies:

Say less, for as Solomon so insightfully declared, "In the multitude of words there wanteth not sin: but he that refraineth his lips is wise" (Proverbs 10:19).

Pray more. "Remove from me the way of lying," David prayed (Psalm 119:29).

Think again. Before you say anything about anyone else, THINK:

   T: Is what you are about to say the whole Truth?

   H: Is it Helpful? Will people be edified?

I: Is it Inspirational? Will God be praised as a result?

N: Is it Necessary?

K: Is it Kind?

The best way to keep from bearing false witness is to simply say less, pray more, and think again.

JUNE 30

Thou shalt not covet thy neighbour's house, thou shalt not covet thy neighbour's wife, nor his manservant, nor his maidservant, nor his ox, nor his ass, nor any thing that is thy neighbour's.

Exodus 20:17

Of all the commandments, the last one is probably taken the least seriously. If a person breaks the sixth commandment, he might be executed. If he breaks the eighth, he might end up in jail. If he breaks the ninth, he might be sued. But if he breaks the tenth commandment, not only is he forgiven, but applauded, for coveting is a key component of our culture.

Essentially, to covet is simply to want more than one possesses. Our economy is based upon this. Society screams at us that the way to have real life is to have this car or that toy. But the Giver of Life, the Author of Life, the One who declared, "I am the Life," said, "That's not true. A man's life does not consist of the stuff he has materially." And to illustrate His point, He went on to give a parable of a man who had so many material goods that it was necessary for him to construct bigger barns to hold it all. Although the financial planners would consider him wise, and his culture might consider him blessed, God considered him a fool for failing to lay up treasure in the only place that matters: heaven (Luke 12:20).

If God blesses you materially, wonderful! God gives us richly all things to enjoy (1 Timothy 6:17). I find it interesting that in Jesus' parable, the rich man was planning to enjoy his wealth in the future (Luke 12:19). In other words, up to that point, he never truly enjoyed what he had. And such is all too often the case. The man living for things, wanting more things, focused on things will never, ever be satisfied; he will always think he needs just a few more things to make him happy.

The solution? Not only are we to enjoy material blessings, but we are to employ them, not to make more money for ourselves, but to help others, to extend the gospel to others.

Abraham, a wealthy man of Ur, left his comfortable life behind to seek a city whose builder and maker was God (Hebrews 11:10). He saw the big picture. He saw the kingdom. And so must we.

JULY 1

And all the people saw the thunderings, and the lightnings, and the noise of the trumpet, and the mountain smoking: and when the people saw it, they removed, and stood afar off. And they said unto Moses, Speak thou with us, and we will hear: but let not God speak with us, lest we die.

Exodus 20:18–19

So powerful was God's power and potency, His glory and grandeur that the people said, "You speak to us, Moses, because if God speaks to us, we'll die." And that's the way it's supposed to be.

The Word of God is powerful, sharper than any two-edged sword. It pierces. It divides. It kills our pride, our self-centeredness, and our flesh (Hebrews 4:12). And because it does, the person who wants to pamper his flesh, the person caught up in the sins of the flesh will often be one who doesn't want to hear from God anymore. If I choose to indulge my flesh day after day, week after week, I won't be at Bible study six months down the road.

If you're at a place where lately it's been hard to get into the Word, I have great news for you: God wants to do something special in you. Satan sees what God desires to do and is trying to keep you from that blessing. It's a big one, a great one. So pick up the Word, let God speak, and discover the blessings in store.

JULY 2

I will not drive them out from before thee in one year; lest the land become desolate, and the beast of the field multiply against thee. By little and little I will drive them out from before thee, until thou be increased, and inherit the land.

Exodus 23:29–30

"I've gone to Bible study for six weeks," some say, "and I'm still depressed, still defeated." Or, "I've been praying for three months, and my situation still hasn't changed."

The Lord, however, says, "I'll not drive out your enemies as quickly as you might think because there's something else in play. If I drove them out in one year, the wild beasts would multiply. Therefore, until you're increased, until you're ready to occupy the land, I'm keeping them there in order to keep the fields tilled and the wild beasts at bay."

This is hard for me because patience doesn't come easy. I like things to happen immediately. But that's not the way God works. "Count it all joy," He says, "when you go through trials, in order that patience might have her perfect work" (see James 1:2–4). I want to get ahead of God, but He says, "If the project was completed, if the answer was given on your schedule, you wouldn't be ready for it. My timing is perfect—any earlier, and it would be disastrous. In the meantime, you'll be increased by talking the situation over with Me, by waiting on Me, and by spending time with Me."

"I want this kind of ministry," we say, or "that kind of girl to marry," or "this type of family."

"Great!" the Lord says. "But I've got a lot of work to do to make you the kind of person who can handle that responsibility. It's not going to happen quickly. Little by little, I'll drive out the obstacles. In the meantime, stay close to Me."

JULY 3

And he said unto Moses, Come up unto the LORD, thou, and Aaron, Nadab, and Abihu, and seventy of the elders of Israel; and worship ye afar off.

Exodus 24:1

"Draw nigh to Me and I will draw nigh to you," God says to us (see James 4:8). Yet to this group, God says, "Come and worship ye afar off." They were told to worship even though they were to worship from afar. I know that because of the work of Christ on the cross, I can come boldly unto the throne of grace. I can draw nigh to God. I can call Him Abba, or Papa. But the fact is, sometimes I don't feel that way emotionally. I feel like I'm worshiping Him from afar. Ever feel that way? Take heart. I have learned that it's okay because God is worthy of worship whether I am emotionally engaged or not.

Worship is not about how I feel. It's all about who God is. And He is worthy to receive glory and honor and power, for He has created all things and for His pleasure they are and were created—whether we feel this or not (Revelation 4:11).

JULY 4

And thou shalt put into the ark the testimony which I shall give thee.

Exodus 25:16

The testimony is the Ten Commandments, the two tables of stone written by the finger of God (Exodus 31:18).

"Come boldly before the throne of grace and find mercy and grace to help in time of need," God says to us (see Hebrews 4:16).

"But I can't," we say. "I haven't prayed in days. I haven't been to church in weeks. I haven't witnessed in months. I haven't kept the commandments."

Where were the commandments kept?

In the ark.

Who kept the commandments?

Jesus. "I do always those things that please [the Father]," He said (John 8:29).

Jesus kept the commandments perfectly. And as believers, we are in Him positionally (2 Corinthians 5:17). Therefore, the Father looks at us and doesn't see our sin. He looks at us and sees His Son (Romans 3:22).

JULY 5

And thou shalt make a mercy seat of pure gold: two cubits and a half shall be the length thereof, and a cubit and a half the breadth thereof. And thou shalt make two cherubims of gold, of beaten work shalt thou make them, in the two ends of the mercy seat. And make one cherub on the one end, and the other cherub on the other end: even of the mercy seat shall ye make the cherubims on the two ends thereof. And the cherubims shall stretch forth their wings on high, covering the mercy seat with their wings, and their faces shall look one to another; toward the mercy seat shall the faces of the cherubims be. And thou shalt put the mercy seat above upon the ark.

Exodus 25:17–21

Most Christians try to meet God at the ark by keeping the commandments, by going to this meeting, by doing those things, by not sinning, by living purely. God, however, says He'll meet us not at the ark, but at that which covers it—the mercy seat.

How do we walk with the Lord practically? Not by anything we do, how long our devotions are, how many chapters of the Bible we've read, how many prayers we offer, but simply and solely by the unmerited, undeserved, unearned favor of God. This is where so many people miss it. Although they know they're saved by grace, they think they're sanctified through works. Big mistake. A true relationship with God is not about witnessing, ministry, or devotional life. It's all about what He did in and through Christ.

On that first Easter Sunday morning, had you looked into the empty tomb, you would have seen two angels sitting, one at the head and one at the foot of the blood-stained slab where the body of Jesus had lain (John 20:12). Leviticus 16:14 tells us that the mercy seat would be sprinkled with blood. Thus, the mercy seat paints a perfect picture of the only way we can have fellowship with God, that being through the finished work of the Son.

JULY 6

And in the ark thou shalt put the testimony that I shall give thee. And there I will meet with thee, and I will commune with thee from above the mercy seat, from between the two cherubims which are upon the ark of the testimony, of all things which I will give thee in commandment unto the children of Israel.

Exodus 25:21–22

It was at the mercy seat that God would meet with man. And we err greatly whenever we forget this . . .

> After capturing the ark, the Philistines eventually put it in the temple of their god Dagon, only to find Dagon face down before it the following day. Setting Dagon aright, they returned the next day to find him toppled over once again, this time with his head and hands severed (1 Samuel 5). While it would seem obvious that they needed a more powerful god to protect them, they instead decided to protect their god by sending the ark back to Israel. Seeing the ark on its way back to their border, the people of God were understandably

excited. But their excitement soon turned to terror when God smote 50,070 of their number when they looked inside the ark, perhaps for no other reason than to see if the commandments were still inside (1 Samuel 6).

"I will meet you at the mercy seat," God says. But sometimes we make a deadly mistake when we set aside mercy to get to the bottom of an issue, to lay down the law on someone. I have done this, and it always leads to death in relationships, in families, in friendships, and in ministry.

"The letter of the law kills," Paul would write, "but the Spirit gives life" (see 2 Corinthians 3:6). Once we set aside mercy, even temporarily, to get to the bottom of an issue, to find out who's right and who's wrong, to get to the letter of the law, the end result will always be death. Always. Friendships will die. Families will divide. Ministry will shut down. No good comes from removing the mercy seat. Therefore, be merciful. To whom? To the person you're angry with. Be gracious. To whom? To the person you feel has wronged you.

Whenever you feel far from God, a practical way you can be brought back into His presence is by remembering the mercy seat. That is, find people to whom you can show mercy. I have discovered over and over again in my own life that there are two uniquely practical ways I truly experience the presence of the Lord. The first is by praising Him. Psalm 22:3 declares that He inhabits the praises of His people. The second is by showing mercy to people, for it was at the mercy seat that God chose to dwell.

JULY 7

Thou shalt also make a table of shittim wood: two cubits shall be the length thereof, and a cubit the breadth thereof, and a cubit and a half the height thereof.

Exodus 25:23

Why was the table of showbread to be two cubits long? Two is the number of union, communion, and agreement (Amos 3:3). True communion with God takes place when we agree with Him and confess our sins. The Greek word translated "confession" is *homologeo*, which means "to speak the same."

Thus, confession in the biblical sense is not a matter of promising not to sin again, but rather of simply agreeing with God and saying of any given sin, "This sin is depressing and defeating me, Lord. And it's detrimental to others."

Surely God knows our sins. Why, then, does He want us to confess them? Because every sin I specifically confess loses its grip on me to an ever greater degree. In addition, when I also confess that a specific sin is blotted out by the blood of Calvary, there is a dynamic which takes place in the Spirit that sets me free. Confession is not promising never to sin again, but simply calling sin what it is and acknowledging that it's forgiven. That's two cubits. That's union.

JULY 8

And thou shalt make a candlestick of pure gold: of beaten work shall the candlestick be made: his shaft, and his branches, his bowls, his knops, and his flowers, shall be of the same.

Exodus 25:31

The word translated "candlestick" is the Hebrew word *menorah*. A menorah held oil lamps rather than wax candles. The lampstand was not made of wood covered with gold as were the ark and the table of showbread, but it was made of pure gold.

A few chapters from now, we will see how Aaron made a calf from molten gold. Unlike that false god, this lampstand, which speaks of Jesus Christ as the Light of the Word, was made of beaten gold. Many people say, "You Christians claim that Jesus is the single answer, the only Way, the one true Light. But how do you know what you're declaring is right?" The answer is that, like the gold of the candlestick, He was beaten, yet He rose again from the dead.

Truly, it's when you are beaten and yet continue to burn bright that the beauty, the reality of the Light of the Word is most clearly seen. This means that the point at which you choose to embrace the difficulty that seems to beat upon you is the point where you will see Jesus in ways you've never seen Him before. It is when you're being beaten, when you're in the fiery trial that Jesus is clearer to you than you ever dreamed possible.

Ask Shadrach, Meshach, and Abed-nego. As they were in the furnace, whom did they see? The Son of God in their midst. How real was He? So real they didn't want to leave the furnace (Daniel 3:25–26). A lot of people try to get out of the fire, when in reality, it is the fire itself which causes the Lord to be seen most clearly.

JULY 9

And the tongs thereof, and the snuffdishes thereof, shall be of pure gold. Of a talent of pure gold shall he make it, with all these vessels. And look that thou make them after their pattern, which was shewed thee in the mount.

Exodus 25:38–40

The instruments used to trim the wicks and snuff out the candles were to be pure gold. So too, there will be people in our lives who are there morning and evening, "snipping" and "snuffing." And, although my tendency is to belittle them, I am in error when I do because they provide golden opportunities for me to burn brighter.

I find it interesting that although the weight is given of the lampstand (a talent), unlike the ark and the table of showbread, the dimensions aren't given. Could this be because there is no limit to how brightly we are to shine?

JULY 10

Moreover thou shalt make the tabernacle with ten curtains of fine twined linen, and blue, and purple, and scarlet.

Exodus 26:1

The curtains, which would serve as walls of the tabernacle, were to be made of four colors: white, blue, purple, and scarlet. The number four draws one's mind to the four Gospels which, not surprisingly, correspond perfectly to the four colors of the tabernacle. Luke speaks of the righteous humanity of Jesus, which would be typified by the fine white linen. John portrays Jesus as deity, which would be typified by blue, the color of heaven. Matthew writes of Jesus as King of the Jews, as seen in purple, the color of royalty. Mark speaks of Jesus as the Suffering Servant, seen in the color scarlet . . .

> The Hebrew word, *tola'ath*, can be translated either of two ways: "scarlet" or "worm." Why? Because in Old Testament times when people wanted to dye something scarlet, they would dip the material in ground-up worms and the material would take on a scarlet color.
>
> "I am a worm, and no man," cried the psalmist, prophetically speaking of Jesus on the cross (Psalm 22:6). And the word he used was *tola'ath*, a most fitting word. You see, to reproduce, the *tola'ath*, or worm, would fasten itself on the limb of a tree and die in the process of giving birth. As it died, it left a red spot that, according to the New International Bible Encyclopedia, turned white after three days and flaked off like snow. "Though your sins be as scarlet, they shall be as white as snow," Isaiah declared (1:18). The picture is perfect. Jesus fastened Himself to a tree that we might be born into His family. He sacrificed His life that we might live. Three days later, He rose again, and our sin that was scarlet was washed white as snow.

Is it any wonder that scarlet was one of the colors in the tabernacle and in the garments of the priest?

JULY 11

And thou shalt make staves for the altar, staves of shittim wood, and overlay them with brass. And the staves shall be put into the rings, and the staves shall be upon the two sides of the altar, to bear it.

Exodus 27:6–7

The altar would be carried by staves, or poles, slipped through the rings upon it. I like this because the altar speaks of Communion and the Communion Table ought to be portable. That is, wherever we are, we are to remember and receive the work Christ did for us on the brass altar of Calvary.

The altar was the only piece of tabernacle furniture covered with purple (Numbers 4:13–14). Purple is the color of royalty. Why is Jesus Christ our King? Not because of what He does for me presently, but because of what He already did on the cross. He's not our King so that we'll have a happy day or have our bills paid, so that we'll get a newer car or have better relationships. The purple cloth was over the brass altar exclusively because His death is the basis of His kingly authority over our lives. His sacrifice saved us from hell, and even if He never answers another prayer or sends another blessing our way, that is reason enough to praise Him all the days of our lives.

JULY 12

And for the gate of the court shall be an hanging of twenty cubits, of blue, and purple, and scarlet, and fine twined linen, wrought with needlework.

Exodus 27:16

The door into the outer courtyard was made of the same fabric as the veil and as the door into the tabernacle itself. Whether one is talking about the door into the courtyard (the place of salvation), the door into the Holy

Place (the place of service), or the door into the Holy of Holies (the place of worship), it's all the same door. It's all through Jesus.

You see, just as the tabernacle was comprised of three sections—the outer courtyard, the Holy Place, and the Holy of Holies—I believe there are three stages of our lives in Christ.

There are those who are inside the courtyard. They're in Christ, part of the kingdom. They realize Jesus Christ, the Lamb of God, was slain for their sins. They receive His salvation; they embrace His grace.

But there are others who say, "Because God has been so good to me, I want to serve Him." So they go into the Holy Place and serve the showbread, which speaks of the Word of God. They teach Sunday school, lead family devotions, or share the Word with someone at work. They see the golden lampstand and desire to let their light shine through good works (Matthew 5:16), by helping in the nursery, visiting shut-ins, and serving those in need. They smell the incense burning and are reminded that it speaks of intercession. So they pray consistently for the lost and for their brothers and sisters, for their families and their countries.

Yet there are still others who, like the high priest himself, enter into the Holy of Holies in order to simply spend time in the Lord's presence, to consider His character, ponder His nature, give Him praise, express their love, and bring Him pleasure. All too often, we don't understand this. We think if we could lead worship, preach a sermon, or be a missionary, we'd be amazing. But those things don't hold a candle to the highest level, to coming into the presence of the Lord and worshiping Him intimately. And here's the irony: the highest form of ministry, the most satisfying aspect of ministry is available to every single person right now.

> Jesus went to the home of His close friends in Bethany, the home of Mary, Martha, and Lazarus. Lazarus is not mentioned in the Luke 10 account. He was outside, in the outer courtyard, if you will. He was a friend of the Lord to be sure. But he was outside. Martha was in the kitchen, or the Holy Place, as it were, serving. She was baking bread, doing good works, and even praying, "Lord, tell my sister to get in here and help me!" Mary, however, was sitting at the feet of

Jesus. She was in the Holy of Holies. And, of her, Jesus said, "Mary has chosen the better part" (see Luke 10:42).

Nothing compares to being in the Holy of Holies, to being in the Lord's presence. It's the highest calling, the most important aspect of ministry. And it's available to every one of us.

JULY 13

And they shall make the ephod of gold, of blue, and of purple, of scarlet, and fine twined linen, with cunning work.

Exodus 28:6

The ephod was an apron that extended to the knees, a most fitting garment for one involved in the work of preparing animals for sacrifice. The ephod speaks of Christ because, in Old Testament culture, the ephod spoke of authority.

> After Gideon led the people of Israel to victory over their enemies, the Midianites, the people asked him to be their king. Gideon refused, saying it was the Lord who would rule them (Judges 8:23). Not many people would turn down an opportunity for power or privilege or prestige. Gideon did. There are many wonderful lessons to be learned from the life of Gideon, and this is one of the great ones. He did not take advantage of an opportunity to put himself in a place of prominence. But then he made a critical mistake when he melted the golden earrings the men had collected as the spoils of war into a golden ephod. Evidently, he thought a golden ephod would help the people remember they were to get instruction and counsel from God through the high priest. But his plan backfired when the people began worshiping the ephod instead of worshiping God (Judges 8:27).

You and I have a great High Priest in Jesus. Therefore, how careful we must be that we don't begin to say, "I've got some pretty good things to say, some very enlightening counsel to give, my own golden ephod to share with you."

"Woe to the rebellious children, saith the LORD, that take counsel, but not of me," the Lord declares. "In returning and rest shall ye be saved. And thine ears shall hear a word behind thee, saying, This is the way, walk ye in it" (Isaiah 30:1, 15, 21). Jesus alone wears the ephod. Jesus alone is the Anointed One.

JULY 14

And thou shalt put in the breastplate of judgment the Urim and the Thummim; and they shall be upon Aaron's heart, when he goeth in before the LORD.

Exodus 28:30

In the Old Testament, where were the stones—the Urim and Thummim—that would give direction? Over the heart of the high priest. Now, however, the Lord gives direction not by a breastplate worn *over* the heart but by the branding He performs *upon* our hearts.

> But this shall be the covenant that I will make with the house of Israel; After those days, saith the LORD, I will put my law in their inward parts, and write it in their hearts; and will be their God, and they shall be my people.

> Jeremiah 31:33

This is fantastic. Here God declares we'll know what we ought to do not by some external stone, but by impressions and desires within our hearts. That is why David could say, "Delight yourself in the Lord and He will give you the desires of your heart" (see Psalm 37:4). What are we to do to find God's will? Augustine nailed it when he said, "Love [God] and do what you will."[3]

Why do I teach the Bible? Because I enjoy it. You see, I am simple enough to believe God's promise that if I delight in Him, He will put desires in my heart which conform to His perfect plan for me. If you're not delighting in the Lord, don't follow the desires of your heart because they will lead you on a dangerous path. But if you say, "Although I know I have problems and flaws, I do love the Lord and I want to delight in Him," He'll give you light and direction, the Urim and the Thummim, in your heart.

JULY 15

And thou shalt make the robe of the ephod all of blue. And there shall be an hole in the top of it, in the midst thereof: it shall have a binding of woven work round about the hole of it, as it were the hole of an habergeon, that it be not rent. And beneath upon the hem of it thou shalt make pomegranates of blue, and of purple, and of scarlet, round about the hem thereof; and bells of gold between them round about: A golden bell and a pomegranate, a golden bell and a pomegranate, upon the hem of the robe round about.

Exodus 28:31–34

With blue being the color of heaven, we see here a picture of Christ the heavenly One. John tells us it was because He knew where He had come from, and where He was going that He washed His disciples' feet (John 13:3–5). Some people say, "You're so heavenly minded, you're no earthly good." Jesus, however, would show us we can be no earthly good until we're heavenly minded. Why? Because if I'm not heavenly minded, I'll get bogged down taking care of my toys, my trinkets, and my trivial world. But as I choose to be heavenly minded, and live for the big picture of eternity, I will enjoy this life immensely because I won't take it so seriously.

Of all the fruits in the world, none has more seeds than the blood-red interior of a pomegranate. On the cross, Jesus shed His blood in order that His Spirit might bear much fruit through seeds like you and me.

If pomegranates speak of the fruit of the Spirit, bells speak of the gifts of the Spirit. The bells of the ephod were made to have a beautiful sound in and of themselves. But if they hit one another, they would sound like nothing more than a clanging gong or a crashing cymbal. So the bells were to be separated by pomegranates, by the fruit of the Spirit, so as to ring in harmony. That is why in 1 Corinthians 12, Paul talks about the gifts of the Spirit. In chapter 14, he also talks about the gifts of the Spirit. But in between the two is a pomegranate, for in chapter 13, he talks about the fruit of the Spirit, which is love.

JULY 16

And this is the thing that thou shalt do unto them to hallow them, to minister unto me in the priest's office.

Exodus 29:1

In 1 Timothy 1:12, Paul says, "I thank Christ Jesus our Lord, who hath enabled me, for that he counted me faithful, putting me into the ministry." Like Paul, I am amazed at the goodness and grace of God that He would include me in this glorious privilege called ministry.

Ministry is a privilege because of the *present blessings.* "With what measure ye mete, it shall be measured to you," Jesus said (Mark 4:24). That is, what we give out, we'll get back. And I have found that to be oh, so true. When I pray for others, I get blessed. When I share with others, I am confirmed in the truth of the Scriptures. When I witness to others, my own faith grows deeper, stronger, and more powerful.

This should not be surprising. After all, Jesus promised we would receive power to become His witnesses (Acts 1:8). And the word He used for power was *dunamis,* from which we get our word "dynamite." This dynamic experience, this power is like an electrical charge. Therefore, like electricity, it will only enter that from which it can exit. The power, the electricity, and the anointing of the Holy Spirit is given to you that it might flow through you to others. The one who wants to be used by the Lord in the lives of others will experience the electric, dynamic power of the Spirit. That's why I love being in the ministry.

Second, I enjoy being in the ministry because of *future rewards*. What we do in ministry—even as simple as giving a cup of cold water in Jesus' name—will be rewarded by the Lord and will impact us eternally (Matthew 10:42). You might think you don't care about rewards. But you will then. When we get to heaven and rewards are given, you'll say, "I wish I would have taken more seriously the admonitions to strive to run the race, to win the prize, to gain the crown" (see Philippians 3:14).

Third, I love the ministry because of *real needs*. People all around us are lost. Wandering around like sheep without a shepherd, they don't know what to do. They're depressed, discouraged, and worst of all, without Jesus, they're headed for hell. They don't know that God sent His Son not to condemn them, but to save them, to die in place of them that they might be forgiven of their sins and might spend eternity in heaven (John 3:17). So I say, "Lord, thank You for allowing me to be in the ministry because I see people all around me who are confused, and You've given such simple and significant answers for me to share with them."

And He's given the same opportunity to you, for although you might earn a living as a schoolteacher, a carpenter, or an electrician, you are in the ministry every bit as much as I am. The division between the clergy and the laity is a man-made distinction without biblical basis, for Jesus said, "Ye have not chosen me, but I have chosen you, and ordained you, that ye should go and bring forth fruit, and that your fruit should remain" (John 15:16).

JULY 17

Also thou shalt take of the ram the fat and the rump, and the fat that covereth the inwards, and the caul above the liver, and the two kidneys, and the fat that is upon them, and the right shoulder; for it is a ram of consecration: And one loaf of bread, and one cake of oiled bread, and one wafer out of the basket of the unleavened bread that is before the LORD: And thou shalt put all in the hands of Aaron, and in the hands of his sons.

Exodus 29:22–24

The hands of Aaron and his sons—once empty enough to place on the head of the sin offering—are now filled.

> On one mountain ridge stood the people of Israel. On the other were the Philistines. And in the valley between them, Goliath taunted the people of Israel day after day, challenging them to send someone to do battle with him. The Israelites were understandably terrified. After all, Goliath was at least 9'9" and possibly as tall as 11'6". So heavy was his spear that the tip alone weighed thirty pounds. To put that in perspective, shot-putters throw a ball weighing a mere sixteen pounds. The armor he wore to protect his chest was two hundred pounds. Goliath was indeed massive. When the young shepherd boy from Bethlehem arrived on the scene and heard Goliath's jeers, he said, "Give me a chance. Let me take him on." You see, while everyone else thought Goliath was too big to hit, David thought he was too big to miss. Turning down the offer of an armor too large for him, David went into the valley of Elah with the only thing he was accustomed to using: his sling. But it was empty until, there in the very valley in which he would do battle, he found five stones—one of which would slay Goliath (1 Samuel 17:40).

Just as it wasn't until David had already committed himself to the battle that he found the stones, and just as it wasn't until Aaron and his sons were to make an offering to the Lord that they were given bread and meat, it won't be until you start sharing your faith and reaching out to people that you will be given exactly what you need for ministry (Matthew 10:19). Daring to minister is as necessary as preparing to minister, for it's when we are in the valley of confrontation that we'll look down and see five smooth stones waiting to be put to God's use.

JULY 18

Now this is that which thou shalt offer upon the altar; two lambs of the first year day by day continually. The one lamb thou shalt offer in the morning; and the other lamb thou shalt offer at even.

Exodus 29:38–39

A lamb was to be sacrificed every morning and every evening. There seems to be a wonderful principle for which the Lord is laying the groundwork here—we are to start our day with the sacrifice of prayer and praise and end it in the same way. Prayer in the morning opens the door to blessing. Prayer at night locks it in and makes us safe and secure. You see, the Enemy doesn't snooze. Therefore, if you wake up feeling blue and wondering why, it could very well be that you've been a target of his. But you can shield yourself to a large degree from his attacks by turning off the TV and praying before you end your day.

Think of it this way: If I came home from a week away and said, "Tammy, we don't need to sit down and talk. You can just follow me around and we'll talk on the go," what kind of relationship would we have? There needs to be a constant flow of conversation, true. But for a marriage to be strong, there must be not only a quantity of time, but a quality of time, where both people are completely focused on each other.

And I suggest that same thing is true in our relationship with the Lord. While we are to indeed pray without ceasing all through the day, there also must be times when we say, "Lord, I'm here to talk to You, to hear from You, to offer You the sacrifice of thoughtful, articulate, emotional, and intelligent praise. I'm here to press into Your presence, to pour out my heart, to focus exclusively on You." It's not a "got to." It's a "get to."

JULY 19

And thou shalt make an altar to burn incense upon: of shittim wood shalt thou make it. A cubit shall be the length thereof, and a cubit the breadth thereof; foursquare shall it be: and two cubits shall be the height thereof: the horns thereof shall be of the same.

Exodus 30:1–2

Every part of the tabernacle pictures and points to Jesus Christ. And the altar of incense is no exception. The brass altar of chapter 27 portrays Jesus in His first coming. The golden altar of incense speaks of His present work and His second coming. At one cubit by one cubit, or 18" by 18", the altar of incense is much smaller than the imposing brass altar of sacrifice because Jesus doesn't need to go to great lengths, wrestling and pleading with the Father through intercessory prayer on our behalf. No, He's constantly, continually, and consistently bringing us up before the Father in a comfortable confidence.

Sometimes our prayers don't get answered the way we hope because the Lord is answering previous prayers we have forgotten about. For example, we pray, "Lord, make me a godly man. Give me patience. Give me depth. Bring me into holiness."

"Okay," the Lord says. So a challenge comes our way, and what do we say?

"Get me out of here, Lord! Why am I in this predicament? What's going on? Have You forgotten about me? Don't You care?"

That's why we need an Intercessor, a High Priest who loves us, who sees the big picture, who knows what we have asked for and what's coming down the road . . .

"Simon, Simon," Jesus said, "Satan desires to sift you like wheat, but I have prayed for you that your faith fail not. And when you are converted, when you get through this ordeal, strengthen the brethren" (see Luke 22:32).

"But Peter's faith failed," you say.

No it didn't. His hope failed. "Hope maketh not ashamed" (Romans 5:5). That's why when Peter's hope failed, he was ashamed of his link to Jesus (John 18:17). Later on, after Jesus rose again, Peter was unable to tell Him he loved Him because Peter knew Jesus' definition of love was to keep His commandments (John 14:21). Peter's hope failed. Peter's love failed. But his faith never failed. He always believed.

So too, today Jesus says to us, "I know your Simon-like tendencies. I know you get shaken and that you are unstable. But I'm praying for you that your faith doesn't fail. I'm holding you up. So when you get through—and you *will* get through this—strengthen others."

JULY 20

And thou shalt put it before the vail that is by the ark of the testimony, before the mercy seat that is over the testimony, where I will meet with thee.

Exodus 30:6

Upon the golden altar of heaven seen in Revelation 8, the incense speaks not only of the prayers of the Savior on our behalf, but also of our intercessory ministry on behalf of others. Incense was burned on an altar because prayer requires sacrifice. There is nothing harder to do in spiritual life than pray. Why? I believe it's because Satan opposes it so vehemently. Why? He knows that's where the power is. Just as the altar of incense was the piece of furniture closest to the mercy seat, we are never closer to the Father than when we're in prayer.

"Son of David, have mercy on me," cried the Syro-Phoenician woman. Yet Luke tells us Jesus walked by as though He heard her not. "Son of David, have mercy," she cried again. But Jesus kept going. The phrase "Son of David" was a Jewish term used by Jewish people to address the Jewish Messiah. This woman, however, was a Gentile. She had heard stories about what had taken place in Israel, about Jewish people who were blind or leprous crying out to the

Son of David to heal them. So she used their formula. But it didn't apply to her. It was religion. It wasn't real. It wasn't until she said, "Lord, help me," that Jesus stopped in His tracks and healed her daughter (Matthew 15:25).

Keep your prayer simple. Don't think you have to copy how someone else prays or use the phrases someone else uses. The altar of incense was small. It's not the length of your prayers, but their strength and their sincerity that matters (Ecclesiastes 5:2).

JULY 21

The rich shall not give more, and the poor shall not give less than half a shekel, when they give an offering unto the LORD, to make an atonement for your souls. And thou shalt take the atonement money of the children of Israel, and shalt appoint it for the service of the tabernacle of the congregation; that it may be a memorial unto the children of Israel before the LORD, to make an atonement for your souls.

Exodus 30:15–16

There have been groups throughout history who, on the basis of this verse, have said atonement for souls can be made by paying money. Can atonement be purchased? Can man be "at one" with God for a price? No. The entire Bible argues against that. We can't purchase salvation. Yet salvation must indeed be purchased. And it was. Peter tells us we were redeemed not with corruptible things like silver and gold, but by the precious blood of the Lamb (1 Peter 1:18–19).

Great is the day when we realize our lives are not our own, when we say, "If the Lord wants to take me through tragedy or difficulty, if He chooses to make me a pauper, send me to Africa, give me kids or give me none, I'm not my own. And because I've been bought with a price, I who was once headed for hell am destined for heaven."

JULY 22

And the LORD *spake unto Moses, saying, Thou shalt also make a laver of brass, and his foot also of brass, to wash withal: and thou shalt put it between the tabernacle of the congregation and the altar, and thou shalt put water therein. For Aaron and his sons shall wash their hands and their feet thereat: When they go into the tabernacle of the congregation, they shall wash with water, that they die not.*

Exodus 30:17–20

The laver wherein the priests were to wash was to be made of brass. Throughout Scripture, brass is the metal of judgment. Where did the children of Israel get the brass to make the laver? Exodus 38 tells the story. When construction of the tabernacle actually began, the women donated the brass looking glasses they had been given in Egypt. I find this more than coincidental because James likens the Word to a mirror (1:23–25). And therein lies the problem. You see, when we open the Word, we see our reflection, and it's not as it should be. We see our failures and flaws, our sins and shortcomings. And although we understand that the Word brings benefits to those who study it, sometimes we become exhausted by trying to live up to its standards.

But wait, the brass laver was filled with water. Without water, all one would see was the reflection of his flaws and failures, but without a way to rid himself of them. But the addition of water made the laver refreshing and renewing. "All you who thirst, come to Me," Jesus said, "and out of your innermost being shall gush forth torrents of living water" (see John 7:37–38).

I was at a point some years ago when I was reading through the Gospels as I love to do. But I was weary. I came to the portion where Jesus touched a leper and the leper was cleansed. And I heard myself saying, "I need to be helping people physically just like Jesus did."

Then I turned the page and saw how Jesus touched the ears and tongue of a man unable to hear and speak. And I found myself thinking, "I need to find some dumb guys and help them just like Jesus did."

Then I turned the page and read how Jesus had compassion on the multitudes and fed five thousand hungry men. And I said, "That's the way it ought to be. I need to get involved in World Vision or Compassion International and help feed hungry people."

Then I saw Jesus blessing kids and thought, "I need to work with kids."

Then I saw how Jesus calmed the storm on the Sea of Galilee, and was reminded of those I knew whose marriages were on the rocks, whose lives were in turmoil, and decided I should do what I could to see those storms stilled.

Then I read how Jesus defended the woman caught in adultery, and felt that I should stand up for those who are socially or politically oppressed.

And at the end, I was exhausted. Finally, I said, "I just can't read another chapter. I can't do it. Jesus, I'm impressed with You. I see the rightness of what You do. But I can't do all the things You did."

And it was at that moment that the Lord whispered in my heart, "Exactly. You have yourself in the wrong position. I'm the One who touches the leper. I'm the One who blesses the children. I'm the One who feeds the hungry. I'm the One who makes the dumb to speak. I'm the One who stands up for the woman. I'm the One who calms the storms. It's not you. It's Me."

"I get it," I said. "You're the Christ. I'm not. That makes me the leper. I'm being eaten away every day by my sin and carnality. Yet every day You come my way and touch and restore my life. I'm the dumb guy. I say things I shouldn't say. I put my foot in my mouth. Yet You're there to forgive me and straighten me out. I'm the deaf man. But You never give up on me. You open my ears, You renew my thoughts. I'm the little child who needs a touch from You. I'm the hungry one, and only You can meet the need within me. I'm the one caught in adultery, and You're there to forgive me. I'm the one caught in the storm, and You're the One who walks out to rescue me. I've been reading my Bible all wrong. No wonder I've been so weary, so reluctant to keep reading. I've placed myself in the wrong role. You're the Christ; I'm the leper. Thank You for Your mercy. Thank You for Your patience. Where would I be without You?"

And when the Lord adjusted my thinking, Scripture reading became a total joy once again.

JULY 23

Moreover the LORD *spake unto Moses, saying, Take thou also unto thee principal spices, of pure myrrh five hundred shekels, and of sweet cinnamon half so much, even two hundred and fifty shekels, and of sweet calamus two hundred and fifty shekels, and of cassia five hundred shekels, after the shekel of the sanctuary, and of oil olive an hin: And thou shalt make it an oil of holy ointment, an ointment compound after the art of the apothecary: it shall be an holy anointing oil.*

Exodus 30:22–25

Here we see the "recipe" for the anointing oil used throughout Israel's history to anoint three groups of people: prophets, priests, and kings. Oil in Scripture is always emblematic of the Spirit. Therefore, anointing with oil is a picture of the work of the Spirit. As the "Prophet . . . like unto me" of Deuteronomy 18:15, as our great High Priest who ever lives to make intercession for us (Hebrews 7:25), as King of kings and Lord of lords at whose name every knee will one day bow (Romans 14:11), Jesus is the Anointed One. Comprised of the sweet-smelling spices of myrrh, cinnamon, and calamus, this oil was sweet, for Jesus, the Anointed One, is nothing but sweet. He is never grouchy, discouraged, or depressed. He is never out of sorts, under the weather, or in a bad mood. He is the sweetest person you'll ever encounter day after day after day.

"Didn't He call the Pharisees blind guides, hypocrites, and whitewashed sepulchres? That's not very sweet," you may say.

Actually, it was. Knowing it would take that kind of language to break through their thick skulls, hard hearts, and closed minds, Jesus used language intended to jar them into listening. And even though He called them whitewashed tombs, hypocrites, and blind guides, some of their number sensed that He loved them, as seen in their desire to spend time with Him (Luke 11:37; John 3:1).

JULY 24

And the Lord *said unto Moses, Take unto thee sweet spices, stacte, and onycha, and galbanum; these sweet spices with pure frankincense: of each shall there be a like weight: And thou shalt make it a perfume, a confection after the art of the apothecary, tempered together, pure and holy: And thou shalt beat some of it very small, and put of it before the testimony in the tabernacle of the congregation, where I will meet with thee: it shall be unto you most holy. And as for the perfume which thou shalt make, ye shall not make to yourselves according to the composition thereof: it shall be unto thee holy for the* Lord. *Whosoever shall make like unto that, to smell thereto, shall even be cut off from his people.*

Exodus 30:34–38

The perfume Moses was commanded to make was to be sacred. So too, as the fragrance of Christ (2 Corinthians 2:15), we must be holy. The winning combination, as seen in the recipe for the perfume, is to be as gracious to other people as you possibly can be and to seek to be pure and holy in your own life. All too often, we reverse this. We want others to be holy, but we want grace to be poured out upon us. Jesus, of course, is the perfect example of how grace and holiness are to function . . .

While in Samaria—a place Jews didn't usually visit—to whom did Jesus speak? In a day when rabbis didn't even speak to their own wives in public, Jesus talked to a woman. And when she told Him she didn't have a husband, rather than condemn her for her lie, He commended her for the part of her statement that was true (John 4:17). As a result, her heart was touched and her city impacted (John 4:30). Although we might expect Jesus to address the issue of her living situation, that's not what He did. Why? Having been divorced five times, the chances of this woman getting married again were nil. Therefore, leaving the man with whom she was living would have given her no other recourse than prostitution to support herself. Jesus knew this, and no doubt also knew that in due season she would grow in her understanding of who He was and what new life in Him would entail.

Do Samaritans and pagans love to be around you? They loved to be around Jesus. How we need to be like Him: in our own lives to be holy and pure, and in the lives of others to be sweet, to show grace, and to share love.

JULY 25

And I, behold, I have given with him Aholiab, the son of Ahisamach, of the tribe of Dan: and in the hearts of all that are wise hearted I have put wisdom, that they may make all that I have commanded thee.

Exodus 31:6

God empowered, energized, and anointed carpenters, tailors, and perfumers to do this work. Bezaleel was the foreman, but Aholiab was the assistant, along with others who served by his side.

> When asked what was the hardest position in the orchestra to fill, a famous conductor said, "First chair, second violin. I can find all kinds of people who want to play first violin. But it's hard to find someone who wants to be excellent at second violin, someone who wants to play harmony."

Our human tendency is to want to be mediocre at first violin rather than to excel at second. Not so with Aholiab. He was told he would be assistant to Bezaleel. And he was successful in that position. Thus, he is an example for all of history of the way God uniquely and powerfully uses "second fiddles" for His glory.

As chronicled in a 1970s bestseller entitled *The Peter Principle*, all too often the problem in corporate America is that people are promoted to the level of incompetence. That is, a man who does well in his position is promoted to the next level. After doing well there, he is moved to level three. Succeeding there, he is moved to level four. And he keeps being promoted until, toward the top, he's over his head. He was good going up the ladder, but he went one step too far. And when the corporation downsizes, guess who gets the ax? God doesn't want that for us. He wants us to fit into the place He's custom designed for us. Am I saying we are not to take steps of faith? No, I'm saying that we must avoid the folly of taking one step too many.

If God puts you in a number one spot, He will give you the grace and ability to handle it. But if you're in a number two position, rejoice and excel at that. Whether on the job or in ministry, if you're wanting to climb one more rung, be careful. If you're a Bezaleel, great. If you're an Aholiab, wonderful. Just be content and shine in the position the Lord places you.

JULY 26

And Moses took the tabernacle, and pitched it without the camp, afar off from the camp, and called it the Tabernacle of the congregation. And it came to pass, that every one which sought the LORD went out unto the tabernacle of the congregation, which was without the camp.

Exodus 33:7

The Hebrew word *'ohel* is translated "tabernacle" in this passage. The tabernacle spoken of here is not the tabernacle Moses had been given instruction to build; that is called by the Hebrew word, *mishken*. Rather, the tabernacle spoken of here is the meeting tent for the congregation. Moses packs up the meeting tent and re-pitches it outside the camp. Having heard the Lord declare that He would not be in the midst of the camp, it's as if Moses were saying, "If God's not there, I don't want to be there either."

You and I desperately need times of pitching our tents outside the camp of busyness in order to be made aware of God's presence once again. And at times, this takes some effort . . .

A number of years ago, when my three kids were little, I took them camping at Indian Mary campground. As a single dad in those days, I was delighted that my college roommate and his family joined us. But about five hours after we pitched our tents, a massive storm arose. Although we weathered it for a couple of days, staying in the tents and hanging out under whatever coverings we could find, finally it got so wet we packed up everything and all headed home. On my way back to Jacksonville, the kids and I stopped at McDonald's. As they played on the Playland equipment, the sun popped through. At that moment I realized that, although we'd been camping for a couple of days, I missed my objective totally— which was to focus on my kids. We adults were playing games and enjoying fellowship, but I didn't accomplish what I had initially set out to do. So I loaded the kids back in the car, we went back to Indian Mary, re-pitched the tent, hung out all the wet stuff, and shared some of the best four days we have ever spent together.

The same is true in your walk with the Lord. Sometimes you'll have devotions or Bible study, only to realize at the end that a storm blew through, that you were distracted by this, caught up in that, and lost focus. But if you don't give up, if you re-pitch your tent, if you change location and say, "Lord, I really need to be in Your presence," God will meet you there.

JULY 27

And Moses said unto the Lord, See, thou sayest unto me, Bring up this people: and thou hast not let me know whom thou wilt send with me. Yet thou hast said, I know thee by name, and thou hast also found grace in my sight. Now therefore, I pray thee, if I have found grace in thy sight, shew me now thy way, that I may know thee, that I may find grace in thy sight: and consider that this nation is thy people. And he said, My presence shall go with thee, and I will give thee rest.

Exodus 33:12–14

Was it because of the holiness, devotion, or piety of the people that God promised His presence would go with them and give them rest? Obviously not, for just one chapter earlier, they were caught up in idolatry and immorality as they danced around the golden calf. No, God declared His presence would go with them and give them rest, not because they were worthy but because they had a mediator named Moses who stood between their sin and God's holiness. Sin requires judgment, but in Moses, God found a way to bless His people rather than to judge them.

> For there is one God, and one mediator between God and men, the man Christ Jesus; Who gave himself a ransom for all, to be testified in due time.
>
> 1 Timothy 2:5–6

Like the children of Israel, we drop the ball; we fall short; we mess up constantly. But also like them, we experience the presence of God because we too have a Mediator, a greater than Moses—Jesus Christ.

As a result we, like the children of Israel, are given direction by a God who will go "in the way before you, to search you out a place to pitch your tents" (Deuteronomy 1:33).

> As the people were preparing to enter the Promised Land, they were to follow the ark of the covenant, and yet there was to be two thousand cubits—over half a mile—between them and the ark. In commanding this, it's as if God were saying, "Give Me space. I'm going ahead of you to prepare the place for you and to prepare you for the place to which I'm leading you" (see Joshua 3:3–4).

The Lord has promised direction for us. Our part is to give Him space to work.

JULY 28

And he said, I will make all my goodness pass before thee, and I will proclaim the name of the LORD before thee; and will be gracious to whom I will be gracious, and will shew mercy on whom I will shew mercy.

Exodus 33:19

"If you ask anything in My name, I will do it," Jesus said (see John 14:14). For many years, I thought this meant I was to simply add the phrase "In Jesus' name" to the end of my prayers, sort of like, "over and out." But when I understood that praying in Jesus' name means to pray according to His nature, I found I couldn't pray a lot of prayers I had been praying, prayers like, "Lord, deal with that guy who just cut me off on the highway," prayers like, "I want this to happen *now*."

"Am I unmerciful, impatient, or short-fused?" the Lord asked me. "Or am I longsuffering, merciful, and slow to anger? I only work in ways that reflect who *I* am."

It was because Moses knew the name, the nature, and the character of God that he was able to ask for His presence, His pardon, and His eternal promise. Meditate on God's nature as seen in the person of Jesus. Get a strong, firm grip on this, understand, and your prayers will become those God can answer.

JULY 29

And it came to pass, when Moses came down from mount Sinai with the two tables of testimony in Moses' hand, when he came down from the mount, that Moses wist not that the skin of his face shone while he talked with him.

Exodus 34:29

Going without food for forty days does not usually help one's appearance, especially if he is eighty years old. But this was not true in this case, where, after spending forty days in the presence of the Lord on Mount Sinai, Moses' face actually glowed.

Reflecting the glory he had experienced on the mountain, Moses didn't initially realize his face was glowing. That's always the way it is. When we spend time in the presence of the Lord, when we are at His feet, when we take time to pray, when we worship Him and spend time in the Word, our gloom is replaced by a glow. "I don't feel like I glow," you say, but Moses didn't know he was glowing either.

When the Holy Spirit fell on the one hundred twenty disciples in the upper room, a flame burned above each of their heads (Acts 2:3). This means that if you were one of the one hundred twenty, you would look around and see one hundred nineteen other people ignited, on fire, and illuminated with the power of the Spirit. But you would not see the flame on top of your own head. And such is our tendency, to think everyone but us is aflame. Actually, it's the goodness and grace of God that doesn't allow us to see our own flame . . .

"Come and see the zeal I have for the Lord," boasted Israel's King Jehu. In reality, however, Jehu was a hypocrite—as evidenced by his statement two verses later, "Ahab served Baal a little; but Jehu shall serve him much" (see 2 Kings 10:16, 18).

Unlike Jehu, Moses was a man of integrity, of humility. And it was a good thing there was a glow on his face, for he held the law of the Lord in his hands. The children of Israel needed to hear the commands, the exhortations, and the instructions of the Lord. But you know how kids are. They're not always receptive to commandments, instructions, or exhortations. We all tend to be rebellious by nature. Yet when Moses came down from the mountain and talked to the children of Israel, what could they say? After all, his face was glowing.

Mom and Dad, if your kids aren't being very receptive to your instructions, it might be because there's a glare instead of a glow on your face. Moses glowed, and it made the Word he shared acceptable, the things he said palatable.

Why did Moses glow? Having been in the presence of the Lord, he was simply reflecting the glory inherent in the Lord. In other words, just by hanging out with the Lord, Moses' face glowed. So too, spending time in the presence of the Lord will impact you in a very real and special way even today. But here's the problem: Moses' glow began to diminish, decrease, and decline. It wasn't until he spent time with the Lord that he began to glow once again.

And that's what needs to happen in our lives. We need to realize that we need to be renewed and recharged constantly. Oh, we can do well for a while, but then our glow turns to a glower or a glare. And we find ourselves dull. But when we return to the presence of the Lord, we get recharged and refueled constantly and consistently through prayer, through worship, and through His Word.

JULY 30

And Moses called Bezaleel and Aholiab, and every wise hearted man, in whose heart the LORD had put wisdom, even every one whose heart stirred him up to come unto the work to do it.

Exodus 36:2

Bezaleel and Aholiab were given ability to do the work that needed to be done practically. But we also read that they came. If you want your life to be impacting, the key is to have both ability and availability. There are people who have great abilities, but they're never available. When there is work to do, when opportunities open, or when needs are presented, they're just not around. Bezaleel and Aholiab go down in history as models, their names recorded for eternity, as men who used the practical gifts God had given them for His glory. How the church of Jesus Christ needs men who will say, "I can't preach or sing, but I can fix an engine," or "I can't evangelize, but I can pour cement." We need you! Make yourself available, and your name will be added to the roster of Bezaleel and Aholiab.

JULY 31

And he reared up the court round about the tabernacle and the altar, and set up the hanging of the court gate. So Moses finished the work.

Exodus 40:33

Moses was able to finish the work of the tabernacle because he knew precisely how to build it. How did he know? As he spent forty days on Mount Sinai in fasting and prayer, God laid out a perfect pattern for him to follow.

"I wish God would give me a blueprint," we say. "If He would give me a plan, I would follow it." But do we take forty days to seek Him for it? How about four days, or even four hours? Paul spent three years in the deserts of Arabia getting the divine pattern for his life. Jesus spent thirty years tuned into the Father before He ministered publicly for three years. So too, we need times where we seek God fervently and expectantly.

For an example of how this happens, turn to the book of Habakkuk . . .

Habakkuk's name means "wrestler"—an appropriate name for this one who wrestled with why God wasn't doing more to combat the evil in the world around him. And in his life, we see three characteristics of those who seriously seek specific vision from God.

> I will stand upon my watch, and set me upon the tower, and will watch to see what he will say unto me, and what I shall answer when I am reproved. And the LORD answered me, and said, Write the vision, and make it plain upon tables, that he may run that readeth it.
>
> Habakkuk 2:1–2

The first characteristic is determination. Habakkuk didn't say, "I should stand upon my watch," or "I think I'll stand upon my watch." He said, "I *will* stand upon my watch."

"You will find Me when you search for Me with all your heart," God declared (see Jeremiah 29:13). As with Habakkuk, there must come a point in our lives when we are *determined* to seek the Lord if we truly expect to hear from Him.

Second, we see the importance of isolation. I have found that when I'm in desperate need of vision and direction, I must get away from the telephone, radio, television, away from the clamor and clutter of the world. Wherever your "high tower" might be, find a place where you won't be distracted by the needs that incessantly pull at you if you want to hear what it is God would have you do.

Finally, we see Habakkuk's expectation. He didn't say, "I'll watch to see *if* God will speak to me," but, "I'll watch to see what God *will* say to me."

"He that cometh to God must believe that he is, and that he is a rewarder of them that diligently seek him," declares the writer of the book of Hebrews (11:6). James echoes this when he writes,

> If any of you lack wisdom, let him ask of God, that giveth to all men liberally, and upbraideth not; and it shall be given him. But let him ask in faith, nothing wavering. For he that wavereth is like a wave of the sea driven with the wind and tossed. For let not that man think that he shall receive any thing of the Lord.
>
> James 1:5–7

If I approach God but don't expect to receive from Him, I won't.

Determination, isolation, and expectation—as these three components become part of my life, I'll find direction. And if I've dropped the ball, missed opportunities, or failed miserably? I simply go to the cross, where the One who finished the work died to cleanse me completely, and I begin again.

Oh, that we might be a people who find freedom in the finished work of the cross, that we might finish the work God has called us to do, that we might hear Him say, "Well *done*, good and faithful servant."

AUGUST 1

If his offering be a burnt sacrifice of the herd, let him offer
a male without blemish: he shall offer it of his own volun-
tary will at the door of the tabernacle of the congregation
before the LORD. And he shall put his hand upon the head of
the burnt offering; and it shall be accepted for him to make
atonement for him.

Leviticus 1:3–4

In the text before us, we see a man coming to the courtyard of the tabernacle. He stands before the priest and next to him is his bull or lamb, an
innocent, docile, harmless animal. The man would then lay his hand—the
Hebrew language implies that he would press it—upon the animal's head.
Then he would watch the priest slit the animal's throat, and watch as the
animal slumped to the ground. If the man had any kind of compassion, he
would be moved as he realized that, in a very real sense, he was transferring
his sin to the animal, and that the animal was literally dying in his place.

> Short of men in his campaign through Europe, Napoleon began
> to draft heavily in France. However, when approached, one man
> answered, "I can't go. My father is very ill and my mother cannot
> manage the farm alone." So he was allowed to pay someone else to
> go in his place—a common practice of the time. The first day the
> substitute reported for duty, he was killed in battle and subsequently
> buried. A few months later, there was a knock on the door of the
> man who had hired the substitute. Once again, it was a recruiting
> officer who said, "Your number is up."
>
> "You can't take me," said the young man. "I'm already dead and
> buried."
>
> Baffled, the officer hauled him off to a military tribunal. The tri-
> bunal heard the case and sent it all the way to Napoleon himself,
> who, when he heard about the situation, agreed with the would-be
> soldier and said, "You're right. You're already dead. Go home."

The man was free because someone died in his place. So too, I am free because the Lamb of God was slain in my place. It is my sin He bore, the sin of being short with my kids today, the sin of being annoyed with the driver in front of me yesterday, the sin of saying things which shouldn't be said, the sin of thinking things that shouldn't be thought, the sin of doing things which shouldn't be done. My sin was transferred to Jesus, and He died in my place.

Suppose the man came with his bull to the tabernacle, but when the priest told him to put his hand upon the bull, the man said, "Let me teach you the significance of this particular sacrifice."

"I care not how knowledgeable you are theologically or how certain you are doctrinally," the priest would answer. "Put your hand on the bull and press in, for if you don't become involved, the sacrifice will be to no avail."

Many Christians have no shortage of understanding or theological insight about the substitutionary work of Jesus Christ. They have the teaching down, but there's no touching. That is why there will be those who say, "Lord, my theology is impeccable. I can explain to You the whole plan of salvation," only to hear Him say, "Depart from Me. I never knew you. Your teaching was correct, but your touching was non-existent. You were not touching Me, nor were you touched by Me. Your heart was calloused and cold. When the gospel was preached, you slumbered. When the cross was considered, your mind wandered. No longer were you touched by the sacrifice. No longer did you press in."

David was an adulterer, a murderer, and a liar, but after spending one year refusing to acknowledge his sin, David fell down in humility and brokenness. David's was a heart of tenderness, a heart that laid its hand on the sacrifice. No wonder he could say, "Happy is the man whose transgression is forgiven, whose sin is covered. Happy is the man to whom the Lord does not impute iniquity" (see Psalm 32).

AUGUST 2

And he shall kill the bullock before the LORD: and the priests, Aaron's sons, shall bring the blood, and sprinkle the blood round about upon the altar that is by the door of the tabernacle of the congregation. And he shall flay the burnt offering, and cut it into his pieces. And the sons of Aaron the priest shall put fire upon the altar, and lay the wood in order upon the fire: And the priests, Aaron's sons, shall lay the parts, the head, and the fat, in order upon the wood that is on the fire which is upon the altar.

Leviticus 1:5–8

In addition to describing the severity of sin and the grace of God, the book of Leviticus portrays the sacrifice of Christ. Every offering and sacrifice gives us understanding of the unspeakable price the Lamb of God paid, that we might be forgiven, consecrated, and separated.

Burnt offerings were given to consecrate or dedicate one's self. It was a voluntary offering, and had to be so, for true dedication can only be made from a heart filled with desire. True consecration comes not from responsibility, but from response. So too, just as the worshiper voluntarily offered the burnt offering, Jesus laid down His life willingly. When He prayed "If it be possible, let this cup pass from Me," He used a phrase translated into Greek as a first-class conditional clause. This means it was indeed possible that He could bypass the cup of suffering and death. "*Nevertheless,*" He prayed, "not my will, but thine, be done" (Luke 22:42, italics added). Had Jesus demanded to be released from suffering, He would not have had to go to Calvary—but we would be doomed and damned eternally.

Wood was laid on the fire of the altar in preparation for the sacrifice, just as a wooden cross was prepared for Jesus to absorb the fire of God's righteous wrath on our behalf.

The head speaks of the mind. And Jesus' mind is perfect. "Should we pay taxes to Rome?" His enemies asked in a futile attempt to entangle Him in political controversy. A "yes" answer would incense the Jews who abhorred the Roman government. A "no" answer would provide the Romans with grounds to arrest Him for anarchy.

"Whose image is on the coin?" Jesus asked in response. "Give to Caesar that which belongs to Caesar, and to God that which belongs to God." In other words, "The coin bears Caesar's image. Therefore, give the coin to Caesar. But man bears God's image. Therefore, give your life to God" (see Matthew 22:21).

The burnt offering speaks of giving *all* that we are to the Lord. Do this, precious people, and I guarantee you will never, ever be disappointed, because man simply cannot out-give God.

AUGUST 3

And if thy oblation be a meat offering baken in the frying-pan, it shall be made of fine flour with oil. And thou shalt bring the meat offering that is made of these things unto the Lord: and when it is presented unto the priest, he shall bring it unto the altar. And the priest shall take from the meat offering a memorial thereof, and shall burn it upon the altar: it is an offering made by fire, of a sweet savour unto the Lord. And that which is left of the meat offering shall be Aaron's and his sons': it is a thing most holy of the offerings of the Lord made by fire.

Leviticus 2:7–10

As was the case with the burnt offering, the price of the meat offering varied according to possession. If a person had an oven, his meat was to be baked. If he had a covered pan, it was to be baked in the pan. If all he had was a frying pan, it was to be fried. Again, this tells us we are accountable to God according to how He has blessed us. God will use whatever you have, be it an oven, a covered dish, or a simple frying pan.

When Jesus taught the parable of the talents, the indictment was not given to the man with ten talents or even five, but to the man who buried his single talent (Matthew 25:28–29). If you only have one talent, if you possess nothing more than a frying pan, offer that one talent as a meat offering to God, and watch Him be glorified through it.

AUGUST 4

And the priest shall burn them upon the altar: it is the food of the offering made by fire for a sweet savour: all the fat is the LORD's. It shall be a perpetual statute for your generations throughout all your dwellings, that ye eat neither fat nor blood.

Leviticus 3:16–17

In ancient cultures, the fat was considered to be the best part of the animal. Therefore, think of all the people throughout the centuries who read this and thought that the Lord was taking the best part for Himself, when, in reality, He was keeping men from the one part of the animal that causes clogged arteries and heart attacks.

"Why must we have only one partner sexually?" we say.

"I'm saving you from heartbreak, disease, and misery," God answers.

"Why must I give the tithe to You?" we question.

"Because I'm protecting you from the disease of greediness," God answers.

"Why do You get the fat?" we ask.

"So you won't be," God says. "As time goes on, and ultimately when you get to heaven, you'll see everything I did was for your good."

Precious people, everything God does is based on love, for He is love. We might not understand this right now, but as time goes on, we'll see a reason for everything He did in our lives, and the reason that He kept the fat for Himself.

AUGUST 5

And the fire upon the altar shall be burning in it; it shall not be put out.

Leviticus 6:12

The fire on the altar was never to go out. Has the Lord's fire that once blazed in your heart and radiated from your life been somewhat quenched? If so, go back to God and offer Him your body as a burnt offering morning and evening. Dedicate yourself anew to Him and once again He will ignite your soul. Go for it in your witness, in your worship, and in your work for Him. And light up the darkness once again.

AUGUST 6

This is the law of the burnt offering, of the meat offering, and of the sin offering, and of the trespass offering, and of the consecrations, and of the sacrifice of the peace offerings; Which the LORD commanded Moses in mount Sinai, in the day that he commanded the children of Israel to offer their oblations unto the LORD, in the wilderness of Sinai.

Leviticus 7:37–38

In this review of the five sacrifices, notice the portrayal of the life of Christ from His baptism to His crucifixion . . .

In the burnt offering, we see Christ's baptism, for both speak of total dedication. In the meat offering, we see Jesus being tempted, for both show an absence of leaven, an absence of sin. In the peace offering, we see Jesus embarking on public ministry, for both proclaim the good tidings of the gospel. At the cross, we see the sin and trespass offerings, as Jesus died not only for our sin nature, but also for our specific acts of sin.

I find it interesting, however, that in the life of the believer, the sacrifices are illustrated in reverse order . . .

A person gets saved when he realizes he has trespassed. Then he discovers he sins because he's a sinner, because he has a sin nature. He confesses his sin, asks the Lord into his life, and communes with God through the peace offering, at the Lord's Table. Then he says, "Refine me, Lord. Take out the lumps and the leaven in my life." And finally, he says, "Don't only sift me, but consume me, Lord. I'm laying my life down as a burnt offering. I want to be consumed by You."

Where are you in this process? The further you choose to go, the happier you'll be. I can guarantee this because Jesus told us that it's when we lose our lives that we will truly find them (Matthew 10:39).

AUGUST 7

And the Lord *spake unto Moses, saying, Take Aaron and his sons with him, and the garments, and the anointing oil, and a bullock for the sin offering, and two rams, and a basket of unleavened bread; and gather thou all the congregation together unto the door of the tabernacle of the congregation. And Moses did as the* Lord *commanded him; and the assembly was gathered together unto the door of the tabernacle of the congregation.*

Leviticus 8:1–4

There is about to be a presentation of the priests. But before there can be presentation, there must first be preparation. That's always the way it is . . .

God prepared Moses for eighty years—forty years as a prince in the courts of Pharaoh, and forty years as a shepherd on the backside of the desert—before calling him to lead His people away from Pharaoh and to shepherd them across the wilderness.

God prepared Paul for three years in the desert of Arabia before calling him to take the gospel to the Gentiles.

God prepared Jesus for thirty years by having Him grow up under and submit to His earthly father and mother. As a result, He grew in favor with both God and man (Luke 2:52).

To you who, like me, want to be used by God, I would say, as did Zechariah, "Don't despise the day of small things" (see 4:10). You may be on the backside of the desert, going through boring times or difficult situations, but know this: it's all part of God's preparation.

AUGUST 8

And Moses said unto the congregation, This is the thing which the LORD commanded to be done. And Moses brought Aaron and his sons, and washed them with water.

Leviticus 8:5–6

How does the Lord prepare us for service? First, we must be washed with water. Ephesians 5:26 identifies water as the Word of God. "Now ye are clean through the word which I have spoken unto you," Jesus declared (John 15:3). "Thy word have I hid in mine heart, that I might not sin against thee," David proclaimed (Psalm 119:11). The washing of the water of the Word cleanses our souls and purifies our spirits. That's why a person just can't get too much Bible study. Even if you don't understand it all completely, and even if you don't think it's making an impact, it is.

"When the Spirit comes, He shall bring to your remembrance all things I have spoken to you," Jesus promised (see John 14:26). The work of the Holy Spirit is to remind us of the Word. He will not, however, be able to bring to our remembrance what we have not put in our memory. That's why we must read Leviticus, Ezekiel, and Haggai.

"But I don't get those books," you might protest. "They're boring."

Read them anyway because you're putting the Word in your soul, and in due season, at the right time, the Holy Spirit will put the pieces together in such a way that it will blow your mind.

AUGUST 9

And Moses brought Aaron's sons, and put coats upon them, and girded them with girdles, and put bonnets upon them; as the LORD commanded Moses.

Leviticus 8:13

As high priest, Aaron is a picture of our great High Priest, Jesus Christ. Aaron's sons, however, are a picture of you and me—a royal priesthood (1 Peter 2:9). While Aaron wore pomegranates and bells, gems and a gold plate, his sons were attired much more simply, only wearing three items.

The coat, or linen garment, speaks of salvation.

Which robe was placed on the Prodigal Son upon his return?

The best robe.

Whose robe was the best?

The father's.

So too, when you accepted Jesus Christ, you were robed with the Father's best robe, for He robed you with His Son (Isaiah 61:10).

The girdle, or belt, worn around the waist allowed the robes to be tucked in, freeing the legs for service. "Stand therefore, having your loins girt about with truth," Paul would later write to the church at Ephesus (Ephesians 6:14).

Third, we see the bonnets, or turbans, which speak of submission (1 Corinthians 11). In our priestly service, we're to be robed in Christ's righteousness. We're to be doing the work of service. And we're to be submitted to those who are over us. There is no room in the body of Christ for lone rangers or independent agents. There is to be connection and submission, accountability and humility. You'll never be in authority unless you are under authority. And while it is easy for me to submit to those with whom I agree, it is when I submit to a decision that I don't necessarily agree with that a true spirit of submission and humility is worked within me.

AUGUST 10

And he brought Aaron's sons, and Moses put of the blood upon the tip of their right ear, and upon the thumbs of their right hands, and upon the great toes of their right feet: and Moses sprinkled the blood upon the altar round about.

Leviticus 8:24

After being washed in water, robed in righteousness, and anointed with oil, the fourth step of preparation for Aaron and his sons was to be symbolically covered with blood. It was literally applied to the ear, the thumb, and the big toe. Because the things we hear, the things we do, and the places we go can pollute us, we need the blood applied to us, the blood to cleanse us, and the blood to protect us from future sin.

As time went on, these priests applied the blood not only when they entered the tabernacle, but when they exited it as well—a principle I have found to be a real key in ministry. Before I teach or share, or counsel or serve, I need to say, "Lord, I know I am a sinner. I know I am frail. I plead the blood to cleanse me in order that Your Spirit might flow through me." And when I finish teaching, sharing, counseling, or serving, I need to plead the blood as well because when I'm done ministering, one of two things invariably happens: either I am totally discouraged about how badly I did, or I'm proud of how well I did; and that's even more dangerous, for pride goes before destruction (Proverbs 16:18).

Pleading the blood takes care of both of these tendencies as we realize that, because we are sinners through and through, it's only by God's grace that we are allowed to minister at all.

AUGUST 11

Therefore shall ye abide at the door of the tabernacle of the congregation day and night seven days, and keep the charge of the LORD, that ye die not.

Leviticus 8:35

The last step of preparation for the priesthood was isolation. With seven being the number of completion, Aaron and his sons were to remain in the tabernacle for seven days.

Ministry is like the measles. You can't give it unless you get it. You can't give blessing unless you are blessed. And you won't be blessed until you're locked in, tucked away, and set aside. For how long? Until God's preparatory work in you is complete.

Aaron and his sons were no doubt eager to begin, but they had to wait so that they wouldn't die. Many ministries die because people don't know the meaning of a personal devotional life, of spending chunks of time locked away in the presence of God.

AUGUST 12

And they brought that which Moses commanded before the tabernacle of the congregation: and all the congregation drew near and stood before the LORD. And Moses said, This is the thing which the LORD commanded that ye should do.

Leviticus 9:5–6

In Leviticus 9:7–22, we see the procedure that was to be followed by the priests in offering a sacrifice. This passage is studied by Jewish scholars at great length because it's the only time the procedure of a sacrifice is seen. Why does the Lord go into such detail? Why does He take almost an entire chapter to describe this procedure? Because He cares about the details of how He is to be worshiped, just as He cares about the details of how we are to live. Our God is a God of incredible order. Not only does the book of Leviticus attest to this, but His fingerprint can be seen on even the most minute aspect of nature, His concern over each sparrow, His awareness of each hair (Matthew 10:29–30).

The story is told of a lady who approached G. Campbell Morgan with a particular question.

"Why don't you ask the Lord about that?" he asked.

"Oh, it's too small a detail for the Lord," she replied.

"Tell me, madam," he countered, "what in your life is big to the Lord?"

Pray about *everything*, dear saint. Because nothing is big to God, nothing is too small for Him.

AUGUST 13

And Moses and Aaron went into the tabernacle of the congregation, and came out, and blessed the people: and the glory of the LORD appeared unto all the people. And there came a fire out from before the LORD, and consumed upon the altar the burnt offering and the fat: which when all the people saw, they shouted, and fell on their faces.

Leviticus 9:23–24

After a time of consecration and presentation, after a time of going in before the Lord and coming out to bless the people, suddenly fire from heaven came down and consumed the offerings upon the altar. The glory of God was seen and people shouted—an understandable reaction, for the Hebrew word for worship implies a shout of joy.

We see the highest joy in a shout and the deepest reverence in a falling on one's face. So awed and amazed were they by the presence of God, the people's first reaction was to shout, but it was followed by a very quiet reverence before the Lord.

"The LORD is in his holy temple," Habakkuk declared. "Let all the earth keep silence before him" (Habakkuk 2:20). Sometimes the truest sign of an intense move of the Lord is not necessarily a shout, a clap, or even a word, but an awesome, quiet reverence.

AUGUST 14

And Nadab and Abihu, the sons of Aaron, took either of them his censer, and put fire therein, and put incense thereon, and offered strange fire before the LORD, which he commanded them not.

Leviticus 10:1

"Come unto me," Jesus said, "all ye that labor and are heavy laden, and I will give you rest. Take my yoke upon you, and learn of me; . . . and ye shall find rest unto your souls" (Matthew 11:28–29). Why, then, are so many "mature" Christians burned out by their ministry to Him and their service for Him?

I believe Aaron's sons, Nadab and Abihu, give us the answer. Having been eyewitnesses to the glory of God filling the tabernacle, and having seen the flames, having smelled the smoke of the fire from heaven mystically and miraculously igniting the sacrifice upon the altar, it is understandable why Nadab and Abihu would be eager to join their famous father in ministry, to play a pivotal part in the "holy happening" unfolding before their eyes. After all, they had gone through the process of preparation and surely now was the time to begin, their time to shine. So they lit their censers and set out to take part in the celebration.

The problem, however, was that Nadab and Abihu lit their censers with strange fire. Strange fire is from any source other than the altar which burned continually and which speaks of Calvary.

For the love of Christ constraineth us; because we thus judge, that if one died for all, then were all dead: And that he died for all, that they which live should not henceforth live unto themselves, but unto him which died for them, and rose again.

2 Corinthians 5:14–15

What Christ did on the altar of Calvary was that which motivated Paul day after day, year after year—for the love of Christ is a fire that never burns out.

Some people involve themselves in ministry simply because they want to be part of the action. But when the action shifts somewhere else, they shift along with it, leaving ministry behind. Others have a need to be used, so they serve the Lord to fulfill their own need. But when they're needed somewhere else, ministry takes a back seat. Still others serve the Lord out of concern for the lost. But when the lost don't respond as quickly as hoped, they eventually give up ministering altogether.

Ministry for ministry's sake, ministry for fulfillment's sake, or ministry for others' sake is all strange fire that will eventually burn people out.

The only fire that will never burn one out is the fire from the altar of Calvary. Those who, like Paul, are constrained, motivated, and compelled by the love Christ demonstrated on Calvary will still be serving Him with passion, with effectiveness, and with intensity when they draw their last breath this side of eternity.

How can one keep from the Nadab and Abihu mentality? The simplest way is to go to the altar—the Lord's Table—over and over again and remember what Christ Jesus did for us. When we bow our knee and commune with the Lord, when we handle His broken body and drink of His shed blood, all the dials are set back to zero as we remember the price He paid so willingly and lovingly.

AUGUST 15

And Moses called Mishael and Elzaphan, the sons of Uzziel the uncle of Aaron, and said unto them, Come near, carry your brethren from before the sanctuary out of the camp. So they went near, and carried them in their coats out of the camp; as Moses had said. And Moses said unto Aaron, and unto Eleazar and unto Ithamar, his sons, Uncover not your heads, neither rend your clothes; lest ye die, and lest wrath come upon all the people: but let your brethren, the whole house of Israel, bewail the burning which the LORD hath kindled. And ye shall not go out from the door of the tabernacle of the congregation, lest ye die: for the anointing oil of the LORD is upon you. And they did according to the word of Moses.

Leviticus 10:4–7

Neither father nor brother were to mourn the deaths of Nadab and Abihu because the implication would be that God was unfair.

Ezekiel was another who was told not to mourn when, as an illustration to the people, God took his wife (Ezekiel 24). "Righteous and true are thy judgments, O Lord," say the multitudes in heaven (see Revelation 19:2), seeing the full picture, understanding that God's ways are absolutely perfect and without fail.

This side of eternity, our vision is so very limited. Yet even that which appears to be a tragedy to us is part of a bigger plan. After all, do you think Ezekiel and his wife are in heaven right now feeling cheated that her life on earth was cut short, or do you think they're blown away by the goodness of God in allowing her to partake of the unspeakable splendor of heaven early? When you go through a hard time, a setback, or a tragedy, it is oh, so easy to suck sympathy from people, but you always do so at the expense of God's reputation.

AUGUST 16

Whatsoever parteth the hoof, and is clovenfooted, and cheweth the cud, among the beasts, that shall ye eat.

Leviticus 11:3

The Jews were allowed to eat those animals that had a divided hoof and chewed their cud. In other words, cleanliness was determined by how an animal walked and how it ate.

The question for us is obvious. Is there a "dividedness" in our walk? Are we separated from the world, or do we walk like everyone around us? We are new creatures in Christ (2 Corinthians 5:17). Is there a difference in our walk? There should to be.

Second, do we chew the spiritual "cud"? Just as a cow constantly chews and re-chews its food, we are to chew and re-chew the Word, who think it through, pray it in, extract from it every nutrient to feed our inner man. No wonder the Hebrew word for chewing the cud is essentially the same word translated "meditation."

> This book of the law shall not depart out of thy mouth; but thou shalt meditate therein day and night, that thou mayest observe to do according to all that is written therein: for then thou shalt make thy way prosperous, and then thou shalt have good success.
>
> Joshua 1:8

We get to meditate on the Word. We get to look in the book. We get to think it through once more. And as we do, we'll have good success; we'll be healthy; we'll be clean.

AUGUST 17

And these are they which ye shall have in abomination among the fowls; they shall not be eaten, they are an abomination: the eagle, and the ossifrage, and the ospray, and the vulture, and the kite after his kind; every raven after his kind.

Leviticus 11:13–15

Ravens are an unclean bird and a symbol of evil in the Bible. Why, then, did God use them to miraculously deliver food to Elijah in the wilderness (1 Kings 17:6)? I suggest it was to show us that He can use anyone or anything to minister to us. Sometimes we have a tendency to think we can't be instructed by him, or corrected by her because they're "unclean birds." In reality, however, we can learn from anyone God sends our way, even if he or she might appear to be "unclean."

"I'm not going to listen to my parents because they're not as spiritual as I am," some might say. Big mistake. God can use all sorts of interesting creatures and situations to bring food to us, to minister to us, to admonish, nourish, and correct us. Therefore, wise is the one who says, "Lord, give me eyes to see and ears to hear whatever You want to tell me through whatever messenger You choose."

AUGUST 18

And if any part of their carcase fall upon any sowing seed which is to be sown, it shall be clean. But if any water be put upon the seed, and any part of their carcase fall thereon, it shall be unclean unto you.

Leviticus 11:37–38

If an animal fell into a bag of seed, providing the seed was still in its shell, the seed could still be used. But if the shell of the seed was no longer there because water had softened it, that seed was to be thrown out, as the seed itself would have been polluted.

The seed is a picture of the Word (1 Peter 1:23). Therefore, if the seed is not encased by the armor of faith, rats of unbelief will gnaw at it, causing us to question if it truly is infallible, immutable, and applicable. In other words, the Word can lose its potency and power in people who read only to find fault. How much better to read the Word in faith and allow it to find and change the faults within us.

AUGUST 19

But if she bear a maid child, then she shall be unclean two weeks, as in her separation: and she shall continue in the blood of her purifying threescore and six days.

Leviticus 12:5

If she gave birth to a boy, a mother was ceremonially unclean for a total of forty-one days. If she gave birth to a girl, she was ceremonially unclean for a total of eighty days. Why was she unclean twice as long if she gave birth to a girl? Because through circumcision, the sin of the baby boy was addressed, but the sin of a baby girl could not be addressed in that way, leaving the mother alone to deal with the issue of sin.

Why would either mother or baby have to deal with sin? Why would the birth of either son or daughter be considered unclean? When we have babies, people send flowers, buy balloons, and celebrate. What, then, is the meaning of this chapter? Is the birth process something that is unclean? No, for it was God Himself who said, "Be fruitful, and multiply" (Genesis 1:28).

In this passage, God is illustrating something that is difficult for today's world to comprehend or embrace. He is declaring that when a baby is born—as glorious and wonderful an event as that is—it causes uncleanness because another sinner is added to the world.

In Psalm 51, under inspiration of the Spirit, David declares, "In sin did my mother conceive me" (verse 5). At the moment of conception—not in the act of procreation, but at the moment of conception—a sin nature begins. This is the doctrine of the depravity of man—politically incorrect, but true nonetheless. Contrary to current psychological thought, babies don't arrive with a "clean slate." Man is not a sinner because he sins. He sins because he is a sinner. And when I understand this, the implications and applications are profound.

First, an understanding of the depravity of man affects me parentally—how I view my kids and the way I raise my family. To understand that a baby comes into the world as a sinner and not as an innocent little person who is bruised by culture or infected by civilization makes me realize that as great as he is and as much joy as she brings, they're sinners just like me.

Second, an understanding of the depravity of man affects me politically. Communism made great strides as Karl Marx insisted there should be a comradeship, a brotherhood between all men because men are basically, intrinsically good. The Bible says men are basically, intrinsically bad. That is why Communism ultimately collapsed. Capitalism survived because it is actually based on the depravity of man—that man is greedy and will only work to the degree that he is personally rewarded.

Third, an understanding of the depravity of man affects how I see myself personally. In Romans 7, Paul declared, "In my flesh dwells no good thing." Therefore, I don't have to be shocked or down on myself when I am aware of sin within me. Instead, I can say, "Lord, have mercy on me. Lord, take it from me. Lord, deal with me because I know the sin deep within me will destroy me and my family."

> But God commendeth his love toward us, in that, while we were yet sinners, Christ died for us.
>
> Romans 5:8

An understanding of my own depravity actually gives me a great deal of security because I realize who I am and how much God loves me.

AUGUST 20

And if a leprosy break out abroad in the skin, and the leprosy cover all the skin of him that hath the plague from his head even to his foot, wheresoever the priest looketh; Then the priest shall consider: and, behold, if the leprosy have covered all his flesh, he shall pronounce him clean that hath the plague: it is all turned white: he is clean.

Leviticus 13:12–13

Because leprosy that covered a person from head to foot was not active, such a one was pronounced clean. So too, when I realize I am a sinner from head to toe, from top to bottom—that I can't cover my sin, defend myself, explain away my behavior, or justify my actions—then I am on my way to being pronounced clean.

Confession is a real key to salvation . . .

"I was conceived in sin," David said (see Psalm 51:5).

"Woe is me!" Isaiah cried, "for I am undone" (Isaiah 6:5).

"I have sinned," the Prodigal confessed (Luke 15:18).

Confession alone, however, does not guarantee salvation . . .

"I have sinned against the LORD," Pharaoh declared (Exodus 10:16).

"I have sinned," Saul admitted (1 Samuel 15:24).

"I have betrayed innocent blood," Judas confessed (Matthew 27:4).

None of these confessions resulted in salvation. You see, while confession is indeed a key to salvation, the motive for confession is important as well. The second group of men were confessing because they knew they had been caught; the first group confessed because godly sorrow had worked in them a true heart of repentance (2 Corinthians 7:10).

AUGUST 21

As for the living bird, he shall take it, and the cedar wood, and the scarlet, and the hyssop, and shall dip them and the living bird in the blood of the bird that was killed over the running water: and he shall sprinkle upon him that is to be cleansed from the leprosy seven times, and shall pronounce him clean, and shall let the living bird loose into the open field.

Leviticus 14:6–7

When a leper was cured of leprosy, two birds were to be used in the cleansing ceremony. One bird was to be killed in an earthen vessel. The remaining bird would be dipped in the blood of the first. Why? One bird would depict the death of our Savior, our Redeemer. But the story doesn't end there. He ascended to heaven. He rose again. So a second bird was needed to complete the illustration. After being dipped in the blood of the first bird, the second bird was allowed to fly away free. After Jesus died on the cross, the book of Hebrews tells us He took His blood into heaven and sprinkled it in the sanctuary of heaven (9:12–14). Thus, the analogy is perfect.

The resurrection is the hinge on which the door of our faith swings, for if there was no resurrection, Paul was right: we are of all men most miserable (1 Corinthians 15:19).

The resurrection is essential because it provides proof *for* us. "Show us a sign to validate Your claims," Jesus' contemporaries demanded.

"Destroy this body, and in three days, I'll rise again," Jesus answered (see John 2:19). And indeed that continues to be the sign that sets Him apart from all others.

Second, the resurrection tells us He's present *with* us. On that first Easter Sunday, Jesus' followers weren't rejoicing in theological implications or dispensational ramifications but simply in the fact that their friend—the One who had calmed the storm and fed them, the One who had healed and loved them—was with them once again. And the same is true for every believer. What storm is raging around you today? What leprosy is nibbling at you? What problem is pressing down heavily on your soul? You can cast all those cares upon Jesus, for He's with you even now.

Finally, the resurrection reminds us that He's praying *for* us. Jesus ever lives to make intercession for us (Hebrews 7:25). Therefore, if any man sin, we have an Advocate with the Father (1 John 2:1). How does He win His case? Revelation 12 tells us the accuser of our souls is overcome by the blood. That's why, in our text, the leper was sprinkled seven times, for seven is the number of perfection, of completion.

The sparrow of our salvation left His nest in heaven to lodge in a tree called Calvary, to die in place of you and me. But the story doesn't end there. Because He took His blood into heaven to cleanse each of us, we can come boldly before God no matter how inadequate, how unworthy, or how leprous we feel (Hebrews 4:16).

AUGUST 22

And the remnant of the oil that is in the priest's hand he shall pour upon the head of him that is to be cleansed: and the priest shall make an atonement for him before the LORD.

Leviticus 14:18

Only four groups of people were anointed with oil upon the head: kings, prophets, priests ... and lepers. Isn't that just like the Lord to include lepers in such an august group?

> Every day, she made her way to the stream to draw enough water for the two large pots she would carry half a mile back to the manor. Because one of the pots was cracked, by the time she arrived, only a pot and a half were full. After a few years, the cracked pot said, "I'm not worthy. I try to be. I want to be. I mean to be. But I never come through. I only make it half way. Why didn't you discard me long ago?"

"I want to show you something," the servant girl replied. And she took the pots on the walk again. "What do you see?"

"All kinds of flowers," the pot answered.

"That's right," the girl said. "They're there because every day, without you even knowing it, you watered the ground so they could grow."

I think we all feel like cracked pots. We want to do good, but it seems we never do. But here's what we need to know: lepers were anointed to be the bouquet of grace. Lepers like us are producing something in which our Master delights. Sure, there's an anointing on the king and the prophet and the priest. But there's an anointing on the cleansed leper as well, if for no other reason than to be a trophy of God's grace.

AUGUST 23

And this shall be his uncleanness in his issue: whether his flesh run with his issue, or his flesh be stopped from his issue, it is his uncleanness. Every bed, whereon he lieth that hath the issue, is unclean: and every thing, whereon he sitteth, shall be unclean. And whosoever toucheth his bed shall wash his clothes, and bathe himself in water, and be unclean until the even.

Leviticus 15:3–5

In dealing with a chronic discharge of a disease, the key phrase is that there was to be a washing, a scrubbing, a cleansing with water. This predated medical knowledge by thousands of years, for it wasn't until the nineteenth century that doctors understood the importance of cleanliness. Prior to that time, a clean doctor was considered to be about as effective as a clean football player. They wore blood on their clothes and hands as a sign of success. But in 1847, a Hungarian physician by the name of Ignaz Semmelweis made a correlation between the number of autopsies performed and the number of patients who, treated by the same doctors who performed the autopsies hours earlier, died from infectious disease. When he realized it was the doctors themselves who were spreading disease, he came to the revolutionary conclusion that doctors should wash after every operation.

"How shall a young man cleanse his way?" David asked. "By taking heed to the word" (see Psalm 119:9).

"We are washed by the water which is the word" Paul said (see Ephesians 5:26).

"Now ye are clean by the word which I have spoken unto you," Jesus declared (John 15:3).

There is indeed a washing and a cleansing from spiritual disease as we drink of the Scriptures. Like the doctors in the dark ages of medicine, we mistakenly think we don't have to wash ourselves spiritually all that often. Yet we wonder why we remain in an infected condition. God's way is that His Word would be the cleansing agent that would purify and protect us from the infection of lustful thoughts, bad attitudes, cynical spirits, and a host of other diseases we think no one else sees.

It's amazing how much better those who take time to be in the Word personally and fellowship with the Lord intimately do than those who think they don't need to wash. Spending time in Bible study says, "Lord, I'm trusting that something is happening miraculously, supernaturally even now, that Your Word is doing a cleansing work in me."

AUGUST 24

And the LORD spake unto Moses after the death of the two sons of Aaron, when they offered before the LORD, and died; and the LORD said unto Moses, Speak unto Aaron thy brother, that he come not at all times into the holy place within the vail before the mercy seat, which is upon the ark; that he die not: for I will appear in the cloud upon the mercy seat.

Leviticus 16:1–2

Linked to chapter 10, these opening verses of chapter 16 hint that, in addition to burning strange fire, Nadab and Abihu violated God's law by going into the Holy of Holies.

> Suppose you are an Amorite, Ammonite, or a Jebusite watching the Israelites fervently engaged in pitching a huge tent. An Israelite happens across your path and you ask him what he's doing. "Erecting the tabernacle," he would answer, "the tent where God meets with His people."
>
> "I want to go there and meet Him too," you would say.
>
> "Sorry, it's just for Israelites," he would answer.
>
> "Then I wish I were an Israelite," you would say.
>
> "It's not enough to simply be an Israelite," he would answer. "You have to be of the tribe of Levi. They're the only ones who get to put up the tabernacle."
>
> "Then I wish I were a Levite," you would say.
>
> "It's not that simple," he would say. "To go into the tabernacle, you must be a priest, which means you must be of the family of Aaron."
>
> "Then I wish I were of the family of Aaron," you would say.
>
> "It's not that simple," he would say. "Only the oldest member of the family can serve as the high priest. And only the high priest can actually meet with God."
>
> "Then I wish I were the oldest member of the family of Aaron so I could meet with God whenever I wished," you would say.
>
> "It's not that simple," he would say. "The high priest can only meet with God one day each year on Yom Kippur. And if he's not properly prepared, he'll die."

We can have the tendency to read the Old Testament and think it would be wonderful to live in the days when people saw firsthand the parting of the Red Sea, the drowning of Pharaoh's army, and manna falling from heaven. Yet, in reality, we live in much better days because we experience every day that which only one of them could experience on only one day each year:

the *kabowd*, the glory of God. It's an unbelievable privilege God has given to you and me. Thus, these days are better indeed.

AUGUST 25

And when he hath made an end of reconciling the holy place, and the tabernacle of the congregation, and the altar, he shall bring the live goat: and Aaron shall lay both his hands upon the head of the live goat, and confess over him all the iniquities of the children of Israel, and all their transgressions in all their sins, putting them upon the head of the goat, and shall send him away by the hand of a fit man into the wilderness: and the goat shall bear upon him all their iniquities unto a land not inhabited: and he shall let go the goat in the wilderness.

Leviticus 16:20–22

The sin offering required two goats. One was to be sacrificed because the wages of sin is death. But the other goat was brought before Aaron in order that he might lay his hands on its head and verbally, articulately, and carefully confess the sins of the nation and, in a sense, transfer the sin to the goat. Symbolically bearing the sins of the whole nation, the goat was then led to the wilderness, where it symbolically carried the sins of the congregation out of sight.

The scapegoat is an illustration of God's declaration that He will remember our sins and iniquities no more (Jeremiah 31:34). When this understanding finally drops from one's head to one's heart, it is so exhilarating, and so liberating because most of us believe that God, like Santa Claus, is making a list and checking it twice, that God is keeping score. He's not. We remember each other's sin. But God has chosen to erase from His memory bank the sins we confess.

Most people know this doctrinally, but because they don't believe it in the deepest part of their soul, they believe God is disappointed with them due to what happened ten years ago or ten weeks ago or ten minutes ago. In Psalm 103, God says, "As far as the east is from the west, so I have put your iniquities from Me" (see verse 12). In Isaiah, He says, "I have cast your sins behind My back" (see 38:17). Isaiah 44:22 tells us He has blotted out our sins like a thick cloud; Job 14:17 says that He puts our sins in a bag and sews it up; Micah 7:19 declares that our sins are cast into the depths of the sea.

What the scapegoat pictured symbolically and temporarily, the Lamb of God achieved practically and eternally when He died on the cross of Calvary for each and every sin of all of humanity.

AUGUST 26

And this shall be a statute for ever unto you: that in the seventh month, on the tenth day of the month, ye shall afflict your souls, and do no work at all, whether it be one of your own country, or a stranger that sojourneth among you: for on that day shall the priest make an atonement for you, to cleanse you, that ye may be clean from all your sins before the LORD.

Leviticus 16:29–30

The Day of Atonement took place in the seventh month, on the tenth day. Seven is the number of perfection, ten the number of the law. Do we keep the law perfectly? No. And that is the reason for the Day of Atonement.

On the Day of Atonement, how would the children of Israel know if the offering was sufficient? They would know their sins were covered if the high priest emerged from the tabernacle—for if he was not properly prepared, if his offering was unacceptable, he would die in the Holy of Holies, in the presence of a holy, almighty God.

So too, I know with certainty that I am forgiven because our great High Priest, Jesus Christ, came out of the tomb. Therefore, the book of Hebrews declares, "Let us come boldly unto the throne of grace that we might find grace and mercy to help in time of need" (4:16). Because the work of atonement has been accomplished completely and perfectly, God invites us specifically and personally to come into the Holy of Holies, to come before His throne. The question is, will we take advantage of the invitation?

The story is told of a telegraph company in the 1800s seeking to hire an operator. The salary offered being quite substantial, only the most qualified were encouraged to apply. On the day of the invitation, seven men showed up. As they sat outside the boss' office waiting for their interview and listening to the telegraph operators working in the background, suddenly, the last one to arrive suddenly stood up and went into the boss's office without being asked. The boss emerged a few minutes later and said, "Gentlemen, thank you for coming. But there will be no need for an interview. I've hired this man for the position."

"Wait a minute," one of the remaining six protested, "that's not fair. This man was the last to arrive. We should have had our chance to be interviewed for this position."

"You did," the boss said. "While you were sitting here, one of our operators was tapping out a message saying, 'If you receive this message, come into my office immediately. The job is yours.'"

All of the men were trained. All were qualified. All had knowledge of Morse code, but only one of the seven was tuned into the message being tapped out right then.

I can't help but wonder today if there is one in seven who has really heard the message being tapped out that says, "Come boldly to My throne. Talk with Me. Cast your care upon Me. Receive from Me help, strength, and instruction."

Have you heard the message, Mom—the tap, tap, tap of the Morse code of the Master saying, "Come and talk to Me about your son or daughter. This is the moment"?

Have you heard the message, husband? Do you hear the tapping of the Master saying, "Come boldly to the throne of grace that you might find help for your marriage which is presently unraveling"?

If you're wondering whether to go to college, take the job, or move away; if you're struggling with physical affliction or fighting depression, I wonder if there is one in seven who hears the Lord saying, "The stone is rolled away. The veil is rent. The way is open. Come on in!"

AUGUST 27

And thou shalt say unto them, Whatsoever man there be of the house of Israel, or of the strangers which sojourn among you, that offereth a burnt offering of sacrifice, and bringeth it not unto the door of the tabernacle of the congregation, to offer it unto the LORD; even that man shall be cut off from among his people.

Leviticus 17:8–9

Ezekiel 20 tells us that, when the Israelites were in Egypt for four hundred years, they were involved in idolatry. Therefore, because God the Father was very concerned about the tendency of His people to fall into heresy, which often led to idolatry, He said, "I want all sacrifices to be made at the tabernacle."

"We don't like the tabernacle. It's too confining," some might have protested. "Can't five of us just get together and sacrifice in the woods?"

"No," God said.

"Who needs priests?" others might have asked. "Aren't we all spiritual? Can't we all offer sacrifices?"

"No," God said.

There are those today who think they can worship God without going to church. "My church is on the golf course," they say, or "at the lake," or "on the beach." "Why go into a stuffy building?" they ask. "Isn't God the God of creation?"

This passage reveals God's heart concerning the way He wants to be worshiped, not because He is stuffy and contrary, but because He knows what will happen practically. You see, over the years, I have noticed that the people who choose to seek the Lord at their lake house rather than in the sanctuary with the congregation never do well over the long haul. There can be a tendency, especially for older Christians, to say, "church was great for our first ten years, but now we just need some space on Sundays," failing to realize that it's when we're with our brothers and sisters—living stones being fit together for a holy habitation (1 Peter 2:5)—that sometimes we're rubbed the wrong way by necessity. That is, it is the interaction, the fellowship, the seeking of God together that not only smoothes our rough edges, but also gives us stability.

AUGUST 28

And whatsoever man there be of the house of Israel, or of the strangers that sojourn among you, that eateth any manner of blood; I will even set my face against that soul that eateth blood, and will cut him off from among his people. For the life of the flesh is in the blood: and I have given it to you upon the altar to make an atonement for your souls: for it is the blood that maketh an atonement for the soul.

Leviticus 17:10–11

When Peter Marshall, chaplain of the United States Senate in the 1940s, first arrived in Washington, D.C., to pastor the New York Avenue Presbyterian Church, an elderly lady is said to have greeted him by saying, "I do so hope you won't talk too much about the blood, as our previous pastor did."

"I promise I won't talk too much about the blood," the young Scotsman assured her, "because it is impossible to talk too much about the blood."

Peter Marshall nailed it perfectly. It is impossible to talk too much about the blood of Jesus Christ. Why? Because the Bible is soaked in blood, saturated with blood. Ours is a bloody religion indeed. And there's a reason for that. The book of Hebrews tells us that without the shedding of blood there can be no remission of sin (9:22). Therefore, with man's greatest need being forgiveness, it only stands to reason that blood would be spoken of freely and consistently throughout the Word.

Why is blood the key to forgiveness? Because, as seen in our text, the life of the flesh is in the blood. That is why it was blood that cried out when the first murder was committed (Genesis 4:10). There is indeed a potency, a mystery, a power in blood for it is the essence of life. And in Leviticus, God uses these powerful properties of blood to not only show us the seriousness of our sin, but to point to the sacrifice of His Son.

AUGUST 29

Therefore I said unto the children of Israel, No soul of you shall eat blood, neither shall any stranger that sojourneth among you eat blood. And whatsoever man there be of the children of Israel, or of the strangers that sojourn among you, which hunteth and catcheth any beast or fowl that may be eaten; he shall even pour out the blood thereof, and cover it with dust. For it is the life of all flesh; the blood of it is for the life thereof.

Leviticus 17:12–14

Because the blood is sacred, orthodox Jews, as they do to this day, were exceedingly careful not to eat any meat not thoroughly drained of every drop of blood. And then an itinerant Rabbi from Galilee came along one day and had the audacity to proclaim, "Except you drink My blood, you have no life in you" (see John 6:53). No wonder it was at that point that many walked away to follow Him no more (John 6:66).

I know what Jesus was saying. So do you. He wasn't talking about cannibalism, about drinking His blood literally in violation of Leviticus 17. He was talking about intimacy, how we are to devour the Word, how we are to open our hearts, how we are to embrace the work He did when He shed His blood for our sin. Yet, when His followers turned away, Jesus didn't say, "Wait a minute. Let Me explain what I meant. It's not what you think." Why didn't He do that? Why didn't He clarify the issue? I believe it was for three basic reasons . . .

He knew what the Holy Spirit would do. That is, He knew that which He shared could only be made real when the Holy Spirit made it alive. And because it is the work of the Spirit to bring all things to remembrance (John 14:26), Jesus knew the Spirit would bring this occasion to their minds and make application in due season.

Second, Jesus knew what the Father alone could do. Only the Father can cause a person to come to Jesus (John 6:44). The Spirit gives revelation, but it is the Father who determines who will come to His Son.

Third, Jesus knew what the true disciples should do. When asked if he was about to leave with the rest, Peter answered, "Where else would we go? You alone have the words of eternal life" (see John 6:67–68). Jesus didn't hurry to explain His words to those who left because He knew that they must learn to do what you and I must do: walk by faith. Why? Because only faith is strong enough to weather the storms ahead.

When we don't understand what's going on, when we're troubled by a teaching we've heard or a passage we've read, when we're going through a tragedy or a heartbreak, if we're not careful, we will be like those in John 6:66, failing to understand that the only way our faith becomes strong is when, like Peter, we believe in spite of what we don't initially understand.

Jesus knew what the Holy Spirit would do. He knew what the Father alone could do. He knew what His true disciples should do. And knowing these things, Jesus ministered in a way that was wonderfully relaxed and incredibly peaceful.

AUGUST 30

Therefore I said unto the children of Israel, Ye shall eat the blood of no manner of flesh: for the life of all flesh is the blood thereof: whosoever eateth it shall be cut off. And every soul that eateth that which died of itself, or that which was torn with beasts, whether it be one of your own country, or a stranger, he shall both wash his clothes, and bathe himself in water, and be unclean until the even: then shall he be clean. But if he wash them not, nor bathe his flesh; then he shall bear his iniquity.

Leviticus 17:14–16

Here, verse 11 is repeated: the life of the flesh is in the blood. Physiologically, this understanding preceded medicine by thousands of years, for it wasn't until 1628 that an anatomist named Dr. Harvey identified the importance of the red fluid circulating within us. Spiritually, we know that just as our own blood keeps us alive temporarily, the shed blood of the Lamb of God gives us life eternally.

Forasmuch as ye know that ye were not redeemed with corruptible things, as silver and gold, from your vain conversation received by tradition from your fathers; but with the precious blood of Christ, as of a lamb without blemish and without spot: who verily was foreordained before the foundation of the world, but was manifest in these last times for you, who by him do believe in God, that raised him up from the dead, and gave him glory; that your faith and hope might be in God.

1 Peter 1:18–21

When Jesus died on the cross, He paid for each one of our sins specifically. How could He have accomplished this in only six hours two thousand years ago on Calvary? Peter tells us He was slain before the foundation of the world. And John tells us that when we see Him, we'll see Him as a Lamb having just been slain (Revelation 5:6). Therefore, from the perspective of the time/space continuum, the work of salvation was indeed complete in six hours on the cross. But from the eternal perspective, where there is no future and no past (Ecclesiastes 3:15), Jesus' suffering was infinitely greater than anything we can even begin to comprehend. With this being the case, how can I lightly say, "It doesn't matter if I harbor an unforgiving spirit, have a lousy attitude, or engage in a questionable activity. It's all forgiven because of Calvary"?

The work of salvation is complete, finished, done. Yet as true as that is, it is also true that the price Jesus paid for each of our sins individually is unspeakably more than we can understand this side of eternity.

Because the life of the flesh is in the blood, Jesus gave His blood so that we can have life.

AUGUST 31

And the LORD spake unto Moses, saying, Speak unto the children of Israel, and say unto them, I am the LORD your God. After the doings of the land of Egypt, wherein ye dwelt, shall ye not do: and after the doings of the land of Canaan, whither I bring you, shall ye not do: neither shall ye walk in their ordinances. Ye shall do my judgments, and keep mine ordinances, to walk therein: I am the LORD your God. Ye shall therefore keep my statutes, and my judgments: which if a man do, he shall live in them: I am the LORD.

Leviticus 18:1–5

Here, God declares, "I am the Lord your God. You are to behave in a way unlike that which you saw in Egypt." During the four hundred-year period the children of Israel were in Egypt, the Egyptians were the most advanced culture in world history. Although it was impressive in many ways, it was also an immoral culture. To Canaanites, who were even more immoral than the Egyptians, God said, "You are to be neither like those in the land from which you came nor like those in the land to which you are going. I am the Lord your God. I know how you were created. I know what will bring you lasting joy, true peace. If you do what I say, you'll experience life the way it was meant to be."

SEPTEMBER 1

And the LORD spake unto Moses, saying, Speak unto all the congregation of the children of Israel, and say unto them, Ye shall be holy: for I the LORD your God am holy.

Leviticus 19:1–2

Leviticus 19 issues a call to holiness. Holiness is related to wholeness. And God wants us to be a whole people. When you understand this, you'll find that the commands of God are no longer burdensome. You'll find yourself wanting to embrace them, eager to learn them, ready to practice them. The Father wants us to be a blessed people—blessed in our families and our marriages, in our relationships and our occupations. He truly desires us to be happy. Satan, the deceiver and liar, says holiness leads to strangeness. "You'll be miserable," he hisses. "You'll miss out on all the fun." Not so.

God doesn't look in the mirror and say, "I'm not really pleased with this aspect of Myself," or "I wish I was a bit different in this area of My personality." No, because He is holy, God is totally, completely, and absolutely happy with every part of His being. You see, in essence, the word *holy* simply means "whole." And because He's whole, because He lacks nothing, God is supremely happy with who He is. And He wants nothing less for us.

Holiness leads to happiness. That's an absolute, non-negotiable, irrefutable spiritual principle. God wants us to be holy for He is holy. He commands us to be holy, for He wants us to be happy.

SEPTEMBER 2

Thou shalt not curse the deaf, nor put a stumblingblock before the blind, but shalt fear thy God: I am the LORD.

Leviticus 19:14

In addition to the obvious injunction not to be hardened to those who are physically inflicted, blindness and deafness are pictures throughout Scripture of the spiritual insensitivity of a world that's lost.

Cursing the deaf is subtle. Do we have an attitude of cursing those who bother us, those who act worldly because their ears are closed to an awareness of God? How did Jesus deal with the deaf? Consider these words from the gospel of Mark . . .

> And they bring unto him one that was deaf, and had an impediment in his speech; and they beseech him to put his hand upon him. And he took him aside from the multitude, and put his fingers into his ears, and he spit, and touched his tongue; and looking up to heaven, he sighed, and saith unto him, Ephphatha, that is, Be opened. And straightway his ears were opened, and the string of his tongue was loosed, and he spake plain.
>
> Mark 7:32–35

Jesus not only took the deaf man aside from the crowd and gave him individual attention, but He put His fingers in the deaf man's ears and gave him an individual touch. Jesus didn't have to touch him. He could have spoken the word and that would have sufficed, but had He done so, the deaf man wouldn't have heard it. So He related to the man where he was. Then Jesus looked to heaven, showing the man from whence his healing would come. That's the pattern—touching people and relating to them where they are concerning their knowledge and understanding. When Jesus spoke, the man's ears were opened. And as you and I speak the Word of God, spiritually deaf ears are opened as well.

Second, we're not to trip the blind. The concept of being a stumbling block is also seen in 1 Corinthians 8, where a controversy had arisen concerning meat that had been offered to idols before it was sold in discount markets. Looking for a good buy and knowing that idols were powerless to affect meat, some Christians would purchase the meat at discount prices. Others, however, said the meat was defiled and not to be eaten. Paul's answer was that while believers are the freest of men, we're not to use our freedom in a way that causes others to stumble. In any given situation, each of us will either be a stumbling block or a stepping stone. People will either be hindered in coming to Jesus or we'll be stepping stones on their path to Him.

Sometimes I feel we're the ones with blinded eyes, the ones who don't see people properly; we're the ones with deaf ears, unable to hear the cries of lost humanity. How can the Lord make us more like Himself? Look again at Mark's gospel . . .

> And he cometh to Bethsaida; and they bring a blind man unto him, and besought him to touch him. And he took the blind man by the hand, and led him out of the town; and when he had spit on his eyes, and put his hands upon him, he asked him if he saw ought. And he looked up, and said, I see men as trees, walking. After that he put his hands again upon his eyes, and made him look up: and he was restored, and saw every man clearly.
>
> Mark 8:22–25

Sometimes I think we who have been touched by the hand of Jesus Christ, we who have received divine enlightenment, still see men as trees: trees that are in our way, trees that are to be cut down and used for our own purposes. How did Jesus solve this problem? He touched the blind man a second time and made him look up. And then the man saw every man clearly.

You and I also need to look up, for when we fix our eyes on Jesus, we become like Him (1 John 3:2). When I don't look up to the Lord, I'll look down on men. I'll see them as trees. But when I focus on Jesus, I will see people as He sees them.

SEPTEMBER 3

Thou shalt not go up and down as a talebearer among thy people: neither shalt thou stand against the blood of thy neighbour: I am the LORD.

Leviticus 19:16

A talebearer hurts three people: the person he talks about, the person he talks to, and himself.

First, in a very real sense, people are who we say they are, regardless of whether what we say is true. People will either be lifted up or put down in the estimation of others by what we say about them. Jesus draws a direct parallel between murder and the tongue because we have the power to kill another person's reputation with our words (Matthew 5:21–22). Second, telling tales, or gossiping, hurts the person who listens because it affects the way he or she will view the person being talked about. Finally, gossip hurts the talebearer himself because every time we gossip, we become smaller and smaller. As has been wisely said, great minds talk about ideas or ideals; good minds about events; small minds about people. In which company are you?

SEPTEMBER 4

Sanctify yourselves therefore, and be ye holy: for I am the LORD your God.

Leviticus 20:7

"Sanctify," or *qadash* in Hebrew, means "to set apart"—set apart to God and set apart from sin. Can we really be set apart from sin? Can we truly be sanctified?

John Wesley and his brother, Charles, both godly men, believed that if people lived a disciplined life before God, they could achieve a state of sanctity in which they would never sin again. Determined to see this understanding come to fruition, they developed a method to do this, and the Methodist movement was born. On other hand, John Calvin and others said it was impossible to be completely and totally sanctified in this life. And these two views remain in the church to this day.

When Jesus died on the cross, He didn't say, "To be continued," or "This will do for now." He said, "It is *finished*" (John 19:30, italics added). That is why Paul could address the Corinthian believers as those who have been sanctified (1 Corinthians 1:2). Practically, the Corinthian congregation was full of problems. So are we. But positionally, the Corinthians were sanctified. And so are we.

SEPTEMBER 5

*And ye shall keep my statutes, and do them: I am the L*ORD *which sanctify you.*

Leviticus 20:8

Verse 7 begins with "Sanctify yourselves." Verse 8 ends with, "I am the LORD which sanctify you." Is sanctification something we do, or is it something God does for us? It's both. God sanctifies us, yet He won't do it without our participation. We see this illustrated perfectly in 2 Kings 5 . . .

Plagued by leprosy, a Syrian general named Naaman heard there was a prophet in Israel doing miracles. He traveled there and was told by Elisha to dip in the Jordan River seven times.

Naaman was offended. "That dirty river? We have bigger, cleaner rivers in Syria," he protested.

But when his advisors said, "What do you have to lose?" he followed Elisha's instructions, and after his seventh dip, his leprosy was gone.

If we want to be free from the leprosy eating away at our marriages, our families, and our joy, we have a part to play. Seven being the number of completion, and water being emblematic of the Word, we are to dip into the Word over and over and over again. And as we do, God meets us and we begin to see we are indeed sanctified. As we fellowship with Him, listen to Him, and obey Him, we experience the unmistakable sanctifying process. "Sanctify yourselves," God says, "and as you do, I will sanctify you." Without Him, we can't. Without us, He won't.

SEPTEMBER 6

And he that is the high priest among his brethren, upon whose head the anointing oil was poured, and that is consecrated to put on the garments, shall not uncover his head, nor rend his clothes.

Leviticus 21:10

The story is told of a man who, after parking his car, set out for a day hike in the Sierra Nevada Mountains. Three miles into what was to be a relaxing afternoon outing, he noticed ominous storm clouds forming as the temperature dropped dangerously. Realizing a freak snowstorm was headed his way, the man began backtracking toward his car. He had a mile or so to go when the storm became so intense that he couldn't see his hand in front of his face. Losing his way, he walked for two hours until he realized he was freezing. Feeling a deadly lethargy, the man knew that if he sat down, he would never get up, so he fought it for as long as he could. But finally, the desire to rest was just too overpowering, so he sat down at the base of a tree, the snow still falling intensely. As he sat down, he felt something next to him. Brushing away the snow, he discovered the body of a man who had evidently stopped to rest only a few moments earlier. Finding a pulse, the young man stood to his feet and, with a burst of newfound energy, picked up the man who had almost frozen to death, put him on his shoulders, and began walking feverishly. After walking fifty yards or so, he bumped into the side of a cabin. Feeling his way to the front, he banged on the door, which was opened by a man who welcomed the pair inside to warm themselves by his roaring fire.

The application is obvious. In attempting to save someone else, the young man was himself saved. In caring for someone else, he himself was cared for. And that's what Jesus meant when He said, "The measure you give out will be measured back to you" (see Luke 6:38).

When tragedy strikes or when trials come, we'll either say, "This ought not to be. Poor me," or we'll say, "This can be used for Your glory, so pour me, Lord. Pour me out to the people in need all around."

What did our great High Priest do in His time of tragedy, in His time of pain? Even as He hung on the cross in agony, He ministered to a man beside Him, to a woman below Him, and to the crowd around Him . . .

"This day you shall be with Me in paradise," He said to the needy thief beside Him (see Luke 23:43).

"Woman, behold thy son," He said to His grieving mother standing at the foot of the cross below Him (John 19:26).

"Father, forgive them," He prayed concerning the jeering crowd surrounding Him (Luke 23:34).

No wonder Caiaphas rent his garments that day (Matthew 26:65), for he was disqualified from priestly ministry at that moment, superseded by the great High Priest whose garment was not rent (John 19:24).

The garment of Caiaphas was torn. Not so the garment of Jesus, for Jesus will never lose control emotionally or grieve hysterically. Therefore, neither must we. I'm not talking about "keeping a stiff upper lip," having a "positive mental attitude," or a "don't worry, be happy" mentality. I'm talking about the reality of our great High Priest living in you and me through both good days and bad.

Stay in the place of ministry, gang. Follow the example of Jesus. When difficulties come your way, the best thing you can do is go for it more than you ever have previously, in giving out, in sharing with, and in caring for those beside and all around you.

SEPTEMBER 7

What man soever of the seed of Aaron is a leper, or hath a running issue; he shall not eat of the holy things, until he be clean. And whoso toucheth any thing that is unclean by the dead, or a man whose seed goeth from him; or whosoever toucheth any creeping thing, whereby he may be made un-clean, or a man of whom he may take uncleanness, whatso-ever uncleanness he hath; the soul which hath touched any such shall be unclean until even, and shall not eat of the holy things, unless he wash his flesh with water. And when the sun is down, he shall be clean, and shall afterward eat of the holy things; because it is his food.

Leviticus 22:4–7

The remedy for uncleanness is first waiting and then washing. First, the unclean person was to wait until evening. Why evening? Because in Jewish economy, the setting of the sun signaled a new day ...

It is of the LORD's mercies that we are not consumed, because his compassions fail not. They are new every morning: great is thy faithfulness.

Lamentations 3:22–23

The Lord ordered our lives in such a way that every day after about sixteen or eighteen hours, we go to bed and basically "die." To me, His plan is in-genious because I find that after about sixteen hours of living, I've pretty much messed it up. I've dropped the ball once too often and fumbled one too many times. I need to die and start over in a fresh way. So I think it's wonderful that God lets us die every eighteen hours.

How I love the morning hours. Whether I spend them at church, in my place of prayer at home, or walking the streets of town on a spring or sum-mer morning, I love the morning when it's quiet, when I can receive a pip-ing hot batch of mercy fresh from the oven of God's grace.

Second, the priest who was unclean—whether by his own flesh or through contact with the dead things of the world—was to wash. As New Testament priests, the washing refers to the water of the Word (John 15:3). Did you wash today in the water of the Word? We're bombarded every day by creeping things and dead carcasses, by that which would defile us and render us unable to serve or eat that which would satisfy our souls. God would say, "The solution is simple, the remedy is real: wait on Me in this new day and wash in the water of My Word."

SEPTEMBER 8

And the LORD spake unto Moses, saying, When a bullock, or a sheep, or a goat, is brought forth, then it shall be seven days under the dam; and from the eighth day and thenceforth it shall be accepted for an offering made by fire unto the LORD. And whether it be cow or ewe, ye shall not kill it and her young both in one day. And when ye will offer a sacrifice of thanksgiving unto the LORD, offer it at your own will. On the same day it shall be eaten up; ye shall leave none of it until the morrow: I am the LORD.

Leviticus 22:26–30

When an Israelite willingly offered a sacrifice of thanksgiving, it was to be completely eaten on the same day it was offered. Why? First, it was to protect against pollution, against the food becoming spoiled for lack of refrigeration. Spiritually, I believe our thanksgiving can also become spoiled unless offered consistently. Over time, our minds have a way of explaining away God's miraculous hand in any given situation, of attributing His goodness in our lives to our own efforts, to luck, or to coincidence. And thus, our thanksgiving becomes spoiled if not offered immediately, consistently, and wholeheartedly.

Second, I believe this word was given to us to provide satiation. It is as if the Lord is saying, "When you bring Me the sacrifice of thanksgiving, I want you to leave with a full belly. I want you to be deeply satisfied, totally satiated, and completely happy."

> By him therefore let us offer the sacrifice of praise to God continually, that is, the fruit of our lips giving thanks to his name.
>
> Hebrews 13:15

God wants us to offer the sacrifice of praise and thanksgiving not because He needs to be thanked but because we need to be thankful. Why? Thanksgiving is the antidote to depression, the remedy for a cynical spirit. Yes, there are very real battles facing each of us. We are not to pretend they don't exist. But neither are we to indulge in doubt and self-pity. Rather, we're to do what Jehoshaphat did . . .

> With a confederation of Edomite, Ammonite, and Moabite troops arrayed against him, Jehoshaphat, king of Judah, called unto God for help. God responded through a prophet, saying, "Be not afraid nor dismayed by reason of this great multitude; for the battle is not yours, but God's. . . . Ye shall not need to fight in this battle: set yourselves, stand ye still, and see the salvation of the LORD with you, O Judah and Jerusalem: fear not, nor be dismayed; tomorrow go out against them: for the LORD will be with you" (2 Chronicles 20:15, 17).

Jehoshaphat could have said, "What kind of battle plan is that?" Instead, he bowed his head and worshiped. Although all he had was a promise, the next morning, rather than sending his troops to battle, Jehoshaphat sent a choir to praise. And although this made no sense militarily, it disoriented the enemy, they drew their swords in confusion, and they annihilated one another (see verses 20–24).

The same thing is true in the Spirit. We have an Enemy who surrounds us constantly, an adversary who wants to intimidate and depress us daily, whose goal is to rob us of the riches of our joy and peace. But this Enemy is beaten back, confused, and overwhelmed through the power of praise and thanksgiving.

SEPTEMBER 9

And the LORD spake unto Moses, saying, Speak unto the children of Israel, saying, The fifteenth day of this seventh month shall be the feast of tabernacles for seven days unto the LORD.

Leviticus 23:33–34

On the Day of Atonement, the nation confessed their sin and afflicted their souls. The result? A party five days later at the Feast of Tabernacles (five being the number of grace). Every morning during the Feast of Tabernacles, the priests would divide into two processionals. One group would go directly east to the valley of Kidron and gather willow, palm, myrtle, and citrus branches to pass out to the people and to lay in the courtyard of the temple where sacrifices were made. The second group of priests would go south to the pool of Siloam, carrying a golden pitcher, which they would dip into the water. Both companies of priests—those carrying the branches and those carrying the water—would meet at the temple, where the water was poured out from the pitcher before the altar as a reminder of God's provision of water for them during their wilderness wanderings. On the eighth day, the great day of the feast, the priests would go to the pool of Siloam, but they would return with an empty pitcher, acknowledging the fact that because they were now in the Promised Land, there was no longer need for the supernatural provision of water. And as they did, the priests would pray this prayer . . .

> Thus saith the LORD that made thee, and formed thee from the womb, which will help thee; Fear not, O Jacob, my servant; and thou, Jesurun, whom I have chosen. For I will pour water upon him that is thirsty, and floods upon the dry ground: I will pour my spirit upon thy seed, and my blessing upon thine offspring: and they shall spring up as among the grass, as willows by the water courses.
>
> Isaiah 44:2–4

Why would they read this passage? Because they understood that Isaiah 44 was a prophecy of the pouring out of the Spirit that could transpire only when Messiah came to their land.

The year is approximately AD 32. On the great day of the feast, everyone watched as the processional returned from the pool of Siloam, poured out the empty pitcher, and prayed for Messiah to come. Then a young thirty-three-year-old rabbi from Galilee shouts out, "If any man thirst, let him come unto me, and drink. . . . out of his belly shall flow rivers of living water" (John 7:37–38), thereby presenting Himself as Messiah and offering the living water, the rain of the Holy Spirit.

But Jesus' declaration was not yet complete . . .

Every night during the Feast of Tabernacles, the celebration of illumination took place on the temple mount. In this celebration, four huge menorahs, with wicks made of priest's robes which had been worn out, were lit, and shined so brightly that light could be seen one hundred miles away. At the end of the feast, the menorahs would be extinguished, not to be relit until the following year. John tells us that it was on the day after the Feast of Tabernacles, the day after the menorahs were extinguished, that Jesus declared, "I am the light of the world" (John 8:12)—the true Light which would never be extinguished.

Don't lose sight of the fact that the Lord's coming is near, gang. In the meantime, drink deeply of the water of His Spirit and illuminate your life, not with a pillar of fire or a huge menorah which was used and then extinguished, but by the presence and promises of the One who will never leave you nor forsake you as you walk daily with Him.

SEPTEMBER 10

And the son of an Israelitish woman, whose father was an Egyptian, went out among the children of Israel: and this son of the Israelitish woman and a man of Israel strove together in the camp; and the Israelitish woman's son blasphemed the name of the LORD, and cursed. And they brought him unto Moses: (and his mother's name was Shelomith, the daughter of Dibri, of the tribe of Dan:) and *they put him in ward, that the mind of the L*ORD *might be shewed them.*

Leviticus 24:10–12

Here we see the responsibility of the people to protect God's holy name. When, during a fight, the son of an Israelite woman and an Egyptian man blasphemed the name of the Lord, the people of God weren't sure whether he was to be held to the same standards as they were. So they put him in ward, in custody, and sought the mind of the Lord—always a wise thing to do.

Had Moses come to me asking what I thought he should do with a man who was half Egyptian and half Jew and had blasphemed the Lord's name during a fight, my tendency would have been to say, "Let's discuss this. He doesn't have the background the rest of us have had. Here's a chance for us to be merciful, to show grace, to demonstrate to the Egyptian people how kind, big-hearted, and loving we are. Let's not rush into this matter. Let's give him a warning, explain why we don't say those things around here, and let him go. After all, he's half Egyptian."

But verses 13 through 16 show me just how far my thoughts are from God's, that I'm not nearly as wise as I think I am.

And the LORD spake unto Moses, saying, Bring forth him that hath cursed without the camp; and let all that heard him lay their hands upon his head, and let all the congregation stone him. And thou shalt speak unto the children of Israel, saying, Whosoever curseth his God shall bear his sin. And he that blasphemeth the name of the LORD, he shall surely be put to death, and all the congregation shall certainly stone him: as well the stranger, as he that is born in the land, when he blasphemeth the name of the LORD, shall be put to death.

Leviticus 24:13–16

Maybe you're like me. Maybe you think you know what's right and what's wise. But, on the basis of this passage, I encourage you, even as I remind myself, rather than making a decision based upon dialogue, discussion, and debate, to seek the Lord in prayer and see what *He* says concerning any given matter.

God speaks to those who are on their knees seeking Him sincerely, admitting they lack wisdom. God's will is not a mystery. The only question is, will we do what He tells us to do?

SEPTEMBER 11

In the year of this jubile ye shall return every man unto his possession.

Leviticus 25:13

In the year of Jubilee, any land that had been sold was to be returned to its original owner. That is, if a piece of property was sold to cover a debt or to rescue a household financially, it was to be restored to the family of the one who had sold it initially.

With release of debt, rest from labor, and restoration of property, the year of Jubilee seems like a golden opportunity. And yet neither the Bible nor extra-biblical writers give any indication it was ever observed.

Before we chide the Israelites for failing to take advantage of the glorious year of Jubilee, however, we would do well to look in the mirror. If you want to experience jubilee in your own life presently, it begins with releasing people from the captivity in which you hold them because you think they let you down, disappointed, or hurt you. "For if ye forgive men their trespasses," Jesus said, "your heavenly Father will also forgive you: But if ye forgive not men their trespasses, neither will your Father forgive your trespasses" (Matthew 6:14–15). It is the one who doesn't set the debtor free who remains bound in misery. Even though you don't feel it emotionally, you can decide today to do that which Israel never did: to cancel all debts and to experience jubilee in your soul.

SEPTEMBER 12

Ye shall make you no idols nor graven image, neither rear you up a standing image, neither shall ye set up any image of stone in your land, to bow down unto it: for I am the LORD your God.

Leviticus 26:1

If you're a believer in Jesus, Satan knows he's lost your soul. But he'll seek to neutralize and nullify your witness by attacking you, by sending out his demons to cause destruction and deception. What do we do with these images, these powers that plague and haunt us? Consider the following four suggestions ...

In dealing with the entities that war against your soul, there must first of all be *realization*. We are at war. And because we're at war, there will be casualties. When a person sins, the reaction can be, "He has blown it. Shame on him." But we need to realize that he has been attacked and therefore look at him not as vicious but as a victim of the Enemy's attack.

Second, there must be *preparation*. When the disciples were unable to cast out a demon from a boy who was possessed, Jesus told them to do so required prayer and fasting (Matthew 17). Therefore, we must be prepared before the attack comes. How? I suggest one way is by fasting. Before running a marathon, runners stock up on carbohydrates. To prepare spiritually, we are to do just the opposite because something happens when we say "no" to our stomachs. Saying "no" to our appetites physically strengthens the inner man spiritually.

Third, there must be *confrontation* against these entities. We can't run from them. We must move in authority, fervency, and intensity in dealing with them. And yet all too often when we sense a spiritual attack headed our way, we just give up and get depressed. It took a shout to bring down the walls of Jericho (Joshua 6:20). It took a spoken, authoritative command to cast out demons (Mark 5:8). Thus, if we are to wage war against the demonic entities that plague us, we must confront them with authority, and at times even vocally.

Finally, we move in *expectation*, for without faith it is impossible to please God (Hebrews 11:6). We can expect to be victorious knowing that our Enemy and his hordes from hell are doomed to one day be thrown into the bottomless pit forever (Revelation 12).

The victory is ours, gang. All we have to do is take it and act upon it. May we be those who keep ourselves from idols as we recognize them, prepare for them, and confront them in the name of Jesus.

SEPTEMBER 13

And yet for all that, when they be in the land of their en-
emies, I will not cast them away, neither will I abhor them,
to destroy them utterly, and to break my covenant with
them: for I am the LORD their God. But I will for their sakes
remember the covenant of their ancestors, whom I brought
forth out of the land of Egypt in the sight of the heathen,
that I might be their God: I am the LORD.

Leviticus 26:44–45

Even in the time of captivity, even in the place of bondage which was due to their own disobedience, God says, "I won't forget or forsake My people." And that is the Word of the Lord for you and me today. God is saying, "If you walk in My law, you'll be blessed. If you wander from My law, you'll be burned. But even if you're in captivity, know this: I have not forsaken you, for lo, I am with you always" (see Matthew 28:20).

Every broken commandment, every ignored precept can be forgiven because of what Jesus did for us on Calvary. Therefore, even if we're in the land of the Enemy, God still cares about us. If we'll confess our sin to Him, if we'll call upon His name, He'll restore us once again. "If you wander from My ways, terror will come," God says. "If you walk in My ways, I'll bless you. It's your choice. The ball is in your court."

SEPTEMBER 14

And the Lord spake unto Moses in the wilderness of Sinai, in the tabernacle of the congregation.

Numbers 1:1

In Genesis, we see in the person of Abraham God's people waiting—waiting for the son promised to him, the first of a nation which was to number as the stars in the heavens, the sand on the seashore. In Exodus, we see God's people watching, as God raised up a deliverer named Moses to set them free. In Leviticus, we see God's people worshiping, as He outlined for them the way they were to commune with Him. Here in Numbers, we see God's people warring, as they organized into camps to do battle against the enemies they would encounter in the Promised Land.

It was in the wilderness that Moses heard the Word of the Lord. I point this out because sometimes when we go through a wilderness experience, although we try to extract things from the Word, although we spend time in prayer, we don't hear the voice of the Lord. All of us go through such times. But notice exactly where Moses was in the wilderness when the Lord spoke to him—he was in the tabernacle of the congregation when he heard the voice of the Lord. And I believe the best place to hear the Lord speak is still the tabernacle of the congregation, in church.

So many times in my walk when I have been dry, when I haven't heard the heart of the Lord, no sooner would I go into a church service and plop down on a back pew somewhere, than I would begin to listen and wonder, Who told this preacher what I'm going through? The Word spoke directly and specifically to my situation. I say this because sometimes we fail to remember that one of the most effective ways to study the Bible is to consistently and faithfully come to church and travel through the Word with our brothers and sisters in the Lord.

SEPTEMBER 15

But thou shalt appoint the Levites over the tabernacle of testimony, and over all the vessels thereof, and over all things that belong to it: they shall bear the tabernacle, and all the vessels thereof; and they shall minister unto it, and shall encamp round about the tabernacle.

Numbers 1:50

The tabernacle was the place wherein dwelt the *kabowd*, the glory of God—that which every person, whether he knows it or not, craves. You might think you're craving a bigger house, a faster car, or a new boyfriend. But in reality, what you're truly craving is the *kabowd*, the glory of God. And the degree to which you experience the glory of God is the degree to which you will be satisfied in this life presently. Otherwise, you'll fall into the trap of thinking you'll be content as soon as you get the next promotion—failing to understand that it is only the weight, the substance, and the glory of God that will satisfy your soul.

Here we see that the Levites—those who served in the tabernacle—had the privilege of camping closest to the place where the *kabowd* resided. The same is true today. The way to experience the presence of God is to serve—be it teaching a Sunday school class, coaching a Little League team in a way that you are an example of what it means to be a lover of God, raising your kids in the ways of God, serving as a missionary, or being involved in intercessory prayer. Jesus said whatever measure we give out will be given back to us (Matthew 7:2). And I have found this to be oh, so true. The key to experiencing the glory of God is to be involved in service, for if we only take in, we become bloated and groggy; but if we share with others what we're learning, what we've been given, and what we're experiencing, we will receive a continuous fresh supply.

SEPTEMBER 16

These are those which were numbered of the children of Israel by the house of their fathers: all those that were numbered of the camps throughout their hosts were six hundred thousand and three thousand and five hundred and fifty. But the Levites were not numbered among the children of Israel; as the LORD commanded Moses. And the children of Israel did according to all that the LORD commanded Moses: so they pitched by their standards, and so they set forward, every one after their families, according to the house of their fathers.

Numbers 2:32–34

The significance of the camping assignments for the twelve tribes seen in Numbers 2 becomes evident twenty chapters later, for in Numbers 22, we see the children of Israel, en route to the Promised Land, camped in the plain of Moab. This caused consternation in the heart of Balak, the king of Moab, for he had heard of the Israelites' victory over the Ammonites. So, in addition to forming an alliance with the Midianites, Balak persuaded Balaam, a prophet of the Lord, to curse the Israelites.

Accompanied by Balak to the top of a mountain from which he could see the entire Israelite camp, Balaam looked down to see the tabernacle in the midst with a contingent of 108,100 to the west; 186,400 to the east; 157,600 to the north; and 151,450 to the south. In other words, he would have seen the configuration of a cross. No wonder he was unable to curse the Israelites. You see, Balaam thought the Israelites were to be cursed because they were a bunch of complainers and idolaters. God, however, saw no iniquity in them because they were encamped in the cross.

And the same is true for us. Because we're encamped in the cross, because we're in Christ, we can go boldly before the throne of God today and receive what we need (Hebrews 4:16). For whatever battle you're fighting, or whatever issue you're facing, the solution is found at the throne of grace simply because you're encamped in, cleansed by, and forgiven through the cross of Calvary.

SEPTEMBER 17

These also are the generations of Aaron and Moses in the day that the LORD *spake with Moses in mount Sinai.*

Numbers 3:1

A year after Moses received the Ten Commandments on Mount Sinai, he climbed the mountain again to find God's mind, His heart, and His plan. So too, if your life feels disorganized or confused, don't look to a self-help book to solve it for you. The best thing we can do individually, as families or as a church, is to go to the mountain. Although the temptation is to reverse the order, we need to agonize in prayer before we organize a plan. When you feel scattered or out of focus, when your family is frayed by all of its activities, follow the example of Moses. Find a place where you can hear from the Lord.

SEPTEMBER 18

And the LORD *spake unto Moses, saying, And I, behold, I have taken the Levites from among the children of Israel instead of all the firstborn that openeth the matrix among the children of Israel: therefore the Levites shall be mine; because all the firstborn are mine; for on the day that I smote all the firstborn in the land of Egypt I hallowed unto me all the firstborn in Israel, both man and beast: mine shall they be: I am the* LORD.

Numbers 3:11–13

Due to the fact that He created these children, and also spared them at Passover, God owned the firstborn. In other words, they were His, not only by creative right, but also by redemptive right. It was the Lord's original intent that the firstborn of every family in each tribe be a priest. But when only the Levites came forward as those who were on the Lord's side, they became the exclusive tribe God chose to minister to Him. The men of Reuben, Gad, and Naphtali backed away, knowing they would have to deal with their friends and neighbors. The men of Judah, Benjamin, and Zebulun knew that they would have to inflict pain in order to save the nation. In the end, only one tribe was willing to say, "It's not a pleasant task, not an easy thing to do, but we're on the Lord's side and this needs to be done. So we will do it." And, as a result, they were blessed (Exodus 32:29).

In this, I understand why oftentimes we are not used to the degree we would like to be or think we ought to be. Hebrews 4:12 tells us the Word of God is quick and powerful, sharper than any two-edged sword. If the Lord so directs, am I willing to unsheathe the sword of the Word and deal with situations which are detrimental, dangerous, or diseased in the lives of friends, neighbors, or family members? Or will I be like Simeon, Issachar, and Asher who shied away?

It's one thing to say, "I'll take the sword and deal with the Jebusites, the Philistines, and the Canaanites." But will you deal with your own family, your own friends, your own co-workers? Proverbs 29:25 says the fear of man is a snare. It will trip me up. At any given moment, I am living in fear. So are you. The question is, whom do I fear? I will either be walking in the fear of God—not wanting to disappoint Him or disobey Him—or I will be walking in the fear of man—concerned about what others think of me.

The fear of man says, "I care more about you liking me than I do about you doing well." The fear of God, on the other hand, says, "You might not like this, but I'm going to tell you the truth because I care more about you doing well than I do about you not liking me."

Knowing the story of Levi, I would have thought it would be any tribe but his to step up to the task. After all, it was Levi who, along with Simeon, decided to avenge the rape of their sister Dinah by unsheathing the sword and slaying all the men of Shechem (Genesis 34), an offense of such magnitude that Simeon and Levi were cursed and denied an inheritance in the Promised Land (Genesis 49:5–7). Therefore, when Moses asked who would mete out judgment upon Israel, I would have thought Levi would have said, "Not us. We've been down this road before. We're cursed to this day. Let Reuben do it." But that's not what happened, for even though they had failed previously, Levi said, "We will do what's necessary." Amazing.

"How can I correct him?" we say. "I failed in the past the same way he's failing now." Or, "I have no right to confront her. I made the very same mistakes she's making." That's what Levi could have said. Instead, he did what Paul teaches us to do: he forgot that which was behind, pressed ahead, and did what had to be done (Philippians 3:13). As a result (although the curse remained because the Levites chose to stand for the Lord) not only would they be used in ministry, but God Himself would be their inheritance ultimately (Joshua 13:33).

SEPTEMBER 19

And thou shalt give the money, wherewith the odd number of them is to be redeemed, unto Aaron and to his sons. And Moses took the redemption money of them that were over and above them that were redeemed by the Levites: of the firstborn of the children of Israel took he the money; a thousand three hundred and threescore and five shekels, after the shekel of the sanctuary: and Moses gave the money of them that were redeemed unto Aaron and to his sons, according to the word of the LORD, as the LORD commanded Moses.

Numbers 3:49–51

The principle of redemption was to be a life for a life. In place of a life, that which most closely touched a man's life was to be offered: namely, money. Because one's work is where one invests the bulk of his time and energy, that which reveals most about someone's priorities is the way he uses his money. Talk is cheap. The proof of the pudding is not in the song I sing, but what I do when the basket goes by.

Does this mean we can purchase our salvation? No. Our salvation was already purchased, not by our own efforts or money but by the blood of Christ on the cross of Calvary (1 Peter 1:18–19). Therefore, the way we spend money—as well as the way we spend our time, talents, and every other resource given to us—should reflect that which was so freely and sacrificially spent for us when our Lord gave His life to set us free.

SEPTEMBER 20

And the LORD *spake unto Moses, saying, Command the children of Israel, that they put out of the camp every leper, and every one that hath an issue, and whosoever is defiled by the dead: Both male and female shall ye put out, without the camp shall ye put them; that they defile not their camps, in the midst whereof I dwell. And the children of Israel did so, and put them out without the camp: as the* LORD *spake unto Moses, so did the children of Israel.*

Numbers 5:1–4

Those with leprosy, those with a running issue, those defiled by contact with the dead were to be removed from the camp. Why? Not because leprosy was contagious, nor because running issues and dead bodies lead to all kinds of disease. The singular reason God gave for ridding the camp of this kind of impurity was because He dwelt in it.

The trend today in churches is that of being "seeker sensitive." To this end, we're not to sing too many songs, carry our Bibles, or talk about sin and repentance. I wholeheartedly disagree with this trend, for while we are indeed to be seeker sensitive, it is not the sinner who is the seeker, but the Father who seeks those who will worship Him in spirit and in truth (John 4:23). "Behold, I stand at the door, and knock," Jesus declares (Revelation 3:20). And here, God says, "Honor Me. Deal with the leprosy, the issues, and the defilement not only because those things will destroy you, but more importantly because I'm in the camp."

SEPTEMBER 21

*The LORD bless thee, and keep thee: The LORD make his face
shine upon thee, and be gracious unto thee: The LORD lift up
his countenance upon thee, and give thee peace.*

Numbers 6:24–26

To "lift up the countenance" simply means "to smile." Here the priests were
to say to the people, "May the Lord smile upon you and give you peace." In
the blessing of verses 24–26, we see the name of the Lord repeated three
times. In this, there is a suggestion of the Trinity. In verse 24, the reference
is to God the Father, in verse 25, to God the Son, and in verse 26, to God
the Holy Spirit.

In verse 24, we see God the Father as the Giver.

In verse 25, we see God the Son as the Revealer.

In verse 26, we see God the Holy Spirit as the Soother.

These three characteristics correspond to our needs. God is a Trinity. Made
in His image, in a sense, we are as well, for while God is Father, Son, and
Holy Spirit, we are body, soul, and spirit. The body relates to the material—
the realm where the Father blesses us physically. The soul is the mind and
the emotions—that which we think and feel. Sometimes we get confused.
Sometimes we have questions. Sometimes we're disturbed. That's where
God the Son comes in. Any issue I'm wrestling with or any struggle I'm
dealing with will ultimately find its answer in Jesus Christ. The spirit is the
deepest part of my being, the part of me that will live forever. And because
the spirit within me can lack peace, it's the Holy Spirit who inhabits my
spirit, who indwells my spirit, who communes with me in the deepest part
of my being and gives me peace.

SEPTEMBER 22

*And it came to pass on the day that Moses had fully set up
the tabernacle, and had anointed it, and sanctified it, and
all the instruments thereof, both the altar and all the vessels
thereof, and had anointed them, and sanctified them; that
the princes of Israel, heads of the house of their fathers, who
were the princes of the tribes, and were over them that were
numbered, offered: and they brought their offering before
the LORD, six covered wagons, and twelve oxen; a wagon for
two of the princes, and for each one an ox: and they brought
them before the tabernacle.*

Numbers 7:1–3

In our society, we place a high premium on fairness and equality. With that
in mind, look at our text . . .

On the day the tabernacle was dedicated and anointed, the leaders of the
tribes of Israel brought twelve oxen and six wagons as an offering to the
Lord. The wagons and oxen were divided between the three groups of
Levites. The first group, the Gershonites, were given two wagons and four
oxen. So far so good. But when the next group, the sons of Merari, was
given four wagons and eight oxen, the Gershonites must have said, "Wait
a minute. This isn't fair. We only got four oxen and two wagons." But if the
Gershonites didn't like this, imagine how the third group, the Kohathites,
felt when there was nothing left for them. "Unfair!" they must have cried.
And we do the same.

"Wait a minute," we say. "We're all called to serve God, aren't we? Why,
then, does he have four wagons and eight oxen and I have none? Look at
the position he holds, the prosperity she enjoys, the prominence they have.
Why don't I?" And then we fall into the subtle mindset that God is not
truly fair, that He plays favorites. And we're not one of them.

Why were the wagons distributed the way they were? Does God indeed
have favorites? The answer is found in a significant phrase where it says
the wagons were given according to their service (Numbers 7:5). Earlier,

we read that the sons of Gershon were in charge of the fabric and coverings of the tabernacle, to take them up and down and pack them along. But the Merarites had an even heavier load, for they were in charge of the boards, silver sockets, and bars which made up the walls of the tabernacle. In fact, those who study these things say the weight the sons of Merari carried would have been approximately twice as great as that which the sons of Gershon carried. Consequently, called to bear twice as great a burden, it makes sense the Merarites would have twice as many oxen and twice as many wagons.

Of those who appear to be more blessed than we are, we say, "Look at the wagons they have. Look at their oxen." Yes, they may have more oxen and more wagons. But they also have heavier burdens. They have obligations that you and I don't understand. God is fair. With those wagons come added responsibilities and burdens, because to whom much is given, much is required (Luke 12:48).

The Kohathites were to carry the furniture of the tabernacle—including the ark of the covenant—upon their shoulders, which speaks of intimacy, of close proximity. And now I begin to understand. Maybe I don't have four wagons or eight oxen. Maybe I don't even have two wagons and four oxen. Maybe I'm on foot. But maybe that's because the Lord knows that not having the position or possessions others have will result in a deeper intimacy than if there were oxen and wagons rumbling around.

Jesus opted for this when He said, "Foxes have holes, and the birds of the air have nests, but the Son of man hath not where to lay his head" (Matthew 8:20). The priests and Pharisees had an abundance of oxen and wagons. But Jesus chose a different direction. Yet He was so happy and so full of joy that even those with lots of oxen and wagons, so to speak, left everything to follow Him.

He was able to focus on that which mattered. And as a result, there was a sparkle in His eyes, a smile on His face, and a winsome quality to His personality which caused multitudes—of which we are a part—to want to be around Him.

If God has given you four carts and eight oxen, rejoice. But be on guard lest these blessings distract you from walking with Jesus in simplicity. Carts and oxen aren't always as good as they look. Carts lose their wheels; oxen make messes; and life becomes complicated. Thus, it is the wise man who says, "Lord, You set the agenda. You give me what You know is best for me."

My tendency would be to say, "I don't think things are fair. We're going to have a fundraising campaign to buy carts for the Kohathites." But would that truly be best for the Kohathites?

To those with no wagons and no oxen, God says, "You have Me. And I'm all you need."

SEPTEMBER 23

And the LORD spake unto Moses, saying, Take the Levites from among the children of Israel, and cleanse them. And thus shalt thou do unto them, to cleanse them: Sprinkle water of purifying upon them, and let them shave all their flesh, and let them wash their clothes, and so make themselves clean.

Numbers 8:5–7

Although Moses sprinkled water on the priests, they were to shave themselves. The first part of their cleansing was passive, the second part required their participation. So too, although I am clean positionally, I must participate in my cleansing practically. "How shall a young man cleanse his ways?" David asked. "By taking heed to the Word" (see Psalm 119:9). "Thy word have I hid in mine heart, that I might not sin against thee" (Psalm 119:11).

Positionally, I'm being cleansed every day by the blood of Jesus Christ. But practically, there's a bunch of sin in my life and the only way it will be worked out is by the working in of the Word. I've got to wash myself in the water of the Word, take in the Scriptures, meditate on the Word, listen to the Word, and learn the Word.

SEPTEMBER 24

And when the cloud was taken up from the tabernacle, then after that the children of Israel journeyed: and in the place where the cloud abode, there the children of Israel pitched their tents.

Numbers 9:17

Isaiah 63:14 tells us the cloud by day and the pillar of fire by night was the Holy Spirit. Thus, it was the Spirit of God that told the children of Israel where to stop and settle in, when to pack up and move out. Yet although we think it would be wonderful to have a visible, tangible cloud leading us, the children of Israel murmured and complained. And this shows me there's a better way to be led than by the external, the visible, or the tangible.

"I'm going to do something new," God told Jeremiah. "I'm going to write My will on the tables of the hearts of My people" (see Jeremiah 31:33).

I'm so thankful for the new covenant, for God directing us by placing impressions on our hearts. And I have found that the most satisfying, adventurous, and fulfilling life is experienced when I am led by the Spirit, as He writes His will upon my heart.

SEPTEMBER 25

Also in the day of your gladness, and in your solemn days, and in the beginnings of your months, ye shall blow with the trumpets over your burnt offerings, and over the sacrifices of your peace offerings; that they may be to you for a memorial before your God: I am the LORD your God.

Numbers 10:10

One reason the trumpets were to sound was for the purpose of celebration, to signal the feasts and festivals as well as the solemn days.

Everything in the Old Testament is an illustration of New Testament truth, and the trumpets made of silver, the metal of redemption, are no exception, for they give us understanding about that which Paul called a mystery . . .

> Behold, I shew you a mystery; We shall not all sleep, but we shall all be changed, in a moment, in the twinkling of an eye, at the last trump: for the trumpet shall sound, and the dead shall be raised incorruptible, and we shall be changed.
>
> 1 Corinthians 15:51–52

The idea of being changed is that of being metamorphosed, like caterpillars miraculously changed into butterflies. Paul says the same thing is true concerning people. We're not all going to die. But we're all going to be metamorphosed. When? At the last trumpet.

Here in Numbers 10, we see two trumpets. So too, although the Bible is filled with trumpets, there are only two trumpets of God: the first trump and the last trump. The first trump was sounded in Exodus 19 when God gathered His people at the base of Mount Sinai and gave them the Ten Commandments. It was during that convocation that Israel became a nation.

But there is a second trumpet, called the last trump. And it has not yet been heard. When it is, even as Numbers 10 illustrates, it will signal a grand convocation as the dead in Christ shall rise, and we who are alive will be caught up—or raptured—to meet the Lord in the air.

This leads us to mobilization, the second reason the trumpets were sounded here in Numbers 10. When the last trumpet sounds, we'll leave the snares and entanglements of this world behind as we pull up stakes, pack up our tents, and move on to heaven. Oh, what a glorious day that will be!

This leads us to the third reason the trumpets were sounded, for war also is part of the equation. After we are reunited and taken on our journey to our new home in heaven, Revelation 6–19 describes the war that will break out on earth during the horrendous seven-year period of the tribulation.

But this leads to celebration, the last reason the trumpet was to sound. At the end of seven years, when Jesus comes back to the earth and we come back with Him, the earth enters into a new day, a day of unparalleled peace and prosperity.

As I read Numbers 10, I realize that these folks in the wilderness were instructed to keep their ears tuned toward the sound of the trumpet. And I need to do the same in the wilderness I'm in. So do you. We need to remind others to do the same, to keep focused on eternity, to keep their ears tuned for the final trumpet which will sound on a day I believe is not far away.

SEPTEMBER 26

And Moses said unto Hobab, the son of Raguel the Midianite, Moses' father in law, We are journeying unto the place of which the LORD said, I will give it you: come thou with us, and we will do thee good: for the LORD hath spoken good concerning Israel.

Numbers 10:29

How long has it been since you took someone by the hand, looked him in the eye, and said, "You need to be saved. We're going to heaven. If you don't come with us, the alternative is awful. And on the way, we'll do you good. It will be good for you to travel with us. I know you feel more comfortable in the world, but we need you in the kingdom. Would you pray with me right now?"

Maybe you've invited your unsaved brother-in-law or your nephew to church five Christmases in a row, only to have them decline every time. But do you fully comprehend that they are going to hell unless they understand that God has prepared a mansion for them, that God places great value upon them, that they can be helpful to the believing community, that we'll be good to them? We can't let go. We can't give up. We can't stop. The stakes are too high.

One writer said, "If heaven and hell are true, nothing else matters. If heaven and hell aren't true, then nothing matters at all."

I have found that the most effective way to bring people to Jesus is not by discussing doctrine endlessly, debating evolution passionately, or even inviting them to church repeatedly. It is to share with them the way of salvation clearly and to pray with them immediately. I begin by opening my Bible and showing them Romans 3:23 . . .

> For all have sinned, and come short of the glory of God.

"You and I and everyone have fallen short of the glory, the standard, the requirement of God," I say. Then I turn a few pages to Romans 5:6 . . .

> For when we were yet without strength, in due time Christ died for the ungodly.

"When we were pulled down, wiped out, done in by sin, Christ died for us," I say. "It was when we were hopelessly lost that Christ died for you and me." Then I turn the page and show them Romans 6:23 . . .

> For the wages of sin is death; but the gift of God is eternal life through Jesus Christ our Lord.

"The wages of sin is certain death," I say. "You'll be dead in your heart internally. Your marriage will fall short of what it was supposed to be. Your family will be dead relationally. And most importantly, sin brings death eternally. But the gift of God is eternal life, which begins now and lasts through eternity." From there, I take them to Romans 8:1 . . .

> There is therefore now no condemnation to them which are in Christ Jesus, who walk not after the flesh, but after the Spirit.

"Once we change direction and follow Jesus," I explain, "we experience a resurrection of relationships and emotions as the sentence of death is removed from our lives." Finally, we turn to Romans 10:8–10 . . .

> The word is nigh thee, even in thy mouth, and in thy heart: that is, the word of faith, which we preach; that if thou shalt confess with thy mouth the Lord Jesus, and shalt believe in thine heart that God hath raised him from the dead, thou shalt be saved. For with the heart man believeth unto righteousness; and with the mouth confession is made unto salvation.

"If you confess that Jesus is Lord, you'll be saved," I tell them. "And you'll never regret it."

Known as the "Romans Road," I have found this to be a most effective way to share the gospel.

"What if they don't believe the Bible is God's Word?" you ask. "Don't you have to convince them?"

Not necessarily. When asked how to defend the Bible, C. H. Spurgeon, the "Prince of Preachers," answered, "Defend the Bible? I would just as soon defend a lion. Just turn the Bible loose. It will defend itself."

The greatest blessing on earth is to lead someone into eternal life. The Bible says that when one soul is saved, all of heaven breaks out in a cosmic celebration (Luke 15:10). And the same thing will happen in your heart. The issues, problems, and concerns facing you will suddenly matter no longer when you've seen someone take their first step toward heaven.

SEPTEMBER 27

And when the people complained, it displeased the LORD: and the LORD heard it; and his anger was kindled; and the fire of the LORD burnt among them, and consumed them that were in the uttermost parts of the camp. And the people cried unto Moses; and when Moses prayed unto the LORD, the fire was quenched. And he called the name of the place Taberah: because the fire of the LORD burnt among them.

Numbers 11:1–3

The Lord had given instruction to His people. He had appeared unto them. He had been patient with them. And now at last, the trumpets are sounding. Moses says, "Rise up, O Lord, and go before us." Now, the children of Israel are on their way, and the first thing they do is complain about something evidently so insignificant that Scripture doesn't even bother to record the reason. Oh, it must have seemed important to the Israelites at the time, but from God's perspective, it wasn't.

After hearing their complaints, it's as if the Lord gave His people something to complain about through the fire that broke out in their midst. The lesson is a good one for me because through it I understand that complaining causes confusion. If I'm complaining about something in one part of my life, a fire is sure to flare up in another part.

In his letter to the Galatians, Paul tells us that if we bite and devour one another, we ourselves will be consumed (5:15). And here at the outset of the Israelites' journey, God reminds us that we'll get burned if we're a people given to complaining.

SEPTEMBER 28

And while the flesh was yet between their teeth, ere it was chewed, the wrath of the LORD was kindled against the people, and the LORD smote the people with a very great plague. And he called the name of that place Kibroth-hattaavah: because there they buried the people that lusted. And the people journeyed from Kibroth-hattaavah unto Hazeroth; and abode at Hazeroth.

Numbers 11:33–35

Many speculate that it was actually the overindulgence of the people that brought about this plague. And they could be right . . .

They soon forgat his works; they waited not for his counsel: But lusted exceedingly in the wilderness, and tempted God in the desert. And he gave them their request; but sent leanness into their soul.

Psalm 106:13–15

The Lord sent the children of Israel that which they desired, but it killed them. That's important for me to understand. I think I know what I want, but only God sees what is truly best for me. And He promises to withhold no good thing from them who walk uprightly (Psalm 84:11). Therefore, we can be the most peaceful people on the planet because, while everyone else is trying to figure out how to get ahead and how to make it happen, we get to say, "Father, You know my situation. You know what's best for me. I trust You."

I'm so glad we don't have to figure out what's best and make our demands accordingly, but rather we can simply say, "Lord, Your will be done today," fully confident that He will do what's best.

SEPTEMBER 29

And Miriam was shut out from the camp seven days: and the people journeyed not till Miriam was brought in again. And afterward the people removed from Hazeroth, and pitched in the wilderness of Paran.

Numbers 12:15–16

After Miriam questioned Moses' authority, the Lord struck her with leprosy, and the children of Israel were unable to journey until she was healed. In one way or another, envy always holds others back. The entire congregation was stuck for seven days, waiting for Miriam to be healed of her leprous, envious condition.

The book of Romans says we are to rejoice with those who rejoice and weep with those who weep (12:15). Moses modeled this as he rejoiced for Eldad and Medad and wept for Miriam.

Do we rejoice with those who rejoice? Moses did. Envy weeps over those who rejoice and rejoices over those who weep. Moses did just the opposite. Do we?

SEPTEMBER 30

And Moses sent them to spy out the land of Canaan, and said unto them, Get you up this way southward, and go up into the mountain: And see the land, what it is; and the people that dwelleth therein, whether they be strong or weak, few or many; and what the land is that they dwell in, whether it be good or bad; and what cities they be that they dwell in, whether in tents, or in strong holds; and what the land is, whether it be fat or lean, whether there be wood therein, or not. And be ye of good courage, and bring of the fruit of the land. Now the time was the time of the firstripe grapes.

Numbers 13:17–20

Watch out, Moses. Don't send in the spies. Just step out in faith and follow the command of the Lord who promised to give you the land of destiny.

I believe Moses made a mistake the moment he sent in the spies.

"Wait," you say. "Wasn't it the Lord who told Moses to send men in to search out the land?"

In the book of Deuteronomy, we see what really happened that day . . .

And ye came near unto me every one of you, and said, We will send men before us, and they shall search us out the land, and bring us word again by what way we must go up, and into what cities we shall come. And the saying pleased me well: and I took twelve men of you, one of a tribe: and they turned and went up into the mountain, and came unto the valley of Eshcol, and searched it out.

Deuteronomy 1:22–24

The people said, "Send spies to scope out the land to which we're headed."

"Sounds good to me," Moses said of the plan which originated in the hearts of the people.

So finally, God said, "If that's what you want to do, then that's the plan."

The same thing can happen to you and me. If we set our own agenda, if we demand our own way, God very likely will say, "Okay. If that's your plan, go ahead."

That's why it's the wise man or woman who increasingly prays, "Not my will but Your will be done. Here's how I see the situation, Lord, but I lay it before You. Please adjust, modify, or correct it as You desire."

OCTOBER 1

And Caleb stilled the people before Moses, and said, Let us go up at once, and possess it; for we are well able to overcome it. But the men that went up with him said, We be not able to go up against the people; for they are stronger than we. And they brought up an evil report of the land which they had searched unto the children of Israel, saying, The land, through which we have gone to search it, is a land that eateth up the inhabitants thereof; and all the people that we saw in it are men of a great stature. And there we saw the giants, the sons of Anak, which come of the giants: and we were in our own sight as grasshoppers, and so we were in their sight.

Numbers 13:30–33

Ten spies had an evil report. Two believed God. People can't name one of the ten spies, but all of us know the names of Joshua and Caleb. Here's a key to being forgotten in history, by your family, or in the work of the kingdom: Murmur, be cynical, be a doubter, be skeptical, be a critic. Sit back and say, "This isn't right and that will never happen." On the other hand, the men, women, and congregations who leave an imprint on history are those who say, "We believe God will do great things."

Ten of the spies saw the foes.

Joshua and Caleb saw the fruit.

Ten of the spies saw the giants.

Joshua and Caleb saw God.

Ten of the spies saw the walls and their faith crumbled.

Joshua and Caleb had faith and knew the walls would crumble.

It's all a matter of perspective. We will have faith in that which we fear. The ten spies had faith in the giants because they feared them. But Joshua and Caleb feared God, and therefore, had faith in Him.

I saw a nature movie years ago in which, seeing a mountain lion headed his way, a little bear cub stood on its back legs, raised its little paws, and let forth a high-pitched growl. The mountain lion immediately stopped in his tracks, turned around, and ran away, leaving the little bear cub thinking, This is great! Look what I did! And then the camera panned back to show that standing behind the little bear was his mama—a huge grizzly!

We have a great big God standing with us who makes any giant seem like a grasshopper in comparison. The spies lifted up their eyes to the giants. Joshua and Caleb lifted them higher and saw the Father.

OCTOBER 2

And the LORD spake unto Moses and unto Aaron, saying, How long shall I bear with this evil congregation, which murmur against me? I have heard the murmurings of the children of Israel, which they murmur against me. Say unto them, As truly as I live, saith the LORD, as ye have spoken in mine ears, so will I do to you.

Numbers 14:26–28

"Would to God that we die in the wilderness," the children of Israel repeatedly said (see Numbers 14:2).

And, because life and death are in the power of the tongue (Proverbs 18:21), God said, "Okay. As you have spoken, so shall it be."

Faith and words go hand in hand, for out of the abundance of the heart, the mouth speaks (Matthew 12:34). That is why to be saved, we must believe in our hearts as well as confess with our mouths (Romans 10:9–10).

The longer I live, the more I realize that what I say has a huge impact on the unseen world around me. I'm beginning to understand more and more that if I speak critically and cynically even only to my wife, the impact is sure to boomerang back on me. Conversely, if I speak words of faith, I open the door for the Lord to work miraculously.

OCTOBER 3

And Moses said, Wherefore now do ye transgress the commandment of the LORD? but it shall not prosper. Go not up, for the LORD is not among you; that ye be not smitten before your enemies. For the Amalekites and the Canaanites are there before you, and ye shall fall by the sword: because ye are turned away from the LORD, therefore the LORD will not be with you. But they presumed to go up unto the hill top: nevertheless the ark of the covenant of the LORD, and Moses, departed not out of the camp. Then the Amalekites came down, and the Canaanites which dwelt in that hill, and smote them, and discomfited them, even unto Hormah.

Numbers 14:41–45

When God said, "Go," His people refused. Yet now they're saying, "We've learned our lesson. We're going to do it now." But God had already spoken. He had already told them they would wander forty years in the wilderness until the entire generation died.

There can be a presumption that looks like faith but in reality is folly. What's the difference between faith and presumption? Simply this: God's Word. Are you launching out because you're trying to prove your spiritual prowess, or because of some fantastic fantasy, or do you have God's Word on the matter? Faith comes by hearing and hearing by the Word of God (Romans 10:17). Therefore, it is the promise of God found in the Word of God upon which we are to stand.

OCTOBER 4

And the LORD spake unto Moses, saying, Speak unto the children of Israel, and say unto them, When ye be come into the land of your habitations . . .

Numbers 15:1–2

Even after God said that the entire generation was to die, even though He knew they wouldn't be obedient to Him, He reiterates His intention to bring His people into the Land. He doesn't say, "*If* you come into the land . . ." He says, "*When* you come into the land . . ." And to the nineteen-year-olds, sixteen-year-olds, and eight-year-olds hearing this, it would be just as God declared, for although His people could delay His blessings, they could not destroy His purpose.

So too, I can delay God's blessings in my life for forty minutes or forty hours, forty days, forty weeks, or even forty years. But I cannot delay His purpose . . .

> Having made known unto us the mystery of his will, according to his good pleasure which he hath purposed in himself: that in the dispensation of the fulness of times he might gather together in one all things in Christ, both which are in heaven, and which are on earth; even in him.

Ephesians 1:9–10

God's ultimate plan is that in the fullness of time, everything and everyone will be brought into unity in Christ, intimacy with Christ, and conformity to Christ. That is where life is going. Therefore, because God created everything to be brought together in Christ, focused on Christ, united by Christ, the degree to which I do that today will be the degree to which I will move in the same direction as all of creation. Conversely, the degree to which I do anything other than that is the degree to which I'll go against the flow of that which God has predetermined for all of creation.

It's so wonderful to relax in an inner tube in the center of the river. As you cruise along in the sun, it's refreshing and wonderful with some thrills along the way. If, on the other hand, you're trying to go upstream against the flow, it's miserable. You get tired and go nowhere.

Gang, go with the flow of what God determined all of history to do. Be one with Christ; focus on Christ; live for Christ.

OCTOBER 5

And while the children of Israel were in the wilderness, they found a man that gathered sticks upon the sabbath day. And they that found him gathering sticks brought him unto Moses and Aaron, and unto all the congregation. And they put him in ward, because it was not declared what should be done to him. And the LORD said unto Moses, The man shall be surely put to death: all the congregation shall stone him with stones without the camp. And all the congregation brought him without the camp, and stoned him with stones, and he died; as the LORD commanded Moses.

Numbers 15:32–36

Six days shall work be done, but on the seventh day there shall be to you an holy day, a sabbath of rest to the LORD: whosoever doeth work therein shall be put to death. Ye shall kindle no fire throughout your habitations upon the sabbath day.

Exodus 35:2–3

For gathering sticks to kindle a fire, the man in our text was put to death. Working on the Sabbath killed him physically just as it will kill us spiritually. You see, although I realize that Jesus died for my sins, that He paid the price, that He secured my salvation, I can mistakenly think that I need to stoke things up a bit, that I can get things hotter by my own efforts. So I begin to gather sticks by promising to pray four minutes every day and to read my Bible at least once a month. And if I do that, I can think I'm pretty hot. But, like any fire, the fire I've kindled demands more. So I find myself thinking that I better read a chapter a week and pray an hour a day, which then becomes a chapter and two hours of prayer every day and pretty soon fifteen chapters and six hours of prayer a day, until finally, I say, "I can't do this anymore. I can't follow through with these obligations and commitments. I'm so burned out, I'm going to forget the whole thing."

That's what legalism does. That's what this man in our text was doing. He should have been resting, enjoying the Sabbath—but instead he was gathering wood to stoke the fire. And he died in the process because legalism always kills (2 Corinthians 3:6). That's why the Christian life is all about grace. It's not about the sticks I gather or the fire I ignite. It's all about what Jesus did, not with sticks, but on two beams of wood that formed the cross of Calvary.

"It is finished," He said.

And so it is. The person who finally gets it is the one who is truly blessed. This person says, "I'm going to learn to receive grace graciously. I'm going to rest. Instead of trying to impress God, I'm going to enjoy Him." Our Enemy would have us believe that our Father is a stern God who over-reacts in rage to a man innocently picking up sticks, when in fact, He is a Father who wants us to rest in Him because He is a God of immeasurable grace.

OCTOBER 6

And the LORD spake unto Moses, saying, Speak unto the children of Israel, and bid them that they make them fringes in the borders of their garments throughout their generations, and that they put upon the fringe of the borders a ribband of blue: and it shall be unto you for a fringe, that ye may look upon it, and remember all the commandments of the LORD, and do them; and that ye seek not after your own heart and your own eyes, after which ye use to go a whoring: that ye may remember, and do all my commandments, and be holy unto your God. I am the LORD

your God, which brought you out of the land of Egypt, to be
your God: I am the LORD your God.

Numbers 15:37–41

Any Israelite over the age of twenty would not enter the Promised Land because, although there is forgiveness of sin, there are also repercussions; although God forgives and forgets, the scars remain. This is the message of Numbers 15, the first of ten chapters that will chronicle God's dealings with a group of people who had not only failed miserably, but who would continue to do so over the next fifty years.

And yet at the end of this chapter, God says this: "Here's what will make the wilderness wandering which you've brought upon yourselves bearable: around your garments make a border of blue." In Scripture, blue is the color of heaven. Therefore, God was essentially saying, "Never forget that you're on your way to heaven."

"Let not your heart be troubled," Jesus would echo centuries later, "Believe in God, believe also in Me. In My Father's house are many mansions" (see John 14:1–2). My heart can be troubled. So can yours. But because Jesus will never ask us to do that which He doesn't empower us to do, I don't have to let my heart be troubled. What's the key? Heaven—to think about heaven, to be focused on heaven, to be constantly aware that heaven is close at hand. The children of Israel were to have borders of blue on their hems so that when they looked down at their feet as they trudged through the wilderness, they would see a dusty border of blue, reminding them of their higher calling, their grand destination.

The same is true today. From the time I get dressed each morning until the time I undress each night, I am to see the border of blue. That is, I'm to remember that I'm headed for heaven, where all those things I wish I could redo, where all the opportunities I've missed and the mistakes I've made will be set right.

If you remove the border of blue from your garments, if you remove heaven from the equation, you'll be depressed in the wilderness, for the key to being happy and joyful on earth is to live for heaven.

OCTOBER 7

And they took every man his censer, and put fire in them, and laid incense thereon, and stood in the door of the tabernacle of the congregation with Moses and Aaron.

Numbers 16:18

Like Miriam before them, Korah, Dathan, and Abiram questioned Moses' position of authority. That they, along with two hundred fifty leaders, came to the tabernacle with censers in hand indicates that they thought they had a case, they thought they would be vindicated, and they thought God would justify their rebellion.

As I look back over my life, I am amazed by the times I thought I was right only to find out how wrong I was. "We all see through a glass darkly," Paul said (see 1 Corinthians 13:12). And perhaps he understood this better than anyone. "I know this is the right thing to do," he no doubt said as he dragged Christians from their homes, believing they were ruining Judaism and polluting the people of God. What a shock it must have been when, on his way to Damascus one day to imprison more believers, he was knocked to the ground. In that moment, this intellectual giant, this spiritually passionate man, must have realized that he had been absolutely, completely, and 100 percent wrong (Acts 9).

Korah, Dathan, and Abiram thought they were right, but what they failed to factor into the equation was God's sovereignty. God is on the throne. God is in control. Therefore, it's not up to us to pull people down or prop people up. Sometimes I mistakenly think, "I need to straighten this guy out or pull that group down because if it's gonna happen, it's up to me."

God, however, says, "Promotion does not come from the east, the west, or the south. I am the Lord who raises up one and puts down the other" (see Psalm 75:6–7).

It's a great day when a person finally realizes that because God is on the throne and is in control, he can simply say, "Lord, You're the One who will raise up one and put down another, be it the boss of my company or the leaders of our country. Therefore, I'm going to be submitted to You as I submit to those in authority over me."

We can't learn to be humble without being humiliated, to be forgiving without being wronged, to be sweet without bitter experiences. Therefore God uses people and situations in our lives to allow us to experience these things personally rather than just to propound them philosophically.

OCTOBER 8

And it came to pass, that on the morrow Moses went into the tabernacle of witness; and, behold, the rod of Aaron for the house of Levi was budded, and brought forth buds, and bloomed blossoms, and yielded almonds. And Moses brought out all the rods from before the LORD unto all the children of Israel: and they looked, and took every man his rod. And the LORD said unto Moses, Bring Aaron's rod again before the testimony, to be kept for a token against the rebels; and thou shalt quite take away their murmurings from me, that they die not.

Numbers 17:8–10

Not only did Aaron's rod blossom, but it yielded fruit. So too, no one before Jesus and no one since Him has borne the fruit of the Spirit like He did. He perfectly personified a love characterized by joy, peace, and longsuffering; gentleness, goodness, and faith; and meekness and temperance (Galatians 5:22).

Second, we can recognize those to whom we are to be linked, those to whom we are to listen, those to whom we are to submit by the presence of the fruit of the Spirit in their lives.

Mom and Dad, if you're wishing you had more impact on your teenage daughter or junior high grandson, the key is not to beat them with the rod, but to let them see your passion for God, to let them see the fruit of the

Spirit in your life. Kids and adults alike can sense if a person is walking with the Lord and is full of the Spirit because such a life manifests itself in love.

When you have decisions to make about people who claim to have authority, remember Numbers 17 and look for the budding, the blossoming, and the fruit.

OCTOBER 9

And Moses did so: as the LORD *commanded him, so did he. And the children of Israel spake unto Moses, saying, Behold, we die, we perish, we all perish. Whosoever cometh any thing near unto the tabernacle of the* LORD *shall die: shall we be consumed with dying?*

Numbers 17:11–13

God's Word is very dangerous. Why? Because Hebrews 4:12 says it is living and powerful, sharper than any two-edged sword. No wonder, then, that we feel cut up. The Word divides the soul and the spirit—my intellect and emotions from my true self that will live forever. It divides my joints and marrow, an act that, if done physically, would immobilize and kill me. It divides the thoughts and intents of my heart, as it gets to the center of any given matter.

No wonder when I hear or read the Word, I can feel pierced and poked, sliced and diced. That's what the Word does, not only to those who hear it, but to those who speak it . . .

> Mistakenly thinking Jeremiah was coming down on them, the people captured him and threw him into a pit. "That's it," Jeremiah said. "I quit. I'm tired of the pit. Enough is enough. I will speak no more in the name of the Lord" . . . until the Word was like fire in his bones and he couldn't keep quiet (see Jeremiah 20:9).

We've all felt that way. When you share the Word, you can be convicted by the very things you share. Because the Word is a two-edged sword, it cuts both ways. Yes, it comforts, inspires, and delights. But because it's a two-edged sword, it also pierces and penetrates, prods and provokes.

"Shall we be consumed in dying?" the children of Israel asked.

The answer is "Yes."

Jesus said, "If any man come after Me, let him deny himself, take up his cross, die daily, and follow Me" (see Luke 9:23).

"I die daily," said Paul (1 Corinthians 15:31).

The flesh must die before the Spirit can live. And because my flesh seems to reawaken every day, like Paul, I must die daily.

How?

The only way I know to deal with the flesh is with the sword of the Spirit. That's why I need to allow the Word to kill my flesh day after day. And as it does, like the resurrected Jesus, I find I am able to walk through walls and locked doors (John 20:26).

"My son won't talk to me," a father sighs.

"My daughter has shut me out," a mother cries.

"My wife has locked the door," says a weary husband.

"He's built a wall," says the devastated wife.

I suggest that when I allow my flesh to be sliced and diced by the piercing and poking of the Word every day, although it's painful in some ways, humbling and difficult in others, the end result is that I have entry into places I would never have had otherwise. High walls, locked doors, and pulled shades begin to open as my critical, cynical, and harsh nature softens, giving me access into places that were previously closed.

I'm convinced it's our own flesh that keeps us out of places we long to enter. There's no resurrection without death. There's no Easter Sunday without Good Friday. There's no way to enter in without first being broken down. It's a process that must happen daily and continually. And the way it happens is through the Word of God very simply, very powerfully, and very definitely.

OCTOBER 10

And the LORD spake unto Aaron, Behold, I also have given thee the charge of mine heave offerings of all the hallowed things of the children of Israel; unto thee have I given them by reason of the anointing, and to thy sons, by an ordinance for ever. This shall be thine of the most holy things, reserved from the fire: every oblation of theirs, every meat offering of theirs, and every sin offering of theirs, and every trespass offering of theirs, which they shall render unto me, shall be most holy for thee and for thy sons. In the most holy place shalt thou eat it; every male shall eat it: it shall be holy unto thee.

Numbers 18:8–10

Concerning the offerings given to the Lord, He said to those who were serving Him, "This has been offered to Me, but now I'm giving it to you." That is, when a heave offering was made, God didn't receive it physically, but rather gave it to the priests. And when a sin offering or trespass offering was made, although a portion of it went up in smoke to the Lord, the majority of meat remained and was given to the priests.

In offering meat to the Lord on behalf of the people, the priests themselves would be fed. That's always the way it is. If you feel like you're not being fed, teach Sunday school, start a Bible study at work, disciple someone, have family devotions. The priests would be fed to the degree they fed others. And the principle is still true.

OCTOBER 11

Then came the children of Israel, even the whole congregation, into the desert of Zin in the first month: and the people abode in Kadesh; and Miriam died there, and was buried there. And there was no water for the congregation:

and they gathered themselves together against Moses and against Aaron. And the people chode with Moses, and spake, saying, Would God that we had died when our brethren died before the Lord! And why have ye brought up the congregation of the Lord into this wilderness, that we and our cattle should die there? And wherefore have ye made us to come up out of Egypt, to bring us in unto this evil place? it is no place of seed, or of figs, or of vines, or of pomegranates; neither is there any water to drink.

Numbers 20:1–5

Look at what the children of Israel said when they were here at Kadesh thirty-eight years earlier . . .

And all the children of Israel murmured against Moses and against Aaron: and the whole congregation said unto them, Would God that we had died in the land of Egypt! or would God we had died in this wilderness! And wherefore hath the Lord brought us unto this land, to fall by the sword, that our wives and our children should be a prey? were it not better for us to return into Egypt?

Numbers 14:2–3

This sobers me because I realize it is possible for a man or congregation to murmur or complain in the same way we murmured or complained a generation earlier. When we're younger, we think we'll outgrow certain tendencies. "When I'm seventy, I'm going to be a patriarch," we tell ourselves. "My family will highly esteem me. People will want to listen to me. Sure, I'm busy now at age thirty-five or forty. But when I'm seventy, I'll have made a mark spiritually."

Time itself does not make one mature. The only way we will be wise at age seventy is to make wise decisions at age forty. You're making that choice by studying the Word right now, for God has determined that people grow in wisdom by taking heed to His Word chapter by chapter, verse by verse. How I pray that if the Lord tarries, I will not be as foolish at age seventy as I am now. "Lord," I pray, "deepen me." How does that happen? By spending time in and obeying the Word.

OCTOBER 12

And the LORD spake unto Moses, saying, Take the rod, and gather thou the assembly together, thou, and Aaron thy brother, and speak ye unto the rock before their eyes; and it shall give forth his water, and thou shalt bring forth to them water out of the rock: so thou shalt give the congregation and their beasts drink. And Moses took the rod from before the LORD, as he commanded him. And Moses and Aaron gathered the congregation together before the rock, and he said unto them, Hear now, ye rebels; must we fetch you water out of this rock?

Numbers 20:7–10

Without question, Moses was one of the greatest men in history. He had an awesome responsibility. He led 3 million people out of slavery on a journey toward the land of their destiny. He also had a glorious opportunity, for he heard from the Lord directly (Numbers 12:8). Moses was a uniquely blessed and godly man, but he was still a man. And here we see the humanity of Moses in what would be his greatest sin.

If you were to ask Moses' contemporaries what his great sin was, some would point to his murder of the Egyptian in Exodus 2. Others might point to his failure to tend his own children in Exodus 4. Others might point to his marriage to the Ethiopian woman in Numbers 12. But none of those things disqualified Moses in the way this sin does.

The people were thirsty. They were murmuring. They wanted water to drink. In response, God told Moses to take the rod that had blossomed and budded three chapters earlier and to *speak* to the rock. Moses took the rod but then looked at the people and called them rebels. In the Greek Septuagint, the word translated "rebels" is *moros*, from which we get the word "moron." "You morons, must we fetch you water?" Moses cried as he *struck* the rock twice (see verse 11).

And although God provided water, He said, "Because of this, Moses, you will not be allowed into the Promised Land."

Moses had been leading this congregation for decades. He had put up with the murmuring, the complaining, the sin of 3 million people. How, then, can it be that God would disqualify him when he's so close to the finish line? What was the sin Moses committed that marred his record? The sin was obviously related to anger. We know this not only from the context, but from the Psalms . . .

> They angered him also at the waters of strife, so that it went ill with Moses for their sakes: because they provoked his spirit, so that he spake unadvisedly with his lips.
>
> Psalm 106:32–33

As I read the Bible, I understand that the point of a man's greatest strength is more often than not the point of his greatest failure. Known for his meekness, which the Greeks defined as "strength under control," Moses failed when he lost control and lost his temper. Peter was a man known for his courage, as one who walked on water in the midst of a storm and who chopped off Malchus' ear. But where did he fail? He failed when he became a coward before a servant girl (Matthew 26:69). Job was a man who was abundantly patient, and yet he was rebuked by the Lord for a lack of patience (Job 40). David was a man after God's heart, a lover of God, and yet he fell because he lusted after a woman (2 Samuel 11). Unlike the others around him, Noah was a righteous man, yet he failed when he got drunk in his tent (Genesis 9:21).

The same is true of us. Where we think we are strongest will be the point of our greatest vulnerability. If you think your marriage is so strong that you will never be in danger, be careful. If you think you have so much integrity that you would never cheat on your taxes, wait a minute. If you think you're so honest that you would never tell a lie, beware. Where I'm weak, I'm aware of my vulnerability. I know I've got to pray about it. I know I've got to keep my guard up. But when I think I'm together, I fail to pray and I don't watch as carefully as I ought to. I rely on my own strength, not realizing that my own strength is limited.

OCTOBER 13

And Moses lifted up his hand, and with his rod he smote the rock twice: and the water came out abundantly, and the congregation drank, and their beasts also. And the LORD spake unto Moses and Aaron, Because ye believed me not, to sanctify me in the eyes of the children of Israel, therefore ye shall not bring this congregation into the land which I have given them.

Numbers 20:11–12

Moses misrepresented the nature and character of the Father. In blowing his top, Moses signaled to the people that God must be angry with them. But He wasn't. Psalm 103 says our Father has compassion on us, remembering our frames, knowing that we are dust. Our God is a God of incredible mercy, a Father of intense compassion. And because Moses misrepresented Him, he would not be able to lead the congregation into the Land of Promise.

> Moreover, brethren, I would not that ye should be ignorant, how that all our fathers were under the cloud, and all passed through the sea; and were all baptized unto Moses in the cloud and in the sea; and did all eat the same spiritual meat; and did all drink the same spiritual drink: for they drank of that spiritual Rock that followed them: and that Rock was Christ.

1 Corinthians 10:1–4

When the children of Israel began their journey, God told Moses to smite the rock. And out of the rock came water (Exodus 17:6). The Rock is Christ. Christ was smitten once, never to be smitten again. Yes, our sin demanded the Rock be smitten. But He died once for all—for all sin, for all time, for all men. The price has been paid, and now Moses was to speak to the rock. The rock was only to be smitten once because Christ's sacrifice is sufficient. But Moses ruined the picture by striking the rock again.

It's not our job to beat people up or straighten them out. Yes, we are to share the truth with them in love, but anger or bitterness will disqualify us from true leadership, for the wrath of man never works the righteousness of God (James 1:20). Moses no doubt thought, "This is it. It's been almost forty years and these people never stop complaining. Certainly, God, You must have had it up to here with Your people." God's mercy, however, is inexhaustible. It extends all the way to the heavens (Psalm 36:5).

"Your mercies are new every morning," the prophet proclaimed (see Lamentations 3:22–23). Like Moses, we can think God surely must be exhausted, upset, or angry with us and the rest of the sinners surrounding us. But He's not. His mercy is new every morning, and where sin abounds, grace abounds much more (Romans 5:20).

OCTOBER 14

And the LORD sent fiery serpents among the people, and they bit the people; and much people of Israel died.

Numbers 21:6

Why would it be here—only weeks away from their entering the Promised Land—that God would have poisonous serpents bite His people? Because if they're not taught in the wilderness, they will be distraught in the Land of Promise. So too, God is willing to go to great extremes to get us to understand that if we're not happy today, we'll not be happy tomorrow regardless of what comes our way or where we might be. Happiness is an inside job.

God allows His children to feel a lot of pain and even to die in order that they might see and understand that He is with them, that He is enough for them, that He will take care of them. If they don't learn to quit their complaining here, they'll not experience His presence even in the Land of Promise.

How about you? Has it been a week of complaining? Have you heard yourself say, "This is hard right now, but as soon as I get the job or as soon as I retire, as soon as she marries me or as soon as my wife leaves me, as soon as we have kids or as soon as the kids move out, I'll be happy"?

If you're not happy today, you'll not be happy tomorrow unless you get to the root issue. We get so deceived about this. We think we're going to be happy "just as soon as," but "just as soon as" never comes.

OCTOBER 15

And the Lord said unto Moses, Make thee a fiery serpent, and set it upon a pole: and it shall come to pass, that every one that is bitten, when he looketh upon it, shall live. And Moses made a serpent of brass, and put it upon a pole, and it came to pass, that if a serpent had bitten any man, when he beheld the serpent of brass, he lived.

Numbers 21:8–9

What does this mean? Jesus explained it perfectly . . .

"Master, I know no man can do the works You do except God be with Him," Nicodemus said to Jesus.

"Truly, I say unto you, unless a man is born again, he cannot see the kingdom of God," Jesus answered, as if to say, "Let's not talk about miracles, Nicodemus. I want to get to the root: you must be born again."

"Born again?" Nicodemus asked. "Can a man enter into his mother's womb a second time?"

"That which is born of flesh is flesh, but that which is born of Spirit is spirit," Jesus said. And then He reached back to this story in Numbers 21 when He said, "And as Moses lifted up the serpent in the wilderness, even so must the Son of Man be lifted up: that whosoever believeth in him should not perish, but have eternal life" (John 3).

Jesus likens Himself to the serpent—the very creature that caused Eve to question God's goodness in the garden of Eden. Why? Because He who knew no sin would be made sin for us that we might be made the righteousness of God in Him (2 Corinthians 5:21).

Here in Numbers 21, there were no doubt those who said, "You're telling me all I have to do to be healed is look at a pole and see a brass snake? What good will that do? I need some anti-venom." Or, "If I can get the right prescription, I can get over this infection." And, because of their stubbornness, they would die unnecessarily.

So too, there are people today who will not look to the One who hung on the pole of the cross. "All I need is some Prozac," they say, or "a beer, or a hot fudge sundae. All I need is something to fill up the hole in my soul."

God said the only thing we must do is to realize we've been bitten and look to the serpent—the Son of Man—on the cross. The one who does so will be made whole. It's just that simple.

OCTOBER 16

. . . And at the stream of the brooks that goeth down to the dwelling of Ar, and lieth upon the border of Moab. And from thence they went to Beer: that is the well whereof the LORD spake unto Moses, Gather the people together, and I will give them water. Then Israel sang this song, Spring up, O well; sing ye unto it: the princes digged the well, the nobles of the people digged it, by the direction of the lawgiver, with their staves. And from the wilderness they went to Mattanah.

Numbers 21:15–18

The children of Israel sang and water gushed forth. That's always the way it is. When we come to dry times and difficult days in our pilgrimage, we can either choose to murmur or to make music.

> Sing, O barren, thou that didst not bear; break forth into singing, and cry aloud, thou that didst not travail with child: for more are the children of the desolate than the children of the married wife, saith the LORD.

Isaiah 54:1

"Are you barren?" the Lord asks you and me. "I don't want you to grumble about your situation. I want you to sing." An overriding principle seen throughout the Word is that when people are in barren conditions or dry times, power and blessing are released when they choose not to murmur but to praise the Lord. The children of Israel did this, water gushed forth, and they moved on.

OCTOBER 17

And God came unto Balaam at night, and said unto him, If the men come to call thee, rise up, and go with them; but yet the word which I shall say unto thee, that shalt thou do. And Balaam rose up in the morning, and saddled his ass, and went with the princes of Moab. And God's anger was kindled because he went.

Numbers 22:20–22

Why was God's anger kindled? Hadn't He told Balaam to go? When, like Balaam, we beg and insist on our own way, God might say, "Okay." But it's not necessarily His plan or His will.

If you're a parent, you will sometimes let your kids go the way they insist on going, even though you know there will be needless pain and heartache down the road. Sometimes God will do the same with His children. That's why the "name-it-and-claim-it" movement is so frightening to me. I don't want to name and claim anything God knows isn't best for me. I want to pray like Jesus: "Father, . . . not my will, but thine, be done" (Luke 22:42).

OCTOBER 18

And the Lord spake unto Moses, saying, Unto these the land shall be divided for an inheritance according to the number of names. To many thou shalt give the more inheritance, and to few thou shalt give the less inheritance: to every one shall his inheritance be given according to those that were numbered of him. Notwithstanding the land shall be divided by lot: according to the names of the tribes of their fathers they shall inherit. According to the lot shall the possession thereof be divided between many and few.

Numbers 26:55–56

Although the size of the tribe would determine the size of the property given them, the location of the property would be determined by lot, by "drawing straws."

I find the combination of verses 53 to 54, and 55 to 56 fascinating because in the former we see Jesus' parable of the pounds (Luke 19:12–27), in which servants were rewarded according to what they did with an equal number of pounds given to each of them, while in the latter, we see Jesus' parable of the talents (Matthew 25:14–30), in which the servants were rewarded according to what they did with the differing amounts given sovereignly to them. Thus, man's free will and God's sovereignty both enter into the equation.

OCTOBER 19

And the Lord spake unto Moses, saying, The daughters of Zelophehad speak right.

Numbers 27:6–7

Because their father had died, leaving no male inheritor, the daughters of

Zelophehad came to Moses, saying, "It's unfair that we receive no inheritance simply because we have no brother to claim it." In saying that the daughters of Zelophehad were right, is the Lord implying that He neglected to address the question of a lack of a male inheritor, that He simply forgot to put it in the law? Obviously not. I believe the Lord purposely leaves some things unsaid in the Word in order that we might go to Him for further instruction.

When I was younger, I basically thought the Trinity consisted of God the Father, God the Son, and God the Holy Bible. I didn't understand that the real key to vibrant Christianity, to a radical faith, lies in the new covenant, where the Lord says, "I will write My will upon the table of your heart" (see Jeremiah 31:33).

Why was it that the whole known world was impacted, turned upside down by a group of believers who didn't have a single page of the New Testament? It was because even though they didn't have the gospel of Luke or the epistle to the Romans, they knew how to listen to the promptings of the Holy Spirit. And as a result, miracles happened and blessings flowed.

We will be the most radical group of believers in the world to the degree that we say, "Lord, lead me today. Write Your will upon my heart; confirm it by Your Word. And what You tell me, I will do."

OCTOBER 20

And when thou hast seen it, thou also shalt be gathered unto thy people, as Aaron thy brother was gathered. For ye rebelled against my commandment in the desert of Zin, in the strife of the congregation, to sanctify me at the water before their eyes: that is the water of Meribah in Kadesh in the wilderness of Zin.

Numbers 27:13–14

"Your time is about up," God says to His friend, Moses. "It is time for you to be gathered to your people, to be taken to heaven. But first I want you to climb Mount Nebo, where I will show you the Promised Land."

In this, we see both the grace and the discipline of God. God's grace allowed Moses to view the Promised Land. But because he had sinned in misrepresenting God to the people as he struck the rock at Meribah (Numbers 20:11), he would not be able to enter it.

The older I get, the more I realize that although God is indeed gracious and full of mercy, a Father who is inexpressibly patient and kind, there are definite, absolute repercussions of sin. This is why the Bible says the fear of the Lord is the beginning of wisdom (Proverbs 9:10). We ought to walk in the fear of God—not afraid of Him, but afraid of the repercussions of our sin.

OCTOBER 21

And Moses did as the LORD commanded him: and he took Joshua, and set him before Eleazar the priest, and before all the congregation: and he laid his hands upon him, and gave him a charge, as the LORD commanded by the hand of Moses.

Numbers 27:22–23

Called a minister, or servant, of Moses (Joshua 1:1), Joshua played second fiddle to Moses. For forty years, he simply served as number two, faithful in whatever he was to do. "Moreover it is required in stewards, that a man be found faithful," Paul declared (1 Corinthians 4:2). Many want to be men of faith. But rarer, and perhaps more important, is to be a faithful man. Joshua was just that. And in due season, after forty years of faithfulness, God tapped him on the shoulder.

God does that with us, too. It might take forty years, but if we faithfully plug away at what God has called us to do—big or small, noticed or unnoticed—He will tap us on the shoulder one day and say, "You've served faithfully. Now is the time for greater ministry."

OCTOBER 22

And the LORD *spake unto Moses, saying, Command the children of Israel, and say unto them, My offering, and my bread for my sacrifices made by fire, for a sweet savour unto me, shall ye observe to offer unto me in their due season.*

Numbers 28:1–2

It's interesting that the Lord calls the savor of the sacrifices sweet, because if you have ever smelled a burning bull or cow—the hide, the hair, the entire animal, as would be the case in the burnt offering—the odor is anything but sweet. Yet, whenever the flesh is placed upon the altar, it's always sweet to the Father. The flesh speaks of our inclination toward self. Thus, there is nothing sweeter to God than when I lay my flesh on the altar and let it burn.

Why?

Because it sets me free. God knows that sin is only pleasurable for a season (Hebrews 11:25). Consequently, whenever He smells the burning of the flesh, it's sweet to Him because He knows the one making such an offering is set free. "To be carnally, or fleshly, minded is death," Paul writes. "But to be spiritually minded is life and peace" (see Romans 8:6). Do you want to really live, to have abundant peace? Then put your flesh on the altar and be set free.

OCTOBER 23

And ye shall offer a burnt offering, a sacrifice made by fire, of a sweet savour unto the LORD; *thirteen young bullocks, two rams, and fourteen lambs of the first year; they shall be without blemish.*

Numbers 29:13

From the sacrifice of a single lamb in the morning and in the evening, seen in Numbers 28:4, the sacrifice grew to over a ton of flour, one thousand gallons of wine and oil, thirteen thousand oxen, and sixty thousand sheep given annually (Numbers 29:13–39).

"That's an awful lot of giving," you say, "a huge sacrifice."

Wait a minute. Suppose my nine-year-old son Benjamin said to me, "Daddy, can I have ten dollars to get you a Father's Day gift?"

"Sure," I say, and give him a crisp ten dollar bill.

Father's Day morning, sure enough, I get a homemade card from Benny and inside the card is the crisp ten dollar bill.

"Thanks Ben!" I would say excitedly—even though I gave him the money to give to me.

That the Israelites gave thousands of livestock, a ton of flour, and thousands of gallons of wine and oil meant that God had blessed them with these things in the first place. As I did with Benny, God provided His people with everything they would give back to Him.

So too, God gave us all that we have, all that we are. If we lay down our lives for God, it's only because He gave them to us in the first place.

OCTOBER 24

And Moses told the children of Israel according to all that the LORD commanded Moses.

Numbers 29:40

As God is getting His people organized and developing them for their destiny, the sacrificial system is recorded. That is, a lamb was to be sacrificed every morning, every evening, every day. Weekly, an additional lamb was to be sacrificed. Monthly, a greater sacrifice was to be made at the beginning of each month. Annually, there were feasts with accompanying sacrifices that God's people were to celebrate.

In this, I understand that there is a rhythm to spiritual life. Many people have a hard time with this because they view spiritual life as being random. But as we look at God's calendar, it's impossible to deny its rhythm. Therefore, wise is the man, woman, or family who understands God's heart is for us to begin and end our days focused on the Lamb—unlocking the blessings for the day in the morning, closing up the blessings securely in the evening.

In addition, one day a week should be set aside to make twice the expenditure—to be focused on God singularly, offering to Him the day in praise, worship, and fellowship.

In addition, at the beginning of the month, we have opportunity to get away and say, "What's on Your heart for me for the coming month, Lord?" as we carve out time for refreshment and review, for vision and correction.

In addition, the children of Israel observed seven feasts that drew their hearts and minds back to God's goodness to them, to His faithful provision for them. When the people of Israel followed this pattern, they did well. When they deviated from it, they stumbled. God is not wasting pages in His Word to go over arcane, meaningless sacrifices. No, He's teaching us and reminding us that this is the way our lives will count.

Is there a pattern, a rhythm to your spiritual life? Or are you one who is haphazard and inconsistent? As much as we may not like to hear it, God designed us to be disciplined. Therefore, if you want to be prosperous and productive in claiming the promises of the Spirit-filled life, listen to what God told His people on the eve of their entrance into the Promised Land. Follow the pattern, the rhythm of spiritual life as seen here in the book which tells us how to make our lives count, the book of Numbers.

OCTOBER 25

And Moses spake unto the heads of the tribes concerning the children of Israel, saying, This is the thing which the LORD hath commanded. If a man vow a vow unto the LORD, or swear an oath to bind his soul with a bond; he shall not break his word, he shall do according to all that proceedeth out of his mouth.

Numbers 30:1–2

To prepare the children of Israel for the battles that faced them in the Promised Land, in the chapter before us, God deals with the subject of accountability and integrity. After all, if you're headed into battle, it's imperative that the guy next to you means what he says when he declares, "Go one hundred yards ahead and I'll cover you." You've got to be sure that he's not going to change his mind, that he'll come through.

God is serious about vows, promises, and commitments. And that makes me happy because God doesn't hold us to a higher standard than that to which He holds Himself. Therefore, the fact that God tells us we are to keep our word means He keeps His. The Bible is packed with promises—at the very least, three hundred in number. God makes promise after promise to you and me. And what He says, He will do. He told us, for example, that if we believe on Him, we'll not perish but have everlasting life (John 3:16). That's a promise He makes and a promise He will keep.

OCTOBER 26

But if he shall any ways make them void after that he hath heard them; then he shall bear her iniquity. These are the statutes, which the LORD commanded Moses, between a man and his wife, between the father and his daughter, being yet in her youth in her father's house.

Numbers 30:15–16

In Numbers 30 we see God holding men to their word, but making exceptions for women. Is this chauvinistic discrimination? No. It's a wonderful illustration. You see, on one hand, God wants me to be a man of integrity. On the other hand, as the bride of Christ, we are all women. And we have a husband who ever lives to make intercession for us, who steps up, steps in, who's at the right hand of the Father as an Advocate for us (1 John 2:1).

Tempted in all points like us (Hebrews 4:15), Jesus understands our pressures, our frailties, our infirmities, and our desires to keep promises, but He also understands our inability to do so. So He steps in, intercedes, and intervenes on our behalf. It's a wonderful picture and illustration.

This is exactly what happened in Luke 22 . . .

Only hours before He was to be crucified, Jesus told Peter that he would deny Him.

"Not me," Peter argued. "Lord, even if everyone else denies You, I won't. I'll die alongside of You, if it comes to that. You can count on me" (see verse 33).

Hearing Peter's heart, but also knowing he couldn't do what he promised, Jesus said, "Satan has desired to sift you like wheat. But I have prayed for you that your faith fail not. And when you make it through, strengthen the brothers" (see verses 31–32).

From there, Peter would eventually find himself in Jerusalem, preaching at the service in which three thousand were saved (Acts 2:41). Because Jesus prayed for the man who made a vow he couldn't keep, thousands were saved.

You have a friend in Jesus Christ. You have a Bridegroom who knows all about your fickleness. You have One who steps up and steps in on your behalf, who ever lives to make intercession for you (Hebrews 7:25). No matter what vows you have made at any given time, Jesus will see you through. He promised to, and He keeps every promise perfectly. If, however, you turn your back on Him, walk away from Him, and are no longer covered by Him, you're on your own.

Numbers 30 has much to say about integrity, but also about our security as the bride of Christ.

OCTOBER 27

And the Lord spake unto Moses, saying, Avenge the children of Israel of the Midianites: afterward shalt thou be gathered unto thy people.

Numbers 31:1–2

Moses had already been told he was about to die (Numbers 27:12–13). Here, however, the Lord gives him another assignment—to do battle with the Midianites, the people who followed the counsel of Balaam and caused the Israelites to fall.

Hope deferred makes the heart sick (Proverbs 13:12). Therefore, God is a good Father who doesn't want us to be under the illusion that somehow, someday everything will be hunky dory. It doesn't work that way. There are battles until the day we go to heaven. "Moses," God said, "you're going to heaven, but before you do, there's a battle to fight."

So too, we battle against our flesh, against the world's system, and against our Enemy every day until the day we die. This is a key to spiritual maturity, for once we understand this, we'll not be disappointed or depressed by hope deferred.

OCTOBER 28

*And Eleazar the priest said unto the men of war which went to the battle, This is the ordinance of the law which the L*ORD *commanded Moses; only the gold, and the silver, the brass, the iron, the tin, and the lead, every thing that may abide the fire, ye shall make it go through the fire, and it shall be clean: nevertheless it shall be purified with the water of separation: and all that abideth not the fire ye shall make go through the water. And ye shall wash your clothes on the seventh day, and ye shall be clean, and afterward ye shall come into the camp.*

Numbers 31:21–24

The spoils the Israelites had taken from the Midiantes—the gold, silver, brass, and iron—were to be purified by fire and water. So too, in the war we wage daily, everything we have, everything we are must be purified by the trials of fire and by the truth of the water of the Word.

I will not know what is gold, silver, and precious stones versus what is wood, hay, and stubble in my life until I go through trials, for they alone reveal to me where my heart is.

"Abraham, take your son, your only son whom you love, and offer him as a sacrifice to Me," God said. Abraham obeyed, took Isaac to Mount Moriah, put him on the altar, and was ready to plunge the knife in his hand into the chest of his son (Genesis 22:1–10).

"Lay not thine hand upon the lad," God then said, "neither do thou any thing unto him; for now I know that thou fearest God, seeing thou hast not withheld thy son, thine only son from me" (Genesis 22:12).

The result of this incredible trial: Abraham knew that God knew that he loved God more than he loved his son.

How are we purified? By the water of the Word (Psalm 119:9). And we'll see the results by how we react in the trials we face.

OCTOBER 29

And Moses and Eleazar the priest took the gold of them, even all wrought jewels. And all the gold of the offering that they offered up to the LORD, of the captains of thousands, and of the captains of hundreds, was sixteen thousand seven hundred and fifty shekels. (For the men of war had taken spoil, every man for himself.) And Moses and Eleazar the priest took the gold of the captains of thousands and of hundreds, and brought it into the tabernacle of the congregation, for a memorial for the children of Israel before the LORD.

Numbers 31:51–54

The men of war brought 420 pounds of gold to the tabernacle as a memorial to the Lord. We talk a lot about making memories with our kids and our families. But these men made a memory for God. "You've been so good to us," they said. "Let this be a memory for You."

I read this and I say, "Make me that kind of man, Lord—a man who makes memories for You. I'm so calloused and cold. Circumcise my heart. Let me see what You've done for me and my family."

I miss my daughter Jessie. Oh, I'm so glad she's in heaven. And I'm glad for the memories we have. But I miss her a lot. If you have a daughter you're able to tuck in tonight, who's still with you, you need to be thankful. Maybe you've had a bad day, or you are going through hard times; but if you can tuck your daughter in, it's time for you to make a memory for the Lord, a memorial unto Him. It's time for you to bring Him the jewels and gold of thanksgiving and praise for His abundant goodness to you.

OCTOBER 30

And Moses said unto them, If ye will do this thing, if ye will go armed before the LORD to war, and will go all of you armed over Jordan before the LORD, until he hath driven out his enemies from before him, and the land be subdued before the LORD: then afterward ye shall return, and be guiltless before the LORD, and before Israel; and this land shall be your possession before the LORD. But if ye will not do so, behold, ye have sinned against the LORD: and be sure your sin will find you out. Build you cities for your little ones, and folds for your sheep; and do that which hath proceeded out of your mouth.

Numbers 32:20–24

Because God will never take us one step further in our spiritual lives than we want to go, Moses agreed to Reuben's and Gad's proposal, but warned them that if they didn't live up to their agreement, their sin would find them out.

This is a pivotal, foundational principle. Notice Moses didn't say it was God who would track them down, do them in, find them out. No, should Reuben and Gad fail to keep their end of the bargain, it was their sin that would find them out. And the same is true with us.

Due to the finished work of the cross, God not only forgives our sin, but buries it in the sea of His forgetfulness (Micah 7:19; Hebrews 10:17). Yet I must understand that, as Galatians 6:7 declares, whatever I sow, I will reap. It isn't God who says, "Aha! I'm going to expose that sin to embarrass you." That's not the nature of our Father. No, it is the sin itself that will come to fruition. I am firmly persuaded and deeply convinced that there is no exception to this. Every time I sin, that sin will sooner or later track me down, find me out, and humiliate me. But it's not God doing this. Rather, it's the work of the Enemy to not only seduce us into sin, but to expose and humiliate us through it.

OCTOBER 31

And the children of Gad and the children of Reuben spake unto Moses, saying, Thy servants will do as my lord commandeth. Our little ones, our wives, our flocks, and all our cattle, shall be there in the cities of Gilead: but thy servants will pass over, every man armed for war, before the LORD to battle, as my lord saith. So concerning them Moses commanded Eleazar the priest, and Joshua the son of Nun, and the chief fathers of the tribes of the children of Israel: and Moses said unto them, If the children of Gad and the children of Reuben will pass with you over Jordan, every man armed to battle, before the LORD, and the land shall be subdued before you; then ye shall give them the land of Gilead for a possession.

Numbers 32:25–29

Joined by the half-tribe of Manasseh, the tribes of Reuben and Gad did indeed remain on the east side of the Jordan. Oh, they went into the Promised Land occasionally, but they didn't live there. And, as we see in Joshua 22, when they built an altar on their side of the Jordan, the other tribes said, "What are you doing building an altar? There is only to be one altar—at the tabernacle."

"Wait a minute," said the men of Gad. "We're not building an altar to offer sacrifices, but so that in the coming days you won't disavow us. It's not a working altar, but simply a monument so that future generations will know we're linked with you." Yet, although they made peace that day, the problems had begun, leading to suspicion and division in the nation between those who wanted to stay and those who wanted to go on.

Although they established cities, as evidenced by the remainder of the chapter, it would eventually be these who didn't go in, who didn't go on, and who were picked off first by the Syrians and the Assyrians. And it would be they who would become corrupted, for when Jesus came on the scene, the prized property of Reuben and Gad, the land of the Gadarenes, was filled with pigs, demons, and pagan Greek culture.

Why?

Because we either move further and deeper into the presence of the Lord, or we move in the other direction and become more and more interested in the things of the world. Right now, you are either deeper than you were five years ago, or you are more shallow. But you are not the same. Either my knowledge of the Lord is deeper, my walk stronger, my faith larger, or it is less. It's a great misconception to think we can put our spiritual lives on cruise control, to think that, because we know the plan of salvation and basic biblical principles, we can coast from here on out. We can't.

Reuben and Gad made a monumental mistake choosing a place of comfort rather than one of commitment by opting for affluence rather than obedience. "This land is good for our cattle and for our families," they said. And yet, by the time Jesus walked their land, there was not a cow in sight. If you want your cattle to do well, take them into the Promised Land, otherwise they'll turn into pigs. And if you want your kids to do well, take them with you, otherwise they'll be the ones who prefer that Jesus depart from their coasts (Mark 5:17).

Is your praise more fervent, your prayer more intense, your commitment to the kingdom greater, your time in the Word longer, your knowledge of God larger, your love for the Lord deeper than it was two years ago? Press in. Go on. Don't stop.

NOVEMBER 1

These are the journeys of the children of Israel, which went forth out of the land of Egypt with their armies under the hand of Moses and Aaron. And Moses wrote their goings out according to their journeys by the commandment of the Lord: and these are their journeys according to their goings out.

Numbers 33:1–2

Every stop along the way, every place we've pitched our tent, every time we've pulled up stakes to move on, God remembers. I wish that could be said of me. My kids will say, "Dad, remember when we did that?" But I don't. I forget the places we stopped and some of the things we've done. Not our Father. He remembers it all. In Hebrews 6:10, we read that God is not unrighteous to forget our works and our labor of love. God never forgets anything we've done. Whenever we've done what He's led us to do, He records it, remembers it, and eventually rewards it (Matthew 10:42). He never forgets—not a single work.

God has led you from stop to stop, from place to place that you have long since forgotten about, like the time your co-worker was bogged down with a bunch to do and you chose to stay an extra twenty minutes to help him; the time you helped in the nursery when it wasn't even your turn; the time you stood by the one in your seventh grade class whom everyone else was picking on. "I remember when you chose to do what I led you to do, when you pitched your tent where I told you to pitch it," God says. "It's in My scrapbook. It might be boring to others, forgotten by you, but it's important to Me."

NOVEMBER 2

And they removed from Kadesh, and pitched in mount Hor, in the edge of the land of Edom.

Numbers 33:37

In Numbers 33:3 and 4, we see the children of Israel leaving Egypt. In verses 5 through 8, they go to and through the Red Sea. In verses 9 through 15, they go from Marah to Mount Sinai, where they received the law and instructions for building the tabernacle and the sacrificial system. In verses 16 through 36, they go from Mount Sinai to Kadesh-barnea. And in verses 37 through 49, they go from Kadesh-barnea to the Jordan River, into the Land of Promise.

In this account, there is something huge missing, a glaring omission, namely, the thirty-eight years the children of Israel wandered in the wilderness due to their unbelief. In other words, the Father records exactingly and carefully every single spot where they pitched their tents in obedience to His leading. But when they were in sin, there's no mention, no record, no memory as far as He is concerned.

How I like that! He remembers where we've been, but He forgets about our sin. He edits it out of the video, throws away the slide, erases it from His journal. That's the kind of God we serve.

Why doesn't He remember our sins? Because He sent His Son to die on the cross in our place and shed His blood in order that they could be cleansed. What a price the Father paid to eradicate that memory, to clean up my story.

NOVEMBER 3

These are they whom the LORD commanded to divide the inheritance unto the children of Israel in the land of Canaan.

Numbers 34:29

The Israelites never came close to taking all of the territory God had given them. God had so much for them. He had given so much to them. He had such grand plans for them. Yet they never took advantage of them. And as I read this, I can't help but wonder, Lord, how much more do You have in mind for me, for my family, for the church? As I do, I realize I can get very comfortable on this side of the Jordan and miss out on what God wants to do through me and in me. I also realize that if I don't deal decisively with the carnal tendencies of my heart, like the children of Israel, I'll possess only a fraction of what the Lord has for me.

NOVEMBER 4

And the Lord *spake unto Moses in the plains of Moab by Jordan near Jericho, saying, Command the children of Israel, that they give unto the Levites of the inheritance of their possession cities to dwell in; and ye shall give also unto the Levites suburbs for the cities round about them. And the cities shall they have to dwell in; and the suburbs of them shall be for their cattle, and for their goods, and for all their beasts.*

Numbers 35:1–3

Serving as ministers in the tabernacle, the tribe of Levi was not given any portion of the Promised Land. Instead, the Levites were to be scattered throughout the entire country. The rest of the tribes were told to give certain cities to the Levites as places in which they could dwell. These cities would number forty-eight.

If the Levites were only in one tribal region, people who weren't close to them wouldn't get the proper ministry. So they were scattered throughout the entire country. And that's what the Lord does with us. The Lord has snuck His servants into the most amazing places. He sneaks Christian teachers into high schools to be effective, secret agents, Levites, reflections of Jesus Christ. He sneaks Christian salesmen, secretaries, and accountants into the workplace to be examples of what it means to be a believer. He sneaks Christian doctors into hospital rooms as ministers of the gospel.

This is such a key. Each of us who is serious about Jesus is in ministry. We are a royal priesthood (1 Peter 2:9). And He's stationed you in that workplace, that neighborhood, and that family to be a servant of His. It's a great day indeed when a believer looks at his work as his ministry and says, "I'm surrounded by people professional pastors would never have an opportunity to reach. I'm here on campus, at the store, and in the neighborhood not just to work for a paycheck or to raise my family, but to be a minister. So I'm going to keep my eyes open and my antennae up in order to determine the part I am to play in this place for God's glory."

NOVEMBER 5

And the LORD spake unto Moses, saying, Speak unto the children of Israel, and say unto them, When ye be come over Jordan into the land of Canaan; then ye shall appoint you cities to be cities of refuge for you; that the slayer may flee thither, which killeth any person at unawares. And they shall be unto you cities for refuge from the avenger; that the manslayer die not, until he stand before the congregation in judgment.

Numbers 35:9–12

In Bible days, there was no such thing as a police force. There was no constable, no sheriff, no deputy, and no patrolman. It was up to the family to keep law and order. Therefore, the way it worked was as follows: If my brother Jimmy was crossing the street and you accidentally hit and killed him, as his brother, it would be up to me to avenge his death—to track you down and kill you. No matter how long it might take, culture required that I kill you.

The idea of the avenger was neither created nor condoned by God. God here is simply controlling the reality of the day, similar to when He gave rules and regulations concerning practices such as divorce and slavery. Why didn't He simply do away with these practices altogether? Because He's treating His people as a family.

When Ben and Mary were little, I didn't have the same requirements or the same expectations for them that I do now that they're seventeen and eighteen. And they'll have still greater obligations when they're twenty and twenty-one. As our kids grow older, we expect more out of them. But we don't burden them immediately. We let them grow. That's what our Father does with His family. Here in the very early stages of their nationhood, and because these customs were already deeply imbedded in their culture, God placed boundaries around customs like that of the avenger, dealing with them more fully as they grew.

NOVEMBER 6

But if the slayer shall at any time come without the border of the city of his refuge, whither he was fled; and the revenger of blood find him without the borders of the city of his refuge, and the revenger of blood kill the slayer; he shall not be guilty of blood: because he should have remained in the city of his refuge until the death of the high priest: but after the death of the high priest the slayer shall return into the land of his possession. So these things shall be for a statute of judgment unto you throughout your generations in all your dwellings.

Numbers 35:26–29

If someone accidentally killed another, he was to flee to one of six cities of refuge, where he would be safe from those who wanted to avenge the death until a trial could be held. If, however, he left the city of refuge before the high priest died, he was fair game. The avenger would not be found guilty of his death. Once the high priest died, however, he could return home.

The person who was guilty—as we all are—was kept safe in the city by the life of the high priest. But he was declared not guilty by the death of the high priest. The picture should be obvious. We are kept safe by the life of our great High Priest, Jesus Christ. He is the One who intercedes for us, the One who gives instruction to us, and the One who lives through us. But while we are kept safe by His life, we are saved by His death, for our sins have been washed away by His blood.

For New Testament confirmation of this Old Testament illustration, consider Acts 27 . . .

> The storm was raging. The boat was bobbing up and down. The soldiers were panicked and the sailors were frightened. "We're going down!" they cried.

> But as they fought for their lives on the furious sea, Paul said, "Be of good cheer. There shall be no loss of life."

> As the storm continued, however, the sailors let down a lifeboat to escape the impending crash. "Except the sailors abide in the ship," Paul said, "they can't be saved." So the ropes were cut, the lifeboats fell empty into the sea, and all on board the ship were saved.

So too, as long as we're on board the good ship salvation, we'll be saved. As long as we're in Jesus, our refuge, we're okay. But if we choose to wander off, to bail out, to back away and live a life of drunkenness and fornication, of adultery and bitterness, the Bible says we'll not inherit the kingdom of God (1 Corinthians 6:9; Galatians 5:21; Ephesians 5:5).

Am I teaching contrary to the doctrine of eternal security? No. I believe in eternal security. I know I'm eternally secure because I have no intention of going anywhere other than staying on board the ship of faith. I know I need the Lord. I know I can't make it without Him. He is my city of refuge, my ship of salvation. And I have no intention of leaving.

"Make your calling and election sure," Peter writes (2 Peter 1:10). How? It's so simple, as easily accessible as a city of refuge. You don't have to climb a mountain or swim an ocean. You simply confess with your mouth that Jesus is Lord and believe in your heart that He died for your sin and rose from the dead (Romans 10:9).

When I lead people in the sinners' prayer, I pray right along with them. Is it because I doubt my own salvation? No, I know I'm saved, but why not take every opportunity to say, "Lord, I love You and I understand my great need for You. And rather than be doctrinally arrogant, I want to make sure You're in my heart and that You hear from me again. Lord, I confess You as Lord and am so thankful that You died for me, that You live in heaven, interceding for me."

I say this time and time again, not because I'm insecure and worried about losing my salvation, but simply because in Jesus, my refuge, I have reason for great celebration.

NOVEMBER 7

(There are eleven days' journey from Horeb by the way of mount Seir unto Kadesh-barnea.)

Deuteronomy 1:2

We come to the fifth and final book of Moses, the final book of the Pentateuch, the final book of the Torah, and the final address to the people he had led for forty years. It's a lengthy address, but oh, so impacting, for in it Moses reviews and reminds the people of their history—how their fathers failed miserably, but how God saw them through faithfully.

The parenthetical statement in verse 2 must have been particularly painful for Moses to pen. After all, how long would it take a man to walk from Mount Sinai to Kadesh-barnea, the border of the Promised Land? Eleven days. How long did it take the children of Israel? Forty years.

Forty being the number of biblical generations, an entire generation was lost simply for their lack of faith. When God brought them to Kadesh-barnea, they were supposed to go from there and take the territory, and move into the Promised Land. But they lacked faith and were fearful of the giants about which they'd heard.

Quoting from this very story, Paul says, "Learn the lesson" (see 1 Corinthians 10:11). When God puts something on your heart, do it immediately lest you wander around needlessly and waste your days in a desert experience.

NOVEMBER 8

But as for you, turn you, and take your journey into the wilderness by the way of the Red sea. Then ye answered and said unto me, We have sinned against the LORD, we will go up and fight, according to all that the LORD our God commanded us. And when ye had girded on every man his weapons of war, ye were ready to go up into the hill. And the LORD said unto me, Say unto them, Go not up, neither fight; for I am not among you; lest ye be smitten before your enemies. So I spake unto you; and ye would not hear, but rebelled against the commandment of the LORD, and went presumptuously up into the hill. And the Amorites, which dwelt in that mountain, came out against you, and chased you, as bees do, and destroyed you in Seir, even unto Hormah. And ye returned and wept before the LORD; but the LORD would not hearken to your voice, nor give ear unto you. So ye abode in Kadesh many days, according unto the days that ye abode there.

Deuteronomy 1:40–46

The children of Israel didn't do what God had told them to do when He commanded them to take the Land. Then they did what God had told them not to do when they attacked the Amorites. Why? Because they followed their own counsel rather than God's.

What has God told you to do? What has He put on your heart? I can make a strong case against doing what God has told me to do. I can murmur and blame others. But each time I do, I end up wandering and missing the promised land of whatever area the Lord wants me to possess. Life is either a fantastic adventure or it is an endless detour. And the only difference between the two is faith.

NOVEMBER 9

Ye shall buy meat of them for money, that ye may eat; and ye shall also buy water of them for money, that ye may drink.

Deuteronomy 2:6

That the Israelites were to buy meat and water signals a shift in God's provision for them. In their wilderness wanderings, God had fed them manna from the sky and water from the rock. However, now that they're ready to enter the Promised Land, the manna would begin falling sporadically. And after they had celebrated their first Passover in the Promised Land, the manna would stop completely (Joshua 5:12).

The point is simple. God expects us to grow up, to move on. Concerning that which was once given to us, God will say, "You need to participate in the process, not because I'm being mean to you or holding back from you, but because I want to see maturity in you." As we do with our own kids, God expected His children to participate in their own care.

NOVEMBER 10

The Emims dwelt therein in times past, a people great, and many, and tall, as the Anakims; which also were accounted giants, as the Anakims; but the Moabites call them Emims. The Horims also dwelt in Seir beforetime; but the children of Esau succeeded them, when they had destroyed them from before them, and dwelt in their stead; as Israel did unto the land of his possession, which the LORD gave unto them.

Deuteronomy 2:10–12

Like the Anakims, the Emims and Horims were giants—fearful and terrible. Yet here Moses says that the Horims were beaten back by the descendants of Esau. In other words, because the Edomites wiped out the very giants of whom God's people were afraid (Numbers 13:31–33), the Edomites possessed the land that should have been the Israelites'.

Sometimes we as believers can be real wimpy. "I'm going through this trial, this persecution, this difficulty," we whine, failing to realize that the unbeliever has just as many trials, just as many problems, and just as many difficulties (Matthew 5:45). If you think being a Christian is hard, try being an unbeliever. They have the same problems you and I have, but they don't have the opportunity to approach the throne of grace boldly, to pour out their hearts to the Father, to open the Word for inspiration and instruction. The world has the same kinds of problems we do, but without access to the Problem-Solver.

NOVEMBER 11

But Sihon king of Heshbon would not let us pass by him: for the Lord *thy God hardened his spirit, and made his heart obstinate, that he might deliver him into thy hand, as appeareth this day. And the* Lord *said unto me, Behold, I have begun to give Sihon and his land before thee: begin to possess, that thou mayest inherit his land.*

Deuteronomy 2:30–31

Sihon's refusal to give safe passage to Israel set the stage for a battle he was unknowingly destined to lose. Maybe today you have a broken heart because of someone else's obstinate heart. Most of us know what it's like to be rejected by someone we care about. Yet happy is the man or woman who remembers God's sovereignty. We can be happy if we don't lose sight of the fact that God is in control. When someone has a hard heart toward me, I must remember that God is the One who causes all things to work out for His perfect, divine plan. Walking in the realization that every event is part of God's plan produces a radical life. He desires that I possess more of my possession, to be a bigger person, to gain new territory, and to experience greater victory.

NOVEMBER 12

And I besought the LORD at that time, saying, O Lord GOD,
thou hast begun to shew thy servant thy greatness, and thy
mighty hand: for what God is there in heaven or in earth,
that can do according to thy works, and according to thy
might? I pray thee, let me go over, and see the good land
that is beyond Jordan, that goodly mountain, and Lebanon.
But the LORD was wroth with me for your sakes, and would
not hear me: and the LORD said unto me, Let it suffice thee;
speak no more unto me of this matter.

Deuteronomy 3:23–26

After leading the congregation through the wilderness for forty years, Moses desperately desired to see the Land of Promise. But he couldn't go in because of the sin he committed at Meribah when he implied that God was upset with His people (Numbers 20:10). Consequently, because he misrepresented the nature and character, the goodness and grace of the Father, Moses was unable to accompany the congregation into the Promised Land.

Maybe today in your journey through life, you're a bit discouraged and confused by what you cannot do. You're not sure where to go from here. It seems like the plans you once had have been altered, that doors have been shut. Maybe things haven't worked out for you in the way you thought they should or in the way you hoped they would. Moses can relate to you. And he has good news: the solution to your confusion, the prescription for your pain is found at the top of Mount Pisgah.

Although Moses could not accompany the children of Israel into the Promised Land, the Lord told Moses to climb Mount Pisgah, or Mount Nebo, where he would be given a supernatural view of the entire land.

"Where there is no vision, the people perish" (Proverbs 29:18). The Hebrew word translated "perish" is *para`*, which simply means "naked." Without vision, people feel naked, unsure, exposed, and undone. Without vision, people want to hole up and hide away. Without vision, people perish.

From this point on, Pisgah in Scripture is known as the mount of vision.

And it was at this point that Moses knew what he was to do. He was to encourage Joshua, for as a representative of the law, Moses could not be the one to lead the children of Israel into the Promised Land; but as a picture of Jesus, Joshua could and would.

How about you? Is it clear to you what you're to do? Is it clear what those who follow after you are to be? If not, I encourage you to get to a quiet place, away from distractions and interruptions, and say, "Lord, I need vision. I'm perishing. I'm confused. I'm in the dark."

Get away, brothers and sisters, and seek the Lord. Find your Nebo, your Pisgah, and go there regularly.

NOVEMBER 13

Get thee up into the top of Pisgah, and lift up thine eyes westward, and northward, and southward, and eastward, and behold it with thine eyes.

Deuteronomy 3:27

Forty days after shedding His blood for you and me on Mount Calvary, Jesus stood on the Mount of Olives before ascending to heaven triumphantly. And since whatever goes up must come down, guess who is coming back to the Mount of Olives? The Bible says that when He does, He will walk through the Kidron Valley, through the Eastern Gate, and into Jerusalem as the Prince of Peace to rule over all the kingdoms of the world for one thousand years. In other words, by opting to go to Mount Moriah, by doing what was best for the greatest number, Jesus is not only rewarded in heaven and exalted eternally, but He gets the very thing Satan was offering previously (Matthew 4:8–9). It's a win-win situation. It all works out perfectly.

When we choose to take up the cross and say, "It's not about what's easiest for me. It's about what's best for the most people I can possibly reach and help," we'll get whatever Satan may have tried to seduce us with because

Jesus said that if we seek first the kingdom, everything we need would be thrown in (Matthew 6:33).

One day, I spent some time with a bunch of pastors going through the book of Ezra and dealing with some pastoral issues. When I was done, I had a couple of meetings and then did a radio show. On my way home, I felt really fatigued and weary of soul. Yet the Lord, I believe, gave me a very simple vision, a simple stirring, a simple directive to go and see our brother, Jeff, who, at thirty-five years of age, was dying of brain cancer. But after getting lost twice trying to find his house and having been up since before four in the morning, and knowing my kids weren't home that night and that Tammy had a nice dinner planned, I thought, I'm tired. I'll go home and pick it up tomorrow. Yet, even as I made my way home, I knew that it wasn't right. I knew it wasn't the way of the cross for me at that moment in time. So I made a U-turn, and by God's grace, I found the house.

Jeff's three sons were there with a few pastors, worshiping the Lord, praying, and sharing. I talked to him and read the Scriptures because I believe that even though the mind may not be working, the spirit still perceives and receives prayer, praise, and the Word. So we were sharing together, talking to him about heaven, even though he was unable to comprehend mentally. Then, after an hour or so, something happened I'll never forget. As I sat by his bed, suddenly Jeff looked at me. His eyes were crystal clear, his focus laser sharp. He grabbed my hand and held it for forty-five seconds as our eyes met. And I found myself weeping as he gripped my hand with the strongest grip I've felt in a long time. Then he let go and returned to his previous state.

He went to heaven the next day.

"I'm going to go and do this," I had said. "It's the way of the cross." What I didn't know was Mount Calvary turned into the Mount of Olives. I was caught up into heavenly places. That's the way it always is. I was the one who was blessed. Jeff ministered to me in that forty-five-second window of opportunity. I can't explain it, but I went home with tears in my eyes because I was so deeply touched. And to think I might have missed it because I almost opted for what was more comfortable for me. I almost missed the supernatural blessing God had flow through Jeff into my heart at that moment.

Discouraged today? You need a fresh vision. How do you get that? Go to the mountain. I need to go to the mountain constantly and say, "Father, give me *Your* vision because it will ultimately mean resurrection and ecstasy not only for others, but also for me."

NOVEMBER 14

Behold, I have taught you statutes and judgments, even as the LORD *my God commanded me, that ye should do so in the land whither ye go to possess it. Keep therefore and do them; for this is your wisdom and your understanding in the sight of the nations, which shall hear all these statutes, and say, Surely this great nation is a wise and understanding people. For what nation is there so great, who hath God so nigh unto them, as the* LORD *our God is in all things that we call upon him for? And what nation is there so great, that hath statutes and judgments so righteous as all this law, which I set before you this day?*

Deuteronomy 4:5–8

The Israelites were to obey God's Word not only that they might live, but that they might be a light in order that other nations might see the way life was meant to be lived (Isaiah 49:6).

I'm so glad we have God's Word. It's so right. We're so blessed.

Wherein in time past ye walked according to the course of this world, according to the prince of the power of the air, the spirit that now worketh in the children of disobedience: among whom also we all had our conversation in times past in the lusts of our flesh, fulfilling the desires of the flesh and of the mind; and were by nature the children of wrath, even as others. But God, who is rich in mercy, for his great love wherewith he loved us, even when we were dead in sins, hath quickened us together with Christ.

Ephesians 2:2–5

In times past, we didn't have a clue. We didn't have a promise. We didn't have hope. It's good for us to reflect on this from time to time. Paul says, "Remember where you once were and rejoice in where you are now."

We have God. We have Christ. We have the promises of the Word. We have the hope of heaven. I'm so thankful, so grateful, so glad I'm saved. We're so blessed—every one of us.

NOVEMBER 15

Only take heed to thyself, and keep thy soul diligently, lest thou forget the things which thine eyes have seen, and lest they depart from thy heart all the days of thy life: but teach them thy sons, and thy sons' sons; Specially the day that thou stoodest before the LORD thy God in Horeb, when the LORD said unto me, Gather me the people together, and I will make them hear my words, that they may learn to fear me all the days that they shall live upon the earth, and that they may teach their children.

Deuteronomy 4:9–10

Take heed to yourself because it's not just about you, but about your kids and grandkids as well. Here is your job: to be familiar with the Word, to be constantly learning more about the Word so that you can teach your children and grandchildren.

"Your mother and brothers are calling You," the disciples said to Jesus. "My mother and brothers are those who hear and do the Word," Jesus answered (see Matthew 12:47–50).

Jesus' disciples were His family, but those in your family are your disciples. This is so important to understand. "What's my ministry?" people often ask. And my answer to them is, "Do you have kids or grandkids? Pray for them, share the things you're learning about the Lord with them day by day. And in so doing, you will be in ministry."

If you raise godly kids or are involved in seeing godly grandkids raised up, yours is a fruitful, successful, rewarding, fulfilling, thrilling, eternally impacting ministry indeed. There can be no greater blessing.

NOVEMBER 16

Thou shalt keep therefore his statutes, and his commandments, which I command thee this day, that it may go well with thee, and with thy children after thee, and that thou mayest prolong thy days upon the earth, which the LORD thy God giveth thee, for ever.

Deuteronomy 4:40

The phrase, "which I command thee this day," implies that God must be rediscovered each day. Every day we get to rediscover the nature and beauty of our Father. Every day there ought to be a rediscovery of the grace and glory and grandeur of our God.

"Take heed to My Word," God says. "Rediscover Me each day. Listen to what I have to say once more. Go over the Scriptures, pray them in, think them through, act them out, and it will go well for you and for your family."

A story is told in the Mishnah (a collection of Jewish teachings and writings) of a certain Persian king named Arteban who sent to Judah, the prince in Jerusalem, the largest known diamond in existence. Upon receiving this gift, Judah sent back to Arteban a copy of the book of Deuteronomy with the accompanying note: What you sent me requires guards to protect it. What I have sent you will guard and protect you.

I'm so thankful for God's Word because I know, as you do, that it works. When we take heed and do what we're told to, it goes well with us and with our families, too.

NOVEMBER 17

And thou shalt love the LORD thy God with all thine heart, and with all thy soul, and with all thy might. And these words, which I command thee this day, shall be in thine heart: and thou shalt teach them diligently unto thy children, and shalt talk of them when thou sittest in thine house, and when thou walkest by the way, and when thou liest down, and when thou risest up.

Deuteronomy 6:5–7

Can love be commanded? If you think of love only as a noun, the answer is no. But love in the Bible is not a noun. It's a verb, something you do rather than something you feel. Divorce is rampant today because we have lost our understanding of what love is.

A story is told of an anthropologist who asked the Hopi Indians he was studying, "Why do you have so many songs about rain?"

"We live in the desert," they answered. "We sing about rain because it is so rare."

I wonder if that's why most of our popular songs are about love. Love is a fantasy in the way it's being hyped today.

Jesus taught us that wherever our treasure is, there will our heart be also (Matthew 6:21). In other words, first choose to love and then the feeling will follow. So God here commands love. He doesn't say, "I hope you feel love for Me." He says, "I'm commanding you to show love to Me."

When you get up in the morning, when you go to bed at night, when you're walking, when you're relaxing, talk to your kids about loving God. My brother, Dave, modeled this wonderfully. Every time he would go anywhere—to the post office, to 7-Eleven, to the hardware store—he would take one of his boys, knowing he could spend time with him.

If you haven't been teaching your kids, consider the Chinese proverb which says, "The best time to plant a tree was twenty years ago. The second best time is today." We should have done things twenty years ago. All of us know that. But the second best time to do what's required is now. And if your kids have grown up and moved out of the house, there are always grandchildren, nieces, nephews, or neighbor kids with whom you can share the Lord.

NOVEMBER 18

And it shall be, when the LORD thy God shall have brought thee into the land which he sware unto thy fathers, to Abraham, to Isaac, and to Jacob, to give thee great and goodly cities, which thou buildedst not, and houses full of all good things, which thou filledst not, and wells digged, which thou diggedst not, vineyards and olive trees, which thou plantedst not; when thou shalt have eaten and be full; then beware lest thou forget the LORD, which brought thee forth out of the land of Egypt, from the house of bondage.

Deuteronomy 6:10–12

"When you take possession of houses you didn't build, vineyards and olive trees you didn't plant, and wells you didn't dig, beware," Moses warned, "lest you forget the Lord who brought you out of bondage."

There is peril in prosperity. When things are going well, when things come our way which bless and amaze us, there is an insidious danger, for it is in those days that we can forget the Lord and think that it's our energy, our effort, our creativity, ingenuity, or hard work that gets us where we are.

In Deuteronomy 8, God reminds the people that it was He who gave them everything they had. And it is He who does the same for us; for truly, the foundational essence of our Father is that He is a giver . . .

Blessed be the Lord, who daily loadeth us with benefits.

Psalm 68:19

I am the LORD thy God, which brought thee out of the land of Egypt: open thy mouth wide, and I will fill it.

Psalm 81:10

"Ask, and it shall be given you; seek, and ye shall find; knock, and it shall be opened unto you."

Matthew 7:7

"For God so loved the world, that he gave his only begotten Son ..."

John 3:16

He that spared not his own Son, but delivered him up for us all, how shall he not with him also freely give us all things?

Romans 8:32

Now unto him that is able to do exceedingly abundantly above all that we ask or think, according to the power that worketh in us ...

Ephesians 3:20

Every good and every perfect gift is from above, and cometh down from the Father of lights, with whom is no variableness, neither shadow of turning.

James 1:17

"You're in for a treat," Moses said. "God is going to give you cities and houses you didn't build; olive trees, vineyards, and wells you neither had to plant nor dig." And daily He does the same for us.

NOVEMBER 19

When the LORD *thy God shall bring thee into the land whither thou goest to possess it, and hath cast out many nations before thee, the Hittites, and the Girgashites, and the Amorites, and the Canaanites, and the Perizzites, and the Hivites, and the Jebusites, seven nations greater and mightier than thou; and when the* LORD *thy God shall deliver them before thee; thou shalt smite them, and utterly destroy them; thou shalt make no covenant with them, nor shew mercy unto them.*

Deuteronomy 7:1–2

"When you go into the Land," Moses instructs the people, "God will deliver formidable foes into your hand. And you shall smite them."

The same is true for us.

> There hath no temptation taken you but such as is common to man: but God is faithful, who will not suffer you to be tempted above that ye are able; but will with the temptation also make a way to escape, that ye may be able to bear it.

1 Corinthians 10:13

No temptation will ever come our way without the Lord providing a way for victory at that time. But we need to participate. In other words, the Lord will deliver us, but we have a role to play as well. At the moment of temptation, when the battle is raging, when the Enemy is looming, the Lord will give me victory if I choose to participate. There will always be a way of escape, a way of victory.

> Knowing this, that our old man is crucified with him, that the body of sin might be destroyed, that henceforth we should not serve sin.

Romans 6:6

Because the word translated "crucified" literally means "rendered inactive," we can say, "I'm not going to get beaten up by the enemy of temptation, depression, or seduction. Not only has the Lord promised that there is a way of escape, but the sins of anger, hostility, and lust can't dominate me anymore. When Christ Jesus died on the cross, anything contrary to Christ was crucified and paralyzed. Therefore, all the old nature can do is yell at me, scream at me, and try to intimidate me. But it cannot touch me unless I choose to listen."

Some people say, "I just can't seem to get over this. I can't deal with that. Where's the Lord?" The answer is that the Lord has done His part. Now He's waiting for you to do yours and smite the Enemy.

NOVEMBER 20

The Lord did not set his love upon you, nor choose you, because ye were more in number than any people; for ye were the fewest of all people: but because the Lord loved you.

Deuteronomy 7:7–8

I love this Scripture. Moses says, I want you to know the Lord didn't select you to be His, to be holy, or to be different because you were mightier than others. No, He chose you simply because He loved you. God loves you and me not because we are mighty or together or have something awesome to offer. Quite the opposite, He loves us just because He loves us. Period. His love is not based upon how well I'm doing or how much you're doing, how poorly I'm faring or how much you're erring. God's love for us is honestly, truly, and absolutely unconditional. And once we grasp this, we can go through our day expecting the Lord to bless us, to shower grace upon us—not because of who we are or what we've done but simply and solely based upon who He is.

NOVEMBER 21

Thou shalt therefore keep the commandments, and the statutes, and the judgments, which I command thee this day, to do them. Wherefore it shall come to pass, if ye hearken to these judgments, and keep, and do them, that the LORD thy God shall keep unto thee the covenant and the mercy which he sware unto thy fathers: and he will love thee, and bless thee, and multiply thee: he will also bless the fruit of thy womb, and the fruit of thy land, thy corn, and thy wine, and thine oil, the increase of thy kine, and the flocks of thy sheep, in the land which he sware unto thy fathers to give thee.

Deuteronomy 7:11–13

In verse 7, Moses told the people the Lord loved them unconditionally. Here, he tells them the Lord would love and bless them if they obeyed His words. Is this contradictory? No.

I love my kids whether they're good or bad. I love them simply because they're my kids. But if they say, "We're not going to be here for breakfast, lunch, or dinner, for Christmas, Thanksgiving, or Easter," although I'll still love them, they'll not enjoy the blessings that would have come their way had they remained close to me.

That's what Jude meant when he said, "Keep yourselves in the love of God" (verse 21). He didn't mean we are to try to earn or merit God's love. He meant we are to just "keep ourselves under the spout where God's blessings come out."

Here in Deuteronomy, God says, "You'll experience all kinds of blessings if you hearken to the judgments, if you take heed to the Word, if you let Me love you."

NOVEMBER 22

Thou shalt be blessed above all people: there shall not be male or female barren among you, or among your cattle. And the LORD will take away from thee all sickness, and will put none of the evil diseases of Egypt, which thou knowest, upon thee; but will lay them upon all them that hate thee.

Deuteronomy 7:14–15

Having lived in Egypt for four hundred years, the children of Israel were all too familiar with the diseases of Egypt. Egypt being a type of the world, we too see the sickness of the world in which we live.

Keep in mind that everything in the Old Testament is a physical picture of a New Testament spiritual truth . . .

> The children of Israel were delivered from the bondage of Egypt and brought to the Promised Land.
>
>> We've been delivered from the world system and ushered into the Spirit-filled life.
>
> Their citizenship was in the Promised Land.
>
>> Ours is in heaven.
>
> They fought with swords and spears.
>
>> The weapons of our warfare are spiritual.
>
> They were to smite their enemies.
>
>> We are to reckon dead the Enemy of our soul.

If you don't understand this, the Old Testament will be troubling and impractical to you. There are those who say if we walk with the Lord, we'll have no diseases, that we'll never be sick. Yet, Paul had a thorn in his flesh (2 Corinthians 12:7). He left Trophimus sick (2 Timothy 4:20). He told Timothy to take wine for his stomach problems (1 Timothy 5:23). The diseases the Old Testament talks about which were physical for them are spiritual for us. The Lord wants to make us a peculiar, special people, different from the Egyptians that surround us. And He says that will happen if we do what He tells us to do.

NOVEMBER 23

Thou shalt not be affrighted at them.

Deuteronomy 7:21

What do you fear? At any given moment, I am living in fear and so are you—either in the fear of the Lord, which is the beginning of wisdom and success (Proverbs 9:10), or in the fear of man, which is a snare (Proverbs 29:25).

"What are your goals for the coming school year?" I asked my two youngest kids.

About to start seventh grade, Ben looked at me and said, "I have two goals, Dad. The first is to remember where my locker is; the second is to be able to open it."

Ben was kidding—sort of. But remember seventh grade? Lockers and combinations and PE? Remember all those fears? Well, guess what? You made it! You're here. You got through those junior high years. So too, the exhortation of Moses to the congregation at the Jordan was, "Remember how much God has done for you already. He's not going to let you down now."

God loves you, gang. He proved it to us on the cross. So do what He's called you to do and don't fear. Don't listen to the whisper of the Enemy. Instead, say, "Lord, You've loved me so passionately, I'm going to do what You direct me to, let the chips fall where they may."

Jesus put it this way: "Fear not, little flock; for it is your Father's good pleasure to give you the kingdom" (Luke 12:32). Fear not and watch and see how God will bless you.

NOVEMBER 24

And the Lord thy God will put out those nations before thee by little and little: thou mayest not consume them at once, lest the beasts of the field increase upon thee. But the Lord thy God shall deliver them unto thee, and shall destroy them with a mighty destruction, until they be destroyed.

Deuteronomy 7:22–23

Had God driven the enemy out of the land quickly, wild beasts would eat the crops that would otherwise have nourished God's people. So He drove the enemies out a little at a time until the children of Israel were ready to take on more territory.

So too, God is working in you and on me. "But it's going so slowly," you say. "I thought I would be a lot further along by now." I know. I thought I would be too.

But God would say to you and me, "Be patient and trust Me. I'm not going to drive out your enemies immediately. But little by little, I'll give you more territory, more possibilities, more responsibilities. You wait. You watch. You'll see."

NOVEMBER 25

All the commandments which I command thee this day shall ye observe to do, that ye may live, and multiply, and go in and possess the land which the Lord sware unto your fathers. And thou shalt remember all the way which the Lord thy God led thee these forty years in the wilderness, to humble thee, and to prove thee, to know what was in thine heart, whether thou wouldest keep his commandments, or no.

Deuteronomy 8:1–2

"Do what you know is right in God's sight," Moses instructed the children of Israel. "Remember how the Lord took you through the wilderness for forty years to humble you, to prove you, to test you, that you might know where you're truly at, what's really taking place within your hearts."

It's easy to say, "I'm going to keep the commandments of the Lord. I'm going to do what He tells me." The proof, however, is in the wilderness. It's when the days are dry and difficult and when the heat is rising that we get to see if we are truly those who obey what the Lord tells us to do.

Maybe you are in a wilderness season, in the desert of difficulty. If so, this is an important opportunity for you to realize and to see what's going on deep within your heart. Just as we don't know what's in a sponge until it's squeezed, I can't know what's taking place deep within me until I'm squeezed. Oh, I can quote the verses, sing the songs, and say the phrases, but the fact is, I won't know what's truly going on until and unless I'm squeezed by days of difficulty and times of trouble.

NOVEMBER 26

And he humbled thee, and suffered thee to hunger, and fed thee with manna, which thou knewest not, neither did thy fathers know; that he might make thee know that man doth not live by bread only, but by every word that proceedeth out of the mouth of the LORD doth man live.

Deuteronomy 8:3

The Israelites welcomed God's provision of manna because they were in a place of hunger. That's always the way it is. We get hungry in the wilderness, in the day of difficulty. And it is then that we long for God's provision for us. Jesus put it this way: "Blessed are you when you hunger and thirst for righteousness, for then you'll be filled" (see Matthew 5:6). Too often, we don't crave the Bread of the Word or the Bread of Life because we're not hungry. There's a progression seen here: My reaction in the wilderness makes me hungry for righteousness. So I go to church once again, have devotions once more, exchange *Newsweek* for the Word, turn off talk radio, and listen to teaching tapes. But this doesn't happen until I'm hungry. And I don't know I'm hungry until I'm in the wilderness. It's all part of the program.

Jesus quoted this verse in His own wilderness experience. He was tested for forty days as Satan came and said, "If You're the Son of God, turn these stones into bread. Take care of Yourself. Find a way to satisfy Your own needs."

"No," Jesus said, and quoted Deuteronomy 8:3.

In fact, all three times He dealt with Satan in Matthew 4, Jesus quoted from Deuteronomy. That is why I suggest Deuteronomy was where He was having devotions at that time. As a result, He was empowered to withstand the temptation and to obey His Father—the same opportunity each of us has who eats freely of the Bread of Life, who partakes consistently of the manna of the Word.

NOVEMBER 27

And it shall be, if thou do at all forget the LORD thy God, and walk after other gods, and serve them, and worship them, I testify against you this day that ye shall surely perish. As the nations which the LORD destroyeth before your face, so shall ye perish; because ye would not be obedient unto the voice of the LORD your God.

Deuteronomy 8:19–20

Was there ever a time when you were serving the Lord more diligently and more consistently than you are today? If your answer is yes, I plead with you to take this passage to heart, for if you do not, you'll perish. Oh, maybe not physically, but your marriage will diminish, your family will diminish, and your joy will diminish. Your life will get smaller and smaller. On the other hand, when you say, "God's been good to me. Therefore, I'm going to learn His ways, give Him praise, and serve Him with all of my heart and soul, mind and strength," you'll find yourself truly blessed in every way.

NOVEMBER 28

Speak not thou in thine heart, after that the LORD thy God hath cast them out from before thee, saying, For my righteousness the LORD hath brought me in to possess this land: but for the wickedness of these nations the LORD doth drive them out from before thee.

Deuteronomy 9:4

Why did God bring you and me into the Promised Land of His kingdom? Because He saw we would want to be righteous? No. Like the children of Israel, we were stiff-necked and rebellious from the beginning (Deuteronomy 9:7). He did so because of the wickedness of our Enemy.

We have an Enemy who, from before time began, has questioned the goodness and kindness, mercy and grace of God. "Can't you eat of that tree, Eve?" Satan hissed. "God knows that in the day you eat of it, you'll become godly." In other words, "God is not as good as He purports to be. He's holding something back from you, Eve. He knows that if you eat of that tree, it would be wonderful for you. And He doesn't want you to have good things" (see Genesis 3:1–5).

Satan challenged the goodness of the Father not only in the garden, but also in heaven. "Of course Job serves You," he said to God. "You've blessed him. But if those blessings weren't there, he would turn his back on You" (see Job 1:9–11).

Psalm 73:1 says, "God is good."

Satan says, "No, He's not."

So God says, "I will prove My goodness and grace by bringing stiff-necked people like these into My kingdom, by showering rebellious people like Jon Courson with blessing."

Blessed be the God and Father of our Lord Jesus Christ, who hath blessed us with all spiritual blessings in heavenly places in Christ: according as he hath chosen us in him before the foundation of the world, that we should be holy and without blame before him in love:

having predestinated us unto the adoption of children by Jesus Christ to himself, according to the good pleasure of his will, to the praise of the glory of his grace, wherein he hath made us accepted in the beloved.

Ephesians 1:3–6

Paul says we were elected and redeemed not because God saw we were a good, sincere people who wanted to be spiritual, but in order that angels and demons alike would marvel, saying, "Look how gracious God is!"

Whether you're prospering materially or moving into the Promised Land of the kingdom and enjoying blessings spiritually, don't think it's because of your righteousness. The greatest danger to the children of Israel would not be the persecution or the battles in the Promised Land. The greatest danger would occur when things were going well because it would be then that they would forget the Lord.

How do you know when you've forgotten the Lord? It's quite simple: you no longer have time for Him. After all, there are ski boats to use, vacations to take, money to spend. In times of persecution people don't forget God. They gather together. They pray with passion. Their roots sink deep into the soil of the Scriptures. But in times of prosperity, people have toys to play with, places to go, hobbies to pursue. And, although they don't admit it, they forget about God.

Statistics confirm that people forget the Lord in time of prosperity not only by withdrawing from fellowship, but by failing to give sacrificially. Ironically, people give much more generously in times of difficulty than in times of prosperity. In times of prosperity, they say, "I can't tithe because I bought the second house, the newer car, and I'm overextended," failing to remember that it was God who gave them the ability to do what they do, to bless them with every single thing they have.

If we truly believe that God has blessed us, we'll say, "This is not my wealth. It's God's. Therefore, in giving my tithe I recognize that what came my way this week is not because of my cleverness or ability, but because of Him."

NOVEMBER 29

And it came to pass at the end of forty days and forty nights, that the LORD gave me the two tables of stone, even the tables of the covenant. And the LORD said unto me, Arise, get thee down quickly from hence; for thy people which thou hast brought forth out of Egypt have corrupted themselves; they are quickly turned aside out of the way which I commanded them; they have made them a molten image.

Deuteronomy 9:11–12

While Moses was on the mountain alone with God for forty days, the people were sinning down below. "I'm going to destroy these people and make of you a new nation," God said to him (see verse 14). Would Moses accept the offer? Wait a minute. This sounds strangely familiar to another test after a forty-day fast . . .

"Bow down to me," Satan said to Jesus, "and the entire world will be Yours" (see Matthew 4:8–9). The similarities are neither coincidental nor accidental. Rather, they show us that what God uses to test us, Satan uses to tempt us. God tests us to work good in us, to show Himself strong through us. Satan, on the other hand, tempts us in order to destroy us.

Whenever you're tempted, realize that God uses what Satan means as a temptation for a test. Conversely, whenever you're going through a test from God, Satan will jump on it and make it a temptation.

James makes it clear that God does not tempt any man to do evil (1:13). Like a car manufacturer who puts his car through rigorous tests in order to showcase its capabilities, when God tests you, He's not saying, "I hope you don't fall apart." No, He says, "I know what I've built into you. And I will not allow you to be tested above what you're able" (see 1 Corinthians 10:13). The test He sends our way is not Him saying, "I wonder what's going to happen." It's Him saying, "Look what I've done."

This makes murmuring or complaining or whining a sin. "Pipe down," God would say to us. "It's only a test. I know what I've built into you. I know the work I've done deep within you." God knew Moses would pass this test. He wasn't tempting him to sin. Rather, He was testing him, knowing he would come through with flying colors.

If you're tempted by Satan, God intends it as a test to see you through. If you're tested by the Father, Satan will jump on it to tempt you. That's why the Greek word for "test" and "tempt" is the same word. Moses would pass the test. Jesus would beat back the temptation. So when that temptation comes strolling up to you tomorrow, know it's a test from God—and that He won't test you above that which you are able.

NOVEMBER 30

Likewise when the LORD sent you from Kadesh-barnea, saying, Go up and possess the land which I have given you; then ye rebelled against the commandment of the LORD your God, and ye believed him not, nor hearkened to his voice.

Deuteronomy 9:23

When they came to the boundary of the Promised Land, the Lord said, "Take it." The people, however, refused. Why? There were giants in the land.

"Why should we go in there? Our children might die," the fathers might have said.

"I know it's a land that flows with milk and honey," the wives might have said, "but the wilderness isn't such a bad place. We're together as a family. We home-school our kids. God is in our midst. The tabernacle is close by. The *shekinah* glory is seen. Manna comes down every day. This is a fine place to be."

"But it's not the Promised Land," God would say. "There aren't grapes the size of basketballs. There's no milk and honey. There's no destiny."

"Yes," the people would say, "but there's also no risk."

"Trust and obey," we sing. But what we often declare is, "I like it here. Why should I take my kids out of school and make that move? Why should I jeopardize the convenience? I really kind of like the wilderness." Yet, all the while, there's territory to take, work to do, and blessings ahead.

I have observed that when people don't step out and step up and move into the Promised Land—whatever that may be for them—they end up slowly dying in the wilderness. Oh, it's imperceptible at first, but after wandering around for years, they realize they're going in circles. At a certain point, a man says, "Stop this carousel. There's a call upon my life. I know what the Lord wants me to do."

I'm afraid we can be vulnerable to saying, "I'm blessed here. I like this." But in our hearts, we know that God has said, "Step up. Step out. Go where you're needed. There are jobs to do, battles to fight, and people to touch."

I don't know what that means for you personally, but I'll tell you this: we cannot stay the same in our spiritual walk day after month after year. I am either getting more radical for Jesus—taking steps of faith, launching out in service, plunging ahead—or I'm falling back and wandering in circles. Sure, my family might be safe. But something is missing in my soul.

Go in. Possess the land God has told you to take. Yes, you'll take some blows. Certainly there will be challenges and difficulties, but it's only in the Promised Land where the fruit will blow your mind, where the blessings will cause your soul to expand, and where life will no longer be routine.

DECEMBER 1

And the children of Israel took their journey from Beeroth of the children of Jaakan to Mosera: there Aaron died, and there he was buried; and Eleazar his son ministered in the priest's office in his stead. From thence they journeyed unto Gudgodah; and from Gudgodah to Jotbath, a land of rivers of waters. At that time the LORD separated the tribe of Levi, to bear the ark of the covenant of the LORD, to stand before the LORD to minister unto him, and to bless in his name, unto this day. Wherefore Levi hath no part nor inheritance with his brethren; the LORD is his inheritance, according as the LORD thy God promised him.

Deuteronomy 10:6–9

The tribe of Levi was to be the one to minister to the Lord. Why? The story is told in Exodus 32. When Moses came down the mountain the first time, seeing the children of Israel worshiping the golden calf, he said, "Who is on the Lord's side? Who will deal with this situation?" Only one tribe stepped up: the tribe of Levi. From that point on, Levi would be the tribe of ministry because they took the sword in the fear of the Lord. The other tribes said, "We don't want to get involved." And that can all too often be our tendency as well. Yet, if we're not willing to wield the sword of Scripture in love and say, "This cannot go on. This needs to be thought through and cut away," we cannot be servants of the Lord.

Paul said, "If we seek to please men, we cannot be the servants of God" (see Galatians 1:10). We need to be those who are merciful and loving enough to say to the people we care about who are involved in sin, "I care about you and am committed to you. Therefore, I'm not going to hold back the truth from you." This is not anger or hostility, judgment or condemnation. It's love and compassion, kindness and mercy. Only Levi was willing to unsheathe the sword and deal with the cancer that would corrupt the whole congregation. Thus, only Levi would qualify for ministry.

DECEMBER 2

But the land, whither ye go to possess it, is a land of hills and valleys, and drinketh water of the rain of heaven: a land which the LORD thy God careth for: the eyes of the LORD thy God are always upon it, from the beginning of the year even unto the end of the year. And it shall come to pass, if ye shall hearken diligently unto my commandments which I command you this day, to love the LORD your God, and to serve him with all your heart and with all your soul, that I will give you the rain of your land in his due season, the first rain and the latter rain, that thou mayest gather in thy corn, and thy wine, and thine oil. And I will send grass in thy fields for thy cattle, that thou mayest eat and be full.

Deuteronomy 11:13–15

The mention of "latter rain" also appears in Jeremiah 5, Hosea 6, Joel 2, and James 5—where it speaks of the outpouring of the Holy Spirit. "There's coming a time," the Lord says, "when I will pour out My Spirit upon all flesh. Your sons and daughters shall prophesy. Your young men shall see visions, your old men shall dream dreams" (see Joel 2:28).

We are already seeing the beginning of a wonderful last day's outpouring, where people are being filled and empowered by the Holy Spirit. But it's only the beginning. The Lord wants to save souls and bring in a huge harvest in these last days. And He's going to empower us to an even greater degree.

The latter rain is not something we pump up emotionally, but that which the Lord pours out upon those who simply love Him and give themselves in service to Him. "Ye shall receive power, after that the Holy Ghost is come upon you: and ye shall be witnesses unto me both in Jerusalem, and in all Judaea, and in Samaria, and unto the uttermost part of the earth," Jesus said (Acts 1:8).

Power is given for the purpose of service. Therefore, on us who say, "Lord, I love You. That's why I'm here. And I want to serve You. Use me," the Lord will pour out His Spirit in order that we might be His witnesses.

DECEMBER 3

Take heed to yourselves, that your heart be not deceived, and ye turn aside, and serve other gods, and worship them; and then the LORD's wrath be kindled against you, and he shut up the heaven, that there be no rain, and that the land yield not her fruit; and lest ye perish quickly from off the good land which the LORD giveth you.

Deuteronomy 11:16–17

Although the Lord pours out His Spirit to those who give themselves to serve Him, the outpouring will cease if we turn aside and serve the gods of our hobbies, our desires, or our flesh. Once I start serving these gods, the heavens are shut up and my soul gets dry.

Elijah—the one who called down fire from heaven—stormed into wicked King Ahab's court and said, "Be it known unto you, it shall not rain these years but according to my word." And indeed it didn't rain for over three years (see 1 Kings 17:1). James tells us that although Elijah was a man just like you and me, he knew how to pray (James 5:17). Therefore, he evidently knew this text, for Jesus said if His words abide in us, then our prayers will be answered (John 15:7).

That's why we attend Bible studies year after year after year. That's why I read the Word. I want to know what this book has to say that I might pray effectively. Elijah models this. The Word of the Lord was evidently in his heart, enabling him to pray effectively. The more Bible study you take in, the more Scripture you know, the more effectively you can pray. And the effectual, fervent prayer of a righteous man avails, or accomplishes, *much* (James 5:16).

DECEMBER 4

And it shall come to pass, when the LORD *thy God hath brought thee in unto the land whither thou goest to possess it, that thou shalt put the blessing upon mount Gerizim, and the curse upon mount Ebal.*

Deuteronomy 11:29

In Joshua 8, we see half of the tribes of the children of Israel on Mount Gerizim, the other half on Mount Ebal with Joshua, and the priests and Levites in the valley between. Joshua will say a certain commandment to which was attached a blessing, and all the tribes on Mount Gerizim will say, "Amen!" Then he will give a command with a curse—something which they're not to do—and those on Mount Ebal will also say, "Amen!" In so doing, the nation of Israel will acknowledge that if they obey God, they will be blessed. If not, they will be cursed. It was on Mount Ebal that sacrifice was to be made. I love this because where there are curses, an altar is available to make provision. I'm so glad about that because I've been on both sides of the valley. I've experienced the blessings of Gerizim. But I've also wandered over to Ebal. Thus, I am so grateful for the altar, the provision for my sin and stupidity.

Joshua is, of course, a picture of Jesus. Where is Jesus right now? He is between two mountains. He's already been on the mountain of cursing, where He who knew no sin was made sin for us as He hung on the cross of Calvary (2 Corinthians 5:21). But He's coming back to another mountain— the Mount of Olives, which will split in two when He returns as the Prince of Peace (Zechariah 14:4).

"I've heard you talk about being blessed if we obey the commandments," you might say. "I've done my best, tried my hardest. But I'm not being blessed like I thought I would be. You talk about taking territory, but it hasn't happened for me."

Wait. You're in the valley. Wait until Jesus gets back. Oh, we're blessed right now without question, but the Mount of Olives tells me the best is yet to come. When you read these blessings and promises, realize that, although they apply to you, to your marriage, to your family, and to your ministry, the best is yet to come. And I'm so looking forward to that. Obey the Lord. Keep His commandments. Bind His Word before your eyes. Keep it close at hand. Teach your children. And God will bless you, yes in this life; but especially, most importantly, most fully in the age of the kingdom, throughout eternity, in heaven.

DECEMBER 5

Take heed to thyself that thou offer not thy burnt offerings in every place that thou seest: but in the place which the LORD shall choose in one of thy tribes, there thou shalt offer thy burnt offerings, and there thou shalt do all that I command thee.

Deuteronomy 12:13–14

"Tear down their altars. Cut down their groves. Destroy their high places," God declares. "Instead, go to the place I tell and there you shall worship Me. There you shall bring your tithes and offerings to Me. There you shall make your vows to Me. There you shall seek Me."

Where was "there"?

Jerusalem.

"Why do we have to tithe? Why must we go to church on Sunday? I'm going to do what I want to do," some people say. But theirs is a wilderness mentality. They might be sincere, but God says once we have crossed into the Promised Land—which speaks of the Spirit-filled life, the deeper life, the productive life, the fruitful life—it's not up to us what to do.

"Our fathers say we are to worship on Mount Gerizim, yet you Jews say we are to worship in Jerusalem," the woman at the well said to Jesus.

"In reality," Jesus answered, "the Father is seeking those who will worship Him in spirit and in truth" (see John 4:23).

Why do we get together and worship the Lord with uplifted hands, on our knees, at His Table? Because we're worshiping the Lord in spirit. Why do we go through the Bible month after month, year after year, decade after decade? Because we're worshiping Him in truth.

DECEMBER 6

*Thou shalt not do so unto the L*ORD *thy God: for every abomination to the L*ORD*, which he hateth, have they done unto their gods; for even their sons and their daughters they have burnt in the fire to their gods. What thing soever I command you, observe to do it: thou shalt not add thereto, nor diminish from it.*

Deuteronomy 12:31–32

"It's not that simple," the cultist says to the believer. "You can't come boldly before the throne of grace. You've got to prove your sincerity."

In Moses' day, the Canaanites proved they were sincere seekers of their gods by literally burning their sons and daughters. Five-foot-high iron idols dedicated to Molech were constructed with a hole in them in which a fire would burn, causing the idol to become incandescent. Sincere worshipers would place their firstborn child on the red-hot arms of these idols in the valley of Tophet, also known as the valley of Gehenna, which is another name for hell.

Every cult and false religion is based upon man working his way up the ladder of sincerity, good works, and obedience to a system. Christianity alone is not based upon man working up to God, but God reaching down to man. "For by grace are ye saved," Paul declares. And what is grace? It is unmerited, undeserved, unearned favor. It is a gift of God, *not* of works (Ephesians 2:8–9).

What must a man do to be saved? Simply believe in the Lord Jesus Christ (Acts 16:30–31). Period. "It is *finished*," Jesus said (John 19:30, italics added). My standing with God is not about what I do to prove my sincerity, but about what He's already done to prove His love and mercy. And all that's left is for me to respond to His free gift of salvation.

DECEMBER 7

Thou shalt not eat any abominable thing.

Deuteronomy 14:3

In this section, Moses reiterates the dietary laws for the people of Israel—which meats were considered to be clean, which were unclean. These kosher laws served the people of Israel well not only in Moses' generation, but for centuries to come . . .

> In the Middle Ages, when plagues and disease devastated the continent of Europe, the Jewish people were singularly protected from many of them. Mistakenly thinking their protection came from magic or witchcraft, the Jews were persecuted. As time has passed, however, we now know that the reason the Jewish people in Europe were protected was because of their adherence to the sanitary and dietary regulations found throughout the book of Deuteronomy.

The wisdom of God's Word becomes all the more clear in light of the contemporary writings of other cultures. For example, an Egyptian scroll, written at approximately the same time Moses wrote Deuteronomy, is said to have propagated the following: To prevent gray hair, take blood from a black cat, mix it with the fat of a rattlesnake and eat it twice daily. Or to reverse baldness, take fat from a cat, a horse, a crocodile, a hippo, a snake, and an ibex and mix it together and eat it. If you have a severe case of baldness, add to it a tooth of a donkey that has been cooked in honey.

When we read these things, we chuckle because of the absurdity. But when we study the Scriptures, written at the same time as this papyrus, we see them proving to be medically correct and healthy. They are not dated, not absurd—and should the Lord tarry, I have a sneaking suspicion that as we learn more, we'll discover to a greater degree how God's dietary regulations are the best possible plan for the human condition.

When Jesus came on the scene, He said, "The issue is not what you eat physically, but what goes on in your heart" (see Mark 7:15). With this in mind, we can understand that these laws are not only to be followed by the Jewish people of Moses' day, but that they're applicable for you and me spiritually—that we might be careful what we take in, what we put into our soul.

DECEMBER 8

And thou shalt bestow that money for whatsoever thy soul lusteth after, for oxen, or for sheep, or for wine, or for strong drink, or for whatsoever thy soul desireth: and thou shalt eat there before the LORD thy God, and thou shalt rejoice, thou, and thine household, and the Levite that is within thy gates; thou shalt not forsake him; for he hath no part nor inheritance with thee. At the end of three years thou shalt bring forth all the tithe of thine increase the same year, and shalt lay it up within thy gates: and the Levite, (because he hath no part nor inheritance with thee,) and the stranger, and the fatherless, and the widow, which are within thy gates, shall come, and shall eat and be satisfied; that the LORD thy God may bless thee in all the work of thine hand which thou doest.

Deuteronomy 14:26–29

When the children of Israel brought their tithe, it was to be with rejoicing. "For God loveth a cheerful giver," Paul would write to the Corinthians (2 Corinthians 9:7). The Greek word translated "cheerful" is *hilaros*—from which we get the word "hilarious." God loves a person who gives hilariously, cheerfully, or gladly. Therefore, I think it's a mistake to feel obligated to give. It's a privilege to be able to say, "Lord, I'm honoring You in the way You've asked me."

If it's not a privilege for you, don't do it. You'll find, however, that things don't work for you in your budgeting and your own financial situation. Over and over I've watched people miss out on blessings all because of a failure to understand that they couldn't possibly out-give God.

Every third year, a second tithe was taken to take care of people who were poor—the fatherless, the widow, and the stranger. And that money was to be used for their well-being and welfare. If you add together the tithes of Deuteronomy 14, Deuteronomy 16, and Numbers 18, they come to an average of 23 percent annually. While it may be that even in our godless society we are contributing a portion of this through taxes, this we do know for certain: God's ways are right. His heart is *for* us. Therefore, when He asks us to give to Him, it's not only for His glory, but also for our good.

DECEMBER 9

And thou shalt remember that thou wast a bondman in the land of Egypt, and the Lord *thy God redeemed thee: therefore I command thee this thing to day. And it shall be, if he say unto thee, I will not go away from thee; because he loveth thee and thine house, because he is well with thee; then thou shalt take an aul, and thrust it through his ear unto the door, and he shall be thy servant for ever. And also unto thy maidservant thou shalt do likewise.*

Deuteronomy 15:15–17

Sacrifice and offering thou didst not desire; mine ears hast thou opened: burnt offering and sin offering hast thou not required. Then said I, Lo, I come: in the volume of the book it is written of me, I delight to do thy will, O my God: yea, thy law is within my heart.

Psalm 40:6–8

The ear of Jesus Christ was opened, pierced not with an awl but by the wood of the cross of Calvary. Jesus is the perfect bondslave who came not to be served, but to serve (Mark 10:45), who came not to do His own will, but His Father's (Matthew 26:39). For the joy set before Him, He endured the cross, despising the shame (Hebrews 12:2). He knew there would be suffering and bleeding, but He also knew that on the other side, there would be joy which would far outweigh and supersede even the pain.

And such can be the same for you and me . . .

Doulos, the Greek word for servant, refers to an under rower. Think of a ship sailing across the Mediterranean Sea. While the passengers on the deck enjoy the view, below them are men expending great energy, toiling at the oars. That's what it means to be a servant. You slave away hour after hour, day after day in order to get the people above you to their destination. The true servant says, "I want to get you to where you're supposed to be—out of the slough of despondency, out of the place where you're discouraged, confused, or damned eternally. I want to do whatever I can to get you to your destination."

"That sounds awful," you say, "rowing day after day under the deck just to get someone else to his or her destination."

But here's what you must remember: If the people on deck are headed to Maui, guess where you will end up? It's true. If I'm helping someone else to have a better day, I arrive at the same port. If I'm helping someone overcome discouragement, I myself end up overcoming my own discouragement. If I'm helping someone else with their marriage, my own marriage grows stronger, richer, and deeper. If I'm helping someone else who is confused about the nature of the Father, as I row for them, my own understanding of the Father becomes so much clearer.

This should not be surprising. After all, Jesus said, "Give, and it shall be given unto you; good measure, pressed down, and shaken together, and running over, shall men give into your bosom. For with the same measure that ye mete withal it shall be measured to you again" (Luke 6:38).

Next time you have a week where you feel physically, emotionally, spiritually, or mentally fatigued, here's the key: Serve others. Talk to others. Pray with others. Maybe people will notice your labor of love on their behalf. But it may be that your work will take place under the deck where, out of sight, unnoticed by others, as a bondslave, you row faithfully to get them to their destination.

DECEMBER 10

And it shall be, when he sitteth upon the throne of his kingdom, that he shall write him a copy of this law in a book out of that which is before the priests the Levites: and it shall be with him, and he shall read therein all the days of his life: that he may learn to fear the LORD his God, to keep all the words of this law and these statutes, to do them: that his heart be not lifted up above his brethren, and that he turn not aside from the commandment, to the right hand, or to the left: to the end that he may prolong his days in his kingdom, he, and his children, in the midst of Israel.

Deuteronomy 17:18–20

The first act the king was to perform upon taking the throne was not to go to an inaugural ball, throw a party for his donors, or watch a parade in his honor. God declared the first thing a king was to do was to make a copy of the law. Why? Because in writing down every line and every word, the law would be embedded in the king's mind.

I have found that if I have pencil and paper in hand when I have devotions or go to a Bible study, I never come away empty-handed. And even if I never refer to those notes again, taking notes forces me to be engaged in the process of listening.

Not only are we to write the Word down, but we're to pack it around. I have several pocket Bibles I carry not because I'm trying to be a holy Joe or some kind of Pharisee, but because I've found I can redeem a bunch of time— whether waiting for a stoplight, waiting for an appointment, or standing in line at the grocery store. You will be amazed at how much Scripture you can absorb in a single year simply by keeping the Word close at hand.

In addition to writing it down and packing it around, the king was not only to read the Word consistently, but to take it seriously. When I read the Bible, I fear the Lord. Why? Not because I'm condemned, but because I'm convicted. I realize the Word is right and I'm not, that it is good and I'm not, that it is true and I'm not. In other words, when I read the Word, I realize that I need Jesus every single day.

When do I find fault with others? When do I come down on others? When is my heart lifted up above others? When I'm not in the Word. When I'm in the Word, however, I realize how far I have yet to go. In reading the Word, the king would be reminded of his own need for mercy and forgiveness and would thereby be merciful and forgiving toward those he ruled.

If, like Israel's kings were instructed to do, I read the Word consistently and take it seriously, not only will I walk in the ways of the Lord, but also my children will follow. What a simple premise. What a glorious promise.

DECEMBER 11

When thou goest out to battle against thine enemies, and seest horses, and chariots, and a people more than thou, be not afraid of them: for the LORD thy God is with thee, which brought thee up out of the land of Egypt.

Deuteronomy 20:1

To the children of Israel, Moses didn't say, "*If* you see the enemy . . ." He said, "*When* you see the enemy . . ." In other words, battles were inevitable.

So too, if you are facing a battle today, you are neither unique nor alone. Every one of us will have encounters when we feel outgunned and outmaneuvered, when we feel under-prepared and overwhelmed. At such times, we are not to be afraid. Why? Because these challenges provide invaluable opportunities for us to see how God will come through for us.

DECEMBER 12

And it shall be, when ye are come nigh unto the battle, that the priest shall approach and speak unto the people, and shall say unto them, Hear, O Israel, ye approach this day unto battle against your enemies: let not your hearts faint, fear not, and do not tremble, neither be ye terrified because of them; for the LORD your God is he that goeth with you, to fight for you against your enemies, to save you.

Deuteronomy 20:2–4

There is no way to know how great God is until you are in a situation you can't handle, until you don't know what to do, until it is seemingly impossible to solve the problem. We will only know how great and loving our God is when we are in over our heads, completely at a loss. I've been there. So have you. Maybe you're there right now. The priest is to say, "Don't be afraid. The Lord is with you. He brought you out of Egypt, out of the world, out of hell. He's not going to let you go now."

DECEMBER 13

And the officers shall speak unto the people, saying, What man is there that hath built a new house, and hath not dedicated it? let him go and return to his house, lest he die in the battle, and another man dedicate it. And what man is he that hath planted a vineyard, and hath not yet eaten of it? let him also go and return unto his house, lest he die in the battle, and another man eat of it. And what man is there that hath betrothed a wife, and hath not taken her? let him go and return unto his house, lest he die in the battle, and another man take her. And the officers shall speak further unto the people, and they shall say, What man is there that is fearful and fainthearted? let him go and return unto his house, lest his brethren's heart faint as well as his heart. And

> *it shall be, when the officers have made an end of speaking*
> *unto the people, that they shall make captains of the armies*
> *to lead the people.*

Deuteronomy 20:5–9

Three groups of men were exempt from battle: those who hadn't finished building their houses, those who hadn't yet eaten of their vineyards, and those who were engaged, but not yet married. In this, we see God's desire that people delight in His blessings before they devote themselves to battle.

> For ye know the grace of our Lord Jesus Christ, that, though he was rich, yet for your sakes he became poor, that ye through his poverty might be rich.

2 Corinthians 8:9

Jesus left the blessings of heaven in order to bless us. And, while there is definitely a time for battle, there is also a time to delight in the blessings that are ours through the grace of the One who became poor that we might be rich.

A fourth group deferred from battle was comprised of those who were afraid. When people lack faith, they often begin to speak negatively to justify their own fears. Cynicism and criticism are often a cowardly covering for fear. And they're contagious. That's why those who were afraid were to go home.

If you want to be used by the Lord, ask yourself if your household is stable, if the work of your hands is thriving, if your marriage is healthy, if your heart is full of faith. If a man doesn't have a home for his family, he ought to tend to that first. If a man doesn't have a job and wants to be supported by others, he should get a job and succeed at that. If a man has a lousy marriage, he shouldn't be taking on further ministry. If a man is full of fear, he shouldn't try to hide behind ministry or missions. This passage is an important checklist for anyone who wants to be used by the Lord, to be engaged in His work.

DECEMBER 14

When thou shalt besiege a city a long time, in making war against it to take it, thou shalt not destroy the trees thereof by forcing an axe against them: for thou mayest eat of them, and thou shalt not cut them down (for the tree of the field is man's life) to employ them in the siege: only the trees which thou knowest that they be not trees for meat, thou shalt destroy and cut them down; and thou shalt build bulwarks against the city that maketh war with thee, until it be subdued.

Deuteronomy 20:19–20

When the Israelites went to battle, their axes were not to fly indiscriminately. That is, they were not to cut down any fruit-bearing tree. This is a good word for us because in our battle against principalities and powers, against the Devil, our adversary, if we're not careful, we can cut down trees that bear fruit—other believers, denominations, or churches who might have an entirely different flavor than ours, but from which we can be nourished. Wise is the believer who says, "Lord, help me to see what I can glean from that group, what I can learn from those people."

So much of what I've learned has been from trees that, in my own fleshly tendency, I would have chopped down. Wouldn't it be something if all the energy we expended analyzing ministries and criticizing Christians was harnessed against the real Enemy? Yes, there's a war to wage, a battle to fight. And some trees are apostate indeed. But others have fruit that we can glean, through which we can grow, from which we can gain strength for the battle against the Enemy of our souls.

DECEMBER 15

And all the men of his city shall stone him with stones, that he die: so shalt thou put evil away from among you; and all Israel shall hear, and fear.

Deuteronomy 21:21

All the men of the city were to stone the rebellious son. Why? I suggest three reasons . . .

Motivation. With communities being small in Bible times, the men of the city would know the son in question. They would know his family. Therefore, it would be so difficult to stone him, and they would go home resolved to do whatever it took to make sure their own sons didn't follow the same path of rebellion.

Evaluation. Participating in the stoning would cause the men in the community to ask themselves if there was something they could have done to turn him from his rebellious ways.

Proclamation. The stoning proclaimed to the community that rebellion was neither a "stage" nor an inevitable part of growing up. It was simply not to be tolerated.

If you've either been, or raised, a rebellious child, I call your attention to another rebellious son—the Prodigal Son of Luke 15. When this rebellious son returned, his father ran out to meet him not with rocks in his hand, but with a robe for his son. Why? Did God change His mind somewhere between Deuteronomy and Luke about the severity of rebellion?

No. The punishment for rebellion is always death (Romans 3:23). But because a third Son—not the rebellious son, not the Prodigal Son, but the perfect Son—became sin and took my place on the cross, I am forgiven completely.

DECEMBER 16

When a man hath taken a wife, and married her, and it come to pass that she find no favour in his eyes, because he hath found some uncleanness in her: then let him write her a bill of divorcement, and give it in her hand, and send her out of his house. And when she is departed out of his house, she may go and be another man's wife.

Deuteronomy 24:1–2

For centuries, this was a controversial passage in the life and history of Israel. In fact, when Jesus came on the scene, there was a red-hot debate taking place in the culture concerning the definition of "uncleanness." One opinion was voiced by a famous scholar named Hillel. Liberal in his perspective, Hillel said a woman was to be considered unclean—and, therefore, a candidate for divorce—if she caused uncleanness in her home. For example, if she over-salted her husband's eggs, thereby causing him to be angry, the resulting "unclean" atmosphere of the home would be her fault. Hillel went on to say that if a man saw a woman who was "cleaner" than his wife, his wife would become "unclean" by comparison. The other opinion was voiced by a scholar named Shammai, who insisted that uncleanness applied exclusively to immorality.

When asked His opinion on the matter, Jesus answered, "What God has joined together, let not man put asunder."

"Why, then, did Moses give permission to divorce?" the Pharisees asked Him.

"Because of the hardness of your hearts," Jesus explained (see Matthew 19:3–9). As evidenced by Jesus' answer, the answer to the question of divorce doesn't lie in loopholes.

"I want a divorce because I'm being abused," says a wife.

"How are you being abused?" I ask.

"Verbally," she answers.

"I want a divorce because my wife is hindering my spiritual growth," a husband says.

"No," Jesus says. "Go back to the garden of Eden and see that God's plan is that one woman and one man stay together until death separates them."

Does this mean the divorced person has committed the unpardonable sin? Not at all. It means they've committed a sin—just like we all have. But because God hates divorce (Malachi 2:16), it must be an absolute last resort, not a first option. And there must be the admission that it is only the hardness of one's own heart that makes it even a possibility.

DECEMBER 17

Remember what Amalek did unto thee by the way, when ye were come forth out of Egypt; how he met thee by the way, and smote the hindmost of thee, even all that were feeble behind thee, when thou wast faint and weary; and he feared not God.

Deuteronomy 25:17–18

It has been said that the primary task of teaching is not so much to reveal as it is to remind. And evidently Moses would agree, for as we have seen, the entire book of Deuteronomy is a reminder to the children of Israel of what God had done for them, of what He had taught them, and of what He expected of them.

The passage before us is no exception, beginning as it does with the word, "Remember" (verse 17), and ending with the words, "Thou shalt not forget" (verse 19).

What were the children of Israel not to forget? They were not to forget how during their wilderness wanderings the Amalekites attacked them not man-to-man, not face-to-face, but from the back. The Israelites were to remember how the Amalekites would wait in hiding until they passed by, how they would attack those who were weary and feeble.

We, too, have an Enemy who attacks us constantly. "Be sober," Peter said.

"Be vigilant; because your adversary the devil, as a roaring lion, walketh about, seeking whom he may devour" (1 Peter 5:8). It is said that in the jungle, the lion wakes up each day knowing that he simply must outrun the slowest prey. And the same is true spiritually, for like the lion, Satan attacks the weariest or feeblest among us. And, like Amalek, he finds them at the back of the pack.

This is a word we need to remember, a word of which we need to be reminded constantly because we can say, "I've been walking with the Lord for a number of years. I've been involved in a lot of battles. I need to kick back a bit, to cruise awhile," not realizing that those who think they deserve a break are the very ones most vulnerable to an attack . . .

He was a great man, a godly man. Year after year he had led his troops into battle. He was their commander, their king. But at the age of fifty, he said, "I've fought long enough. I'm going to kick back awhile." So he sent another to lead the troops while he stayed behind. On the roof of his palace one night, enjoying the view of the golden city of Jerusalem, his eye came across a woman taking a bath. Intrigued by her, he had an affair with her and tried to cover it up by murdering her husband. He should have been fully engaged. He should have been front and center in the battle. Instead, he thought he deserved a break. And as a result, life was never the same for David, for his family, or for his kingdom.

The same thing can happen to you and me. "I've been walking with the Lord for forty years," we say. "Who says I have to have devotions and go to Bible study? Why not let someone else teach Sunday school? Why not let someone else work in the nursery? Why not let someone else go to the prayer meeting? I'm tired."

We are currently seeing a rash of middle-aged men in our own community falling into immorality. The number of people who have been sucked into sin at this point in life is astonishing to me. And the common thread among them seems to be a misconception that they were justified in pulling away from fellowship, in drifting away from worship because they thought they had paid their dues, because they thought that spending time with the Lord or with His people no longer needed to be a priority.

Precious people, be oh, so careful that you don't grow weary somewhere in middle life, saying, "I've fought the fight. Now it's time to cruise." Amalek attacks the back of the pack. He'll be waiting for you.

DECEMBER 18

Therefore it shall be, when the Lord thy God hath given thee rest from all thine enemies round about, in the land which the Lord thy God giveth thee for an inheritance to possess it, that thou shalt blot out the remembrance of Amalek from under heaven; thou shalt not forget it.

Deuteronomy 25:19

At only thirty years of age, he wasn't weary. But he was feeble. He hadn't always been that way. "Smite the shepherd and the sheep will scatter," the Lord had said.

"Not me," he had boldly answered. "My name is Peter. I'm solid as a rock. You can count on me" (see Matthew 26:31–35).

But hours later, when Jesus was led away to the trial that would ultimately lead to His crucifixion, Peter did what he said he would never do: he ran. And then, feeling feeble, he followed Jesus afar off. He still followed Jesus, but no longer at His side. Now there was a distance between them (Matthew 26:58).

The enemies of Jesus lit fires that night to take the chill away. And Peter was chilled indeed—not only outwardly, but inwardly—to his very soul. He knew he was not where he was supposed to be, where he said he would be, where he used to be. Instead, he stood by the fires of the enemy.

"We know you," one of those who stood by said to him. "You're one of His followers."

"No, I'm not," Peter answered.

"Weren't you with Jesus?" asked a young girl.

"No," Peter insisted.

"I'm sure you're a Galilean," said another.

And at this point Peter swore, the original text indicating that he took an oath as if to say, "My soul be damned if I know that Man" (see Matthew 26:74).

Be careful when you feel feeble that you don't say, "I'm not what I should be or not what I used to be so I'm going to follow Jesus afar off." When you follow Jesus from afar, there's a chill in your soul that will drive you to the fires of the Enemy in search of warmth. You'll visit web sites you know you ought not to look at. You'll turn to movies or to alcohol, to drugs or to fantasies, hoping they'll warm your soul. You'll fall prey to the attack of the Enemy when you allow former sins or tendencies to needlessly drive you to the back of the pack.

What are you supposed to do when you're weary or feeble?

Don't go to the back. Go to the front. Become more engaged than ever, more involved than you ever were before in your spiritual work and devotional life, more committed to service and ministry, to worship and Bible study.

> But they that wait upon the LORD shall renew their strength; they shall mount up with wings as eagles; they shall run, and not be weary; and they shall walk, and not faint.
>
> Isaiah 40:31

Why should we remain front and center in the things of the Lord even when we're tired, even if we're feeble? Because in so doing, our strength is not diminished. It's renewed, replenished, and restored.

We're involved in a battle, to be sure. But there's coming a day when even the memory of Amalek will be blotted out—when Satan is cast into the lake of fire (Revelation 20:10). And Isaiah tells us we're going to "narrowly look" on Satan (14:16–17). That is, with furrowed brow, we'll scratch our heads and say, "Is *this* the one who held people captive, who shook kingdoms, who brought destruction? We were tricked by *him*?" And then we'll see how greatly the lion, seeking whom he may devour, pales in comparison to the Lion of the tribe of Judah (1 Peter 5:8; Revelation 5:5).

Until then, remain fully engaged in your devotional life, in your personal walk, in your service for the King. In so doing, not only will you please Him greatly, not only will your strength be renewed daily, but the arrows of Amalek will never reach you way up there at the front.

DECEMBER 19

And Moses charged the people the same day, saying, These shall stand upon mount Gerizim to bless the people, when ye are come over Jordan; Simeon, and Levi, and Judah, and Issachar, and Joseph, and Benjamin: and these shall stand upon mount Ebal to curse; Reuben, Gad, and Asher, and Zebulun, Dan, and Naphtali.

Deuteronomy 27:11–13

Mount Gerizim and Mount Ebal are each about two thousand feet high. Between them is a valley that served as a natural amphitheater. With six tribes on each mountain and the priests and leaders in between, the stage was set for an illustrated sermon the children of Israel would not soon forget.

As the law was read, the tribes on Mount Ebal would say "Amen" to the curses, while those on Mount Gerizim would affirm the blessings. And lest you think you would rather be on Mount Gerizim affirming the blessings, don't forget that the altar—the place where blood is shed, where forgiveness is made—was on Mount Ebal.

You might be aware of failings and shortcomings in your life, of times you've dropped the ball and cursed yourself or others because of stupidity and sin. But where sin abounds, grace abounds more (Romans 5:20). Therefore, the greater awareness I have of my sin, the more thankful I am for the grace of God. It is not surprising that the one who is forgiven much loves much (Luke 7:47), making Mount Ebal—the place where blood is shed—the place where there is, ultimately, peace and joy.

DECEMBER 20

And it shall come to pass, if thou shalt hearken diligently unto the voice of the LORD thy God, to observe and to do all his commandments which I command thee this day, that the LORD thy God will set thee on high above all nations of the earth: and all these blessings shall come on thee, and overtake thee, if thou shalt hearken unto the voice of the LORD thy God.

Deuteronomy 28:1–2

When I see the blessings in Deuteronomy 28, I can't help but say, "That's exactly what I want. I want to see my family blessed. I want my location to be satisfying to me. I want to see my cupboards full. I want to experience stability and spiritual intimacy. I want to see the work of my hands blessed, to have a daily routine that's fulfilling, to know my future is secure." But this is hardly surprising, for who of us doesn't want these blessings?

So when I hear Moses saying, "If you hearken diligently to the Lord, if you obey all of His commandments, these blessings will be yours," I say, "Wonderful!"—until I try, but inevitably and consistently fail.

You see, the key to success and blessing lies in obeying all of the commandments. It can't be 90 percent or even 99 percent. To get the victory that brings the blessings, one must do it *all* (James 2:10) because the Ten Commandments are interwoven in such a way that to break one is ultimately to break all ten. Think of it this way . . .

> You're out at sea, two miles from shore, when you notice that, although nine of the floorboards in your boat are shipshape, one is rotting away in the salt water. Therefore, even though only one in ten is faulty, even though nine are in perfect order, you're sunk.

So too, Moses said if you want these blessings, you've got to obey *all* the commandments. And therein lies the problem. I want to. I try. But I can't.

There is One, however, who did indeed keep *all* the commandments. In fact, so perfectly did He keep them that even His enemies could find no fault in Him (Luke 23:4). And because Jesus kept all the commandments, because He fulfilled every expectation and requirement of the law, He gets all of the blessings. In other words, every Old Testament blessing, every glorious promise made to those who would walk in God's ways, who would obey God's Word, who would seek God's heart is His because He did all of those things (2 Corinthians 1:19–20).

And here's the amazing news: When you became a Christian, not only did Christ come in you, but you were placed in Him (2 Corinthians 5:17). Therefore, all the promises are yours as well.

DECEMBER 21

Blessed shalt thou be in the city, and blessed shalt thou be in the field. Blessed shall be the fruit of thy body, and the fruit of thy ground, and the fruit of thy cattle, the increase of thy kine, and the flocks of thy sheep. Blessed shall be thy basket and thy store. Blessed shalt thou be when thou comest in, and blessed shalt thou be when thou goest out. The LORD shall cause thine enemies that rise up against thee to be smitten before thy face: they shall come out against thee one way, and flee before thee seven ways. The LORD shall command the blessing upon thee in thy storehouses, and in all that thou settest thine hand unto; and he shall bless thee in the land which the LORD thy God giveth thee.

Deuteronomy 28:3–8

"Why don't I see blessings in my life?" you ask.

Maybe God has blessed you more than you realize. Maybe you haven't taken the time to think through the way He's blessed you in the city and in the country, blessed the fruit of your body, blessed you in the storehouse, blessed you in your basket, blessed you with victory over the Enemy who threatened to crush and destroy you. Maybe He's blessed you more than you think. And maybe part of the issue is to stop and review what He's done for you and to rejoice in that.

But more importantly, maybe you don't see God's blessings in your life because you're working too hard to even notice them . . .

After wasting his father's money in the far country, the Prodigal Son returned, not to punishment, but to a party. "Unfair!" said his older brother to their father. "I've been with you every day, working faithfully. But you never threw a party on my behalf."

"Son," the father answered. "All that I have is yours" (see Luke 15:31), as if to say, "Any time you wanted, you could have had anything and everything you desired. But you were too busy being self-righteous, working in the field trying to impress me, trying to earn something from me to come out of the field and into the party."

So too, many of us have said, "I'm going to pray more. I'm going to work harder. I'm going to worship with greater intensity. I'm going to give more money. I'm going to teach Sunday school or work in the nursery so that I will be blessed," only to find that it never works.

We're blessed, gang, no matter what we do or don't do simply because we're His. But now God wants to use us. Isn't it amazing that God would want to use *us*?

> I am crucified with Christ: nevertheless I live; yet not I, but Christ liveth in me: and the life which I now live in the flesh I live by the faith of the Son of God, who loved me, and gave himself for me.
>
> Galatians 2:20

The more we allow Christ to work in and through us, the more He taps us on the shoulder, saying, "I've already blessed you. Now I want to use you. Go out there and serve for My glory."

DECEMBER 22

For this commandment which I command thee this day, it is not hidden from thee, neither is it far off. It is not in heaven, that thou shouldest say, Who shall go up for us to heaven, and bring it unto us, that we may hear it, and do it? Neither is it beyond the sea, that thou shouldest say, Who shall go over the sea for us, and bring it unto us, that we may hear it, and do it? But the word is very nigh unto thee, in thy mouth, and in thy heart, that thou mayest do it.

Deuteronomy 30:11–14

As we come to chapter 30, nearing the end of Moses' farewell sermon to the children of Israel, I can almost hear Moses pause, sigh, and look the congregation in the eye as he begins to share with them from his soul.

He's been going on and on, repeating the commandments of the Lord. And now he says God's commandment is not secret, mystical, abstract, or hard to reach. It's not in the heavens, but is very near to them. How near? As close as it can be. It's embedded in their hearts and on the tips of their tongues.

After twenty-nine chapters of preaching, Moses pauses and essentially says, "You know what to do. And you know that it's true." People do know. They might not want to admit it, but deep within, they know that the best way to live is to love God and keep His commandments. After all, who does even the unsaved person want to move into the vacant house next to him or her—a person who loves God and honors the Ten Commandments, or one who hates God and believes that murder, adultery, stealing, lying, and killing are acceptable?

Or think of it this way . . .

You run out of gas in the middle of a big city just before midnight. You leave your car by the side of a poorly lit street and begin walking to the nearest gas station. After a block or two, sensing you're not alone, you look over your shoulder and see four big guys following you. Would it make a difference if you knew they were coming out of an evening Bible study and prayer meeting rather than out of a bar?

In our hearts, we know the right way to live is to love God and obey the commands He's given us. "So choose life," Moses says. "Don't violate what you know is true, what you know you ought to do, what you know is best for you."

Jesus said all of the commandments are summed up in a single word: love. "Love the Lord thy God with all thy heart, and with all thy soul, and with all thy mind," He said. "And . . . love thy neighbour as thyself" (Matthew 22:37, 39). We're to love God passionately and love our neighbor compassionately. It's just that simple.

"I know what to do," you might be saying, "I know God's ways are true, that they're best for me and you. But here's the problem: I don't come through. There are times when I don't do what I know is the right thing to do. And there are times when I do things I ought not to do. I understand what is right and good and true. But I fail in so many ways, on so many days."

Wait. There's hope because this very passage pops up again in the New Testament. Paul reaches back to Deuteronomy 30 and look what he says concerning these very things . . .

> But the righteousness which is of faith speaketh on this wise, Say not in thine heart, Who shall ascend into heaven? (that is, to bring Christ down from above:) Or, Who shall descend into the deep? (that is, to bring up Christ again from the dead.) . . .
>
> Romans 10:6–7

Inspired by the Spirit, Paul says, "There's another way. Not the word of the law, but the word of faith . . ."

> But what saith it? The word is nigh thee, even in thy mouth, and in thy heart: that is, the word of faith, which we preach; that if thou shalt confess with thy mouth the Lord Jesus, and shalt believe in thine heart that God hath raised him from the dead, thou shalt be saved. For with the heart man believeth unto righteousness; and with the mouth confession is made unto salvation.
>
> Romans 10:8–10

There's no need to try to attain a spiritual high or dig into the depths of your soul, for salvation is in none of those places. Where is it? It's on the tip of your tongue, if you'll simply confess that you want Jesus to be your Lord.

DECEMBER 23

Be strong and of a good courage, fear not, nor be afraid of them: for the LORD thy God, he it is that doth go with thee; he will not fail thee, nor forsake thee.

Deuteronomy 31:6

Fear is to the Devil what faith is to the Lord. That is, Satan responds to, takes advantage of, and delights in fear the same way our Lord responds to, works through, and delights in faith. When I don't know how the bills will get paid or if the relationship will be restored, the Devil will try to get me to become full of anxiety and fear. God, however, "hath not given us the spirit of fear; but of power, and of love, and of a sound mind" (2 Timothy 1:7).

The disciples were on the Sea of Galilee, toiling at the oars. The wind was howling, the waves were rolling, and the disciples, many of whom were seasoned fishermen, were afraid of the ferocity of the storm. Suddenly they saw Someone walking on the waves, headed in their direction. "It's a ghost!" they shouted, perhaps alluding to the legend that said when a boat was about to go down, a ghost would come to deliver the message that the lives of the men on board were over.

But then they heard the words, "Be of good cheer; it is I; be not afraid" (Matthew 14:27).

Faith is like a muscle. It doesn't grow unless it's exercised. And we need to exercise faith in a most practical way. In the midst of the storm, when it seems as though our boat is sinking, we need to choose to be of good cheer. I have discovered over and over that when I make the decision to be strong, to be of good cheer, to not give into tears and fears, that the Lord is truly near.

Romans 10:17 says faith comes by hearing and hearing by the Word of God. We take faith in as we hear the promises of God's Word and the preaching of the Scriptures. Faith is worked in by the hearing of the Word—but it's worked out by the speaking of the Word. That's why Romans 10 also says we must confess with our mouths (verses 9–10). Faith comes in through the ear, but is worked out through the mouth.

A lot of times we take in a Scripture, but then have a tendency to complain or murmur—and wonder why faith isn't impacting our situation. Jesus said, "*Say* to the mountain, be removed . . ." (see Matthew 21:21). This is such a key, but is forgotten so easily. Faith that works is not only a matter of having devotions in the morning or going to Bible study in the evening, but it's a matter of speaking out that which we have taken in.

If I hear the Word in a Bible study and go my way, saying, "I don't know what's going to happen. I don't know how things are going to work," my faith is short-circuited by my words of fear and frustration. Proverbs 18:21 tells us that the power of life and death is in the tongue. How often we kill our faith either by the words we say or fail to say.

> For he hath said, I will never leave thee, nor forsake thee. So that we may boldly say, The Lord is my helper, and I will not fear what man shall do unto me.
>
> Hebrews 13:5–6

"He hath said . . . that we may boldly say . . ." Next time you are fearful about the future, boldly speak out what He has already said, and watch your faith grow.

DECEMBER 24

He found him in a desert land, and in the waste howling wilderness; he led him about, he instructed him, he kept him as the apple of his eye. As an eagle stirreth up her nest, fluttereth over her young, spreadeth abroad her wings, taketh them, beareth them on her wings: so the LORD alone did lead him, and there was no strange god with him.

Deuteronomy 32:10–12

Eagles can be found on every continent of the world except Antarctica. And the eagle is not only the symbol of America, but was, in czarist days, the symbol of Russia. In Bible times, it was the symbol of the Roman Empire.

The African eagle, with which the children of Israel would have been familiar, makes its home in the Middle East and has a wingspan of up to ten feet.

Once a year, the female eagle lays an egg in a nest high over a bluff or ravine, inaccessible to predators. For the six weeks following its hatching, the eaglet has it made in the shade. He can see lots of things from his vantage point. He's fed hourly by his mother. And he grows fat and plump.

By week five, he has grown quite large. And then something begins to happen. Unbeknownst to him, his mother designed the nest in such a way that sticks point inward. So as he gets fatter, the sticks begin to poke him. And no doubt Ernie Eaglet wonders why his parents didn't make a more comfortable nest—never realizing that its design was all part of the plan to get him to do something he never would have done otherwise: to fly.

The same thing can happen to you and me. We're comfy. We're cozy. We're chubby. But all of a sudden, something begins to happen that agitates us, that pokes at us. "My boss shouldn't treat me this way," we squawk. "My friend shouldn't ignore me that way," we screech.

Wait a minute. It's all part of a divine design, a grand plan. Therefore, wise is the man or woman who doesn't blame the sticks, but realizes they're part of the Father's plan.

At about this time, Mom returns to the nest one day and, with her five-foot wings, stirs it and bumps it. And Ernie is thrown out, causing him to fall hundreds of feet toward the ravine below. Feathers fly. Ernie squawks. The ground gets closer, the rocks bigger—when Mama swoops underneath Ernie and carries him on her back to the nest once again.

Whew! Ernie thinks, That was close! I hope Mom learned a lesson about being clumsy. But a few days later, Mama stirs the nest once again, sending Ernie screeching and tumbling once more. And once again, she swoops underneath him at seemingly the last minute, returning him to the nest at last.

The same process is repeated over and over again. But somewhere after the sixth or seventh time, Ernie catches air. No longer sore at his mother, he soars with her. And he can't believe it. He didn't have any idea that he could fly—until he was dumped out of the nest.

"What are You doing, God?" we cry. "If I'm Your inheritance, if You keep me as the apple of Your eye, then why am I headed for the rocks?" But right before we crash—maybe only a moment or so before we're crushed—He swoops in, bears us on His back, and returns us to the nest. Then, days later, He stirs the nest and begins the process all over again.

You see, God loves you and me too much to allow us to settle into the comfort of mediocrity. So He makes our nest uncomfortable as He gets us ready to do something new. He's not going to let us settle for a perch on a cliff when He knows we could soar in the heavenlies.

DECEMBER 25

He made him ride on the high places of the earth, that he might eat the increase of the fields; and he made him to suck honey out of the rock, and oil out of the flinty rock.

Deuteronomy 32:13

In Israel, bees make their honeycombs, and olive trees take root in crevasses, or fissures, in the rocks. Therefore, what would seem to be an unproductive place actually produces sweetness and sustenance.

"I'm on the rocks," we cry. "This is it. I'm through."

And yet God would say, "There's honey and oil in those rocks, for in them you will discover sweetness you never knew about, empowering and anointing you never would have experienced."

If you're between a rock and a hard place, take hope, dear saint, for it is there you will find honey and oil, sweetness and sustenance for your journey.

DECEMBER 26

For the LORD shall judge his people, and repent himself for his servants, when he seeth that their power is gone, and there is none shut up, or left. And he shall say, Where are their gods, their rock in whom they trusted, which did eat the fat of their sacrifices, and drank the wine of their drink offerings? let them rise up and help you, and be your protection. See now that I, even I, am he, and there is no god with me: I kill, and I make alive; I wound, and I heal: neither is there any that can deliver out of my hand. For I lift up my hand to heaven, and say, I live for ever.

Deuteronomy 32:36–40

We like to think of God as One who heals. And He does. But, as seen in verse 39, He also wounds. When I read about God and study His Word, I realize that He is much bigger than my ability to package Him neatly. He is, after all, God.

"Are you not thirsty?" said the Lion.

"I'm *dying* of thirst," said Jill.

"Then drink," said the Lion.

"May I—could I—would you mind going away while I do?" said Jill.

The Lion answered this only by a look and a very low growl. And as Jill gazed at its motionless bulk, she realized that she might as well have asked the whole mountain to move aside for her convenience.

"Will you promise not to—do anything to me, if I do come?" said Jill.

"I make no promise," said the Lion.

"*Do* you eat girls?" she said.

"I have swallowed up girls and boys, women and men, kings and emperors, cities and realms," said the Lion.

"I daren't come and drink," said Jill.

"Then you will die of thirst," said the Lion.[4]

In his classic series, *The Chronicles of Narnia*, C. S. Lewis drove home a very real point. That is, God doesn't make deals with me or you. He's God. And He can wound, heal, kill, and resurrect whenever He wants. Our God is indeed an awesome God, a fearful and terrible God. He loves us. He proved it by sending His Son to die for us. But never forget this passage in Deuteronomy 32. The people who forget this do so to their own destruction.

DECEMBER 27

And this is the blessing, wherewith Moses the man of God blessed the children of Israel before his death.

Deuteronomy 33:1

Deuteronomy 32 ended with a reiteration of God's refusal to allow Moses to enter the Promised Land with the children of Israel. Chapter 33 begins with Moses blessing the people. And this, among other things, is what qualifies Moses to be called a "man of God," a phrase seen here in Scripture for the first time. When God denied Moses' requests to accompany the people into the Promised Land, Moses could have said, "If after forty years, this is the thanks I get; if after I've given my life for these people and led them through the wilderness to the best of my ability, I'm disqualified because of one mistake, I'm outta here." But he didn't. Rather than running away and licking his wounds, Moses blessed the people.

Greatness is found in what a man does within the boundaries placed around him. Many people say, "If I can't do this, if I can't be that, I won't do anything." Not Moses. He shows us that the way to greatness, to being a man of God, is not to pull back, but to be a blessing.

DECEMBER 28

*And this is the blessing of Judah: and he said, Hear, L*ORD, *the voice of Judah, and bring him unto his people: let his hands be sufficient for him; and be thou an help to him from his enemies.*

Deuteronomy 33:7

"Lord," Moses said, "cause Judah to prosper. May his tribe increase. Help him when he encounters the enemy." As the people of Israel marched through the wilderness and, again, as they will march into the Land of Promise, which tribe leads the way? Judah. *Judah* means "Praise." We enter into His gates with thanksgiving and into His courts with praise (Psalm 100:4). Praise is always the key.

Christian scholar and author Francis Schaeffer reportedly once said that if he had one hour to present the gospel to someone, he would use the first fifty-five minutes to tell him what God is like, and he would use the last five minutes to communicate how he could know Him. The same holds true for the believer. If you want to be victorious and fruitful in your walk with the Lord, praise is absolutely foundational and essential. As we praise the Lord, our focus shifts from what we need to do to what He has already done; from our insufficiency to His all-sufficiency; from our weakness to His all-encompassing strength.

DECEMBER 29

And of Levi he said, Let thy Thummim and thy Urim be with thy holy one.

Deuteronomy 33:8

"I don't know what to do. I don't know which way to go," we are prone to say. Even in these New Testament times, the Urim and the Thummim give us real understanding about finding God's will and getting His direction, for in whose care were the Urim and the Thummim? They were in the charge of the high priest (Numbers 27:21).

"I am the way," said Jesus, our great High Priest. He didn't say, "I'll tell you the way," or "I'll point you to the way." He said, "I *am* the way" (John 14:6, italics added).

One of my tasks as a pastor and teacher is to remind people of this constantly. People come seeking an answer, asking for direction. But what they need to do is simply cling to Jesus every hour, every minute. And then, because He *is* the way, they'll end up in the right place.

At six months old, my granddaughter Bailey doesn't say, "Mommy, how do I get to the mall?" She just stays close to Amanda, and believe me, she'll get there! So too, like Bailey, we can say to the Lord, "I'm not going to be anxious about what I should do tomorrow. I'm just going to abide in You, cling to You today, close to Your heart, right by Your side. And I know I'll end up exactly where I'm supposed to be."

DECEMBER 30

There is none like unto the God of Jeshurun, who rideth upon the heaven in thy help, and in his excellency on the sky. The eternal God is thy refuge, and underneath are the everlasting arms.

Deuteronomy 33:26–27

Having finished the pronunciation of blessing upon the congregation of Israel, this great man of God reminds them again who their God is. If the sun, moon, and stars are the work of God's fingers (Psalm 8:3), what must be the power of His everlasting arms?

When I was three years old, I remember my dad pulling up into our driveway after his day at work at the bank. I would scramble to the top of the wood box on the side of our house each day, and after parking the car, he would walk to the wood box and with outstretched arms say, "Okay, Jon. Jump." And although I was scared, I'd jump. He always caught me. Every time.

Moses is hoping the children of Israel will come to understand the same thing—that their Father has strong arms and that He will never let them fall.

DECEMBER 31

*And there arose not a prophet since in Israel like unto Moses,
whom the LORD knew face to face, in all the signs and the
wonders, which the LORD sent him to do in the land of Egypt
to Pharaoh, and to all his servants, and to all his land, and
in all that mighty hand, and in all the great terror which
Moses shewed in the sight of all Israel.*

Deuteronomy 34:10–12

Stuck in prison, John the Baptist sent messengers to ask Jesus if He was indeed the Messiah. If not, he would look for another. Jesus' answer to the messengers was for them to tell John how He had healed the blind, made the lame to walk, and cleansed the leper, raised the dead. Then Jesus added, "And blessed is he who is not offended in Me" (see Matthew 11:2–6). When John received this message, I wonder if he beat himself for his lack of faith. He had been so bold up to that point; I wonder if he felt his ministry was, after all, a failure.

Certainly Moses would be able to understand. Having been faithful for forty years, his obedience had faltered at a moment of frustration. Yet, because God had shown him the Promised Land, Moses knew the end of his story. John didn't. You see, right after his messengers left, Jesus called John the greatest man ever born (Matthew 11:11).

So too, if you feel like a failure, like you've let the Lord down once too often, like He will never again be able to use you, remember that He sees you as perfect, robed in the righteousness of His Son (Isaiah 61:10). That makes us who are "least in the kingdom" greater even than John the Baptist (Matthew 11:11). Messengers may not tell you this, your prison walls may not confirm it, failure at Meribah may say otherwise—but you, dear saint, are God's prize and His inheritance. And, as seen in the lives of Moses and John the Baptist, those God uses to the greatest degree are often the very ones who question their own effectiveness.

Press on, precious brother; be strong, dear sister. The Promised Land of the Spirit-filled life is yours for the taking. And the Promised Land of heaven is just around the bend.

NOTES

[1] Davis, Robert. "Prayer Can Lower Your Blood Pressure." USAToday.com 11 Aug. 1998. Retrieved January 3, 2005, from <http://pqasb.pqarchiver.com/USAToday/32807200.html?did=32807200&FMT=ABS&FMTS=FT&date=Aug+11%2C+1998&author=Robert+Davis&desc=Prayer+can+lower+blood+pressure>.

[2] Scriven, Joseph M. "What a Friend We Have in Jesus." *Cyber Hymnal.* Retrieved January 6, 2005, from http://www.cyberhymnal.org/htm/w/a/waf-whij.htm.

[3] Augustine. "The Columbia World of Quotations." Bartleby.com. Retrieved January 10, 2005, from http://www.bartleby.com/66/49/4849.html.

[4] Lewis, C. S. *The Silver Chair* (New York: HarperCollins, 1994), 22–23.